The Liturgical Flutist

A Method Book and More

G-6447

The Liturgical Flutist

A Method Book and More

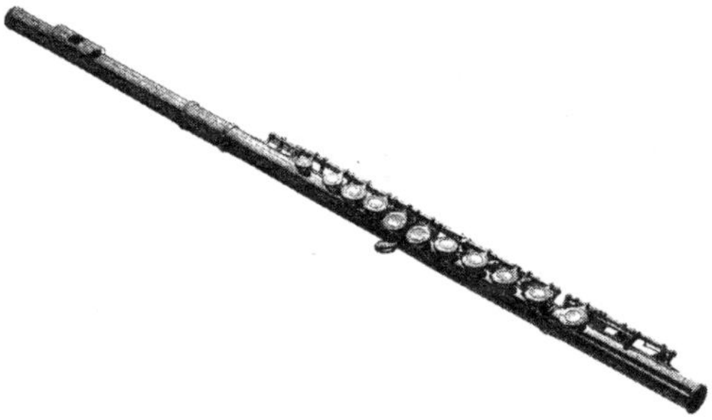

Denise La Giglia
& Anna Belle O'Shea

GIA Publications, Inc.
Chicago

Musical examples written by Anna Belle O'Shea: Chapter 4,
Examples 67, 68, and 69; Chapter 7, Examples 108, 109, 111,
120, 122, 124, 125, 126, 132, 140, 141, 148, 149, 150, 151, and
153; Chapter 8, Example 165; and Chapter 9, Example 170.

Photo credits: Michael J. Griegel, pp. 57 (bottom) and 115 and
Robert Sacha pp. 5, 6, 7, 8, 10, 12, 13, 19, 25, 36, 47, 192, 193,
196, 245, 248, 249, 254, and 255.

The Liturgical Flutist: A Method Book and More
Denise La Giglia and Anna Belle O'Shea

G-6447
ISBN: 1-57999-529-2

Dedication

We give thanks to our all-loving Creator God,
who companions and inspires us,
who draws us ever closer to our deepest truth.
Glory be to God!

I dedicate this book

…to my dad and mom, Joseph and Lorraine Pleshar, who early on gave me the gift of music lessons and a deep sense of being loved.

…to my husband, Frank La Giglia, as well as my children and their families, who lovingly convey pride and value in my work and who are constant in their faithfulness to our family circle—you are my heart and my treasure.

…to my large extended family, who enrich my life and encourage me in every part of the journey, no matter the twists and turns.

…to all my music instructors—band directors, voice and piano teachers, theory instructors—for sharing their love of music; and especially for my first flute teacher, Dorothy Nagl, and my present teacher, Susan Levitin, for inspiring me with their own delight in playing the flute.

…to those at the Institute for Spiritual Leadership and the Institute for Pastoral Studies/Loyola—both the people and places provide me safety, openness, and nurture to expand as well as deepen in spirit.

…to all the many musician friends who have invited me to be a part of their music-making and from whom I have learned so much.

…to my colleagues and wonderful friends who support me not only in my music but in my life.

…to all those with whom I have prayed and for whom I have ministered.

I feel a deep and loving gratitude for how you have all blessed me.
Denise

I gratefully dedicate this book

…to my parents, Anna Belle and Joe O'Shea, and my brothers, Sean and Joseph, for their unconditional love, support, and encouragement; for their example of faith and family; and for instilling in me their strong work ethic.

…to the members of my extended family, who have always stood by me through thick and thin.

…to my colleague, co-author, and special friend Denise La Giglia for proposing to me the idea of this book and inviting me to collaborate as equal partners in this venture.

…to my flute teacher of more than a decade, Phil Sieburg, on whose educational model I have based my own teaching career.

...to my educators at St. Margaret of Scotland School, Maria High School, and De Paul University, who formed me in faith and instilled in me a love for learning.

...to the faculty members of the Rensselaer Program of Church Music and Liturgy, especially founder Father Larry Heiman, C.PP.S., for enabling the realization of my dream of a graduate program for liturgical instrumentalists such as me.

...to my wonderful friends and colleagues with whom I am privileged to minister.

...to my students who have convinced me of the need for this book and who have challenged me by their thirst for further knowledge about church music.

...to the liturgical flutists of days gone by, whose heavenly melodies serve as inspiration.

...to the liturgical flutists of this and future generations for whom this book is offered and with whom we join their hitherto unheard musical prayers.

Thank you for the blessings you are to me.
With love and prayers for each of you,
Anna Belle

Table of Contents

Section I
The Novice Liturgical Flutist
and the Celebration of Sunday Eucharist

Section II
The Experienced Liturgical Flutist:
Exploring the Possibilities

Section III
The Advanced Liturgical Flutist:
Going Deeper

Foreword

The Second Vatican Ecumenical Council (rarely identified by its full name these days) set the Roman Catholic Church on a path of redefining itself, renewing the way it worshiped and encouraging conversation with other Christians. This sudden permission to actively observe Protestant traditions offered many lessons for Catholics, not the least of which was noticing that the person we generally identified as the parish organist and/or choirmaster was in other traditions often known as the minister of music—with the incumbent responsibilities that this title implies.

In the early to mid-1970s, the founders of the organization that bears the name brought the term pastoral musician into the parlance of the Catholic Church—synonymous with, and perhaps becoming the Catholic "brand name" for minister of music. Clearly, these terms gave the church a new way of thinking about the persons who led the music for the church's prayer. These titles implied a responsibility for not only performing the appropriate music correctly, but doing it in such a way that would show a genuine care for the spiritual vitality of the community being served.

Many have said that it is the role of the pastoral musician to maintain the highest possible competence on both sides of this descriptive title. It is insufficient if one is prayerful and service-oriented but does not know the number of flats in the key of D♭, and it is equally insufficient if one plays Bach from memory but never personally enters into the spirit of the corporate prayer. Rather, pastoral musicians must simultaneously develop their ministry skills to the fullest, while striving to become the finest musicians their individual aptitude permits.

In this book, the authors set out to expand our concept of the dual role of musician and pastoral minister by focusing on the flutist. In a manner that is perhaps more comprehensive than any previous work of this genre, this volume systematically examines flute technique, musical development, personal spirituality, and liturgical formation. All who know Denise La Giglia and Anna Belle O'Shea recognize this book as the incarnation of their own spiritual and professional lives. The Liturgical Flutist is a far-reaching source of solid information, direction, and exercise material designed to accompany the flutist of limited experience or study on the road to becoming a fine player; and for a player at any level, it is a rich guide to accompany the journey from being a flutist who merely plays in church to becoming a capable and committed pastoral musician.

This is a book for the flutist; it is a book that enables the music director to have a broader understanding of the use of the flute in liturgical music; and—minus the flute-specific technical portions—it has tremendous worth just for its value as a liturgical handbook and spiritual guide for pastoral musicians of all descriptions.

Robert J. Batastini
August 2005

Acknowledgments

Ideas come from many sources, and the idea for this book is no exception. There are musicians whose names and faces are now gone from memory who planted the seeds of interest for such a project simply through their desire for more information about ministry or their questions about repertoire. I'm grateful for how their inquiries started to shed a little light on a need.

More specifically, there are two persons who had a particular influence on the creation of this book. One is Laurie Pleshar, a professional musician and teacher who is also one of my sisters. She would call me from Boston to check things out regarding liturgical music-making and occasioned any number of interesting discussions. Another is my dear friend Bob Piercy, who in his inimitable way was quite direct and clear about the need for such a resource: "Denise, you have to write it!" I give thanks for their special kind of inspiration.

However, since I know my energies and creativity flow best in collaborative efforts, I invited my cohort, Anna Belle O'Shea, into the project. I still wonder at the synchronicity of our vision, our work habits, our energies, our styles. While I may have initiated the concept, this book would not have happened without Anna Belle as co-creator. To her belongs my deepest gratitude and respect. The real gift to me out of this experience is to have begun in a colleague relationship with her and come to the end realizing that along the way we became good friends. Thank you, Anna Belle.

Denise La Giglia
Evergreen Park, Illinois
April 2005

The writing of a book can be considered the culmination of a lifetime's work to that point, and so it is with this document. The time of its completion brings to mind some of the steps along the way that have been critical to its development.

It was during a relaxed lunchtime conversation many years ago when fellow liturgist/musician and good friend, Sister Jean Phelan, SSND, casually suggested that I use my next "snow day" to jot down some ideas for a hypothetical workshop for liturgical flutists. Little did she know that she was planting a seed that would take several years to germinate.

Workshop opportunities did occur. Denise and I, together with colleague and friend Dominic Trumfio, presented a three-part clinic for liturgical flutists at the 1999 NPM National Convention in Pittsburgh, Pennsylvania. We were awed by the tremendous response and the level of commitment to ministry evidenced by those in attendance. It was only a few months later when Denise approached me with the idea of co-authoring this text. Still riding the wave of enthusiasm from the convention experience, and yet apprehensive about jumping into such a venture, I answered Denise in the affirmative. We little knew that day that it would take countless hours spread over six years to see this project to its completion!

Yet happily I have no regrets. I thank you, Denise, for this opportunity and for the gift of your friendship that has grown throughout the course of this project.

Anna Belle O'Shea
Evergreen Park, Illinois
April 2005

Together we gratefully acknowledge the many people at GIA Publications, Inc., whose expertise has brought this book to fruition, especially

…Alec Harris, President of GIA Publications.

…Bob Batastini, the now semi-retired Vice President and Senior Editor, who believed in us when we first proposed this project, who encouraged us through the ups and downs along the way, and who has journeyed with us to the task's completion.

…Linda Vickers, Executive/Production Assistant, who patiently attended to the innumerable details needed to complete this venture.

…Michael Boschert, Editorial Production Assistant, for his special care and helpful suggestions.

…and Elizabeth Dallman Bentley, Copy Editor, for her expertise in bringing to fruition the long process of editing.

May God bless you!

Denise La Giglia and Anna Belle O'Shea

Preface

Liturgical music is a field all its own, demanding its own focus and attention. The role of the liturgical flutist lies within this field. We believe the time has come for the ministry of the liturgical flutist to be recognized as unique and worthy of being supported with a book of its own.

We began talking about our individual experiences several years ago and realized that we both had a desire to pass on some of the wisdom we have gained in our seventy collective years as liturgical flutists. Although our backgrounds are very different (see Appendix V), it became obvious to us that we shared a similar vision. We found a common bond in the recognition that we had to learn things the hard way and over the course of time. What we now know as instrumentalists is that liturgical music involves more than the ability to play well. It also includes an understanding of ministry, knowledge of liturgy, and openness to one's own spiritual journey. We believe it to be God's good Providence that our lives intersected. Each of us cherishes the willingness of the other to respond so generously with time and energy to see this project to completion.

Our music-making is an expression of our faith life. It is a way of serving God's people. It is a love offering, as expressed in *Music in Catholic Worship #4*.

> *People in love make signs of love, not only to express their love but also to deepen it. Love never expressed dies. Christians' love for Christ and for one another, and Christians' faith in Christ and in one another, must be expressed in the signs and symbols of celebration or they will die.*

It is for this reason that we chose to develop this book both for liturgical flutists and for music directors. There are many music directors who have little to no experience playing flute but who might wish to gain a better understanding of how to communicate more effectively with their parish flutists. Many creative ideas are included to assist music directors in expanding the use of the flute in a variety of prayer contexts. Music directors might also find helpful ideas for assisting other instrumentalists.

This book is designed for those who want to develop their musical gifts into a ministry. Since our expertise lies with the flute, this book is primarily for those flutists who want to go beyond whatever first brought them to use their musical gifts within worship. However, it could also be applied to any instrumentalist (e.g., oboists, string players, etc.).

In this book, the starting point is a flutist who has intermediate to advanced musical skills but may have little to no formal education in liturgy. Perhaps you are a young player with good technical skills or an adult who has played flute fairly consistently throughout your life. Some of you may be returning to playing your flute after a number of years of not playing. Some may have started playing flute as a second instrument. In addition, your memory of music theory may be vague. Depending on your experience, then, the technical aspects of this book can serve as a tutorial or simply a refresher in music theory. They can act as a reminder of already-learned skills or help to expand on these skills by revealing areas that can be further developed, nuanced, and shaped. As a supplement to this book, we encourage you to reference and use some of the wonderful method books on the market for flutists at all stages of musical development. You might even decide that the best way to advance and develop as a flutist is to return to study with an instructor.

We applaud and encourage any and all ways you work to further develop as a player. However, there is a reason you have turned to this book for further study. Our assumption is that, whatever your level of skill or methods for improvement, you have a desire to pray with the flute and deepen a ministerial relationship with the assembly. The technical aspects of this book are designed to support our intentional focus of developing flutists as liturgical ministers within the setting of Catholic ritual. For this reason, each chapter begins with a spirituality component for reflection. In addition, each chapter references liturgical music to help develop skills. Finally, this book includes a compact disc with examples for learning by listening, by playing, and by exploring through improvisation.

We envision this book as a holistic approach to forming THE LITURGICAL FLUTIST. However, a quick look at the table of contents will reveal that you need not proceed methodically through the chapters. Rather, each flutist can choose to use this book as best fits the need or circumstances. While some sections will serve as refreshers or reminders, perhaps others will challenge with something new to consider. Begin at whatever place stretches you beyond where you are. Whatever your approach, our prayers are with you as you open yourself to the Spirit's work within you. We hope you enjoy this journey. May you find many surprises to delight you!

Denise

Anna Belle

Section I

The Novice Liturgical Flutist
and the Celebration of Sunday Eucharist

Chapter 1
Warm-ups

Basic Preparation
Musical Readiness
Discipline and Focus

Rarely do we jump into things without any preparation at all. Think of all the tasks you do throughout your day—taking a shower, brushing your teeth, driving a car, doing a job, cooking. Whatever it is, someone first gave you an example of how to do it, or even literally taught you, or at least explained to you the basic concept. Everything we learn takes a certain amount of time and effort to accomplish. Yet once we learn how to do a task or employ a skill, we sometimes take it for granted as if it were something we always knew.

When you reach a plateau, do you stay there or reach higher? For the flutist, warm-ups (scales, breathing exercises, vibrato studies) are less tedious when done with the mindset of reaching higher. There is recognition of their value, which is not always present when one is comfortably situated on a plateau and questioning the need for more. We know this from our experience. To varying degrees, we have all struggled to consistently do warm-up exercises—and may have even stopped doing them entirely from time to time. If we want our music-making to be an art and a prayer, however, we need to return to the discipline of practicing the basic warm-ups. Think of it as an invitation, but with this caution: Do not get bogged down with the details. Move forward a little at a time, and gradually make each exercise your own. Patience is the best avenue to success.

The aim and final reason of all music should be nothing else but the Glory of God and the refreshment of spirit.

—Johann Sebastian Bach, 18th c.

Let's start with the fundamentals of good technique. This first chapter covers the rudiments of good playing—*posture**, **breathing**, **intonation**, **articulation**, **scales**, **chords**, **vibrato**, and **tone quality**. It is intended to be a refresher, perhaps even a challenge to improve and refine those basic skills that are sometimes taken for granted. Whatever the case, it is important to read these pages with an open mind and a desire to see the familiar through new eyes.

---

* Any terms that appear in **italics and boldface type** are included in the Glossary at the back of this book.

3

You will also find it helpful to have the following basic tools at your disposal:

- A music stand
- A *metronome*
- A *tuner*

Set aside a space for yourself where you can have a focused practice experience free of distractions. Also, always make sure your flute is in good working order and a qualified repair technician maintains it annually.

Posture
open
rooted
balanced

Proper posture ranks among one of the most important elements for achieving musical excellence. Whether standing or seated, posture affects tone quality, intonation, breathing, and technique. It is of equal importance for the jazz musician, the symphonic player, or the church musician.

Standing Position

In the standing position, proper posture is achieved as follows:

- Evenly distribute your weight on both feet. Space your feet apart so they are directly under your hips, and put one foot slightly in front of the other. Be sure to avoid locking your knees by keeping them bent just a bit.
- Hold your head in a natural position; this will keep the airway open for good tone quality. Avoid lowering your head (chin-on-the-chest syndrome) or cocking your head too far back.
- Make sure there is space between your right elbow and your body, giving your lungs room to expand for proper breathing.
- Hold your flute parallel to the floor or at a slight downward angle.
- Place the top of your music stand about chin high so you can maintain eye contact with the music director, accompanist, and assembly. Place the stand itself an arm's distance away from you so you can see the entire page, including the bottom lines, without tilting your head downward.

These habits are absolutely essential for producing a beautiful sound, sustaining long *phrases*, and controlling intonation. Lack of attention to any of these elements will lessen your ability to communicate effectively.

PROPER STANDING POSTURE   POOR STANDING POSTURE

Listen to "God of Day and God of Darkness" on the CD (Track 1). Notice the difference between the first time (played with proper posture) and the second time (played with poor posture).

EXAMPLE 1: EXCERPT FROM "GOD OF DAY AND GOD OF DARKNESS"

BEACH SPRING
The Sacred Harp, 1844

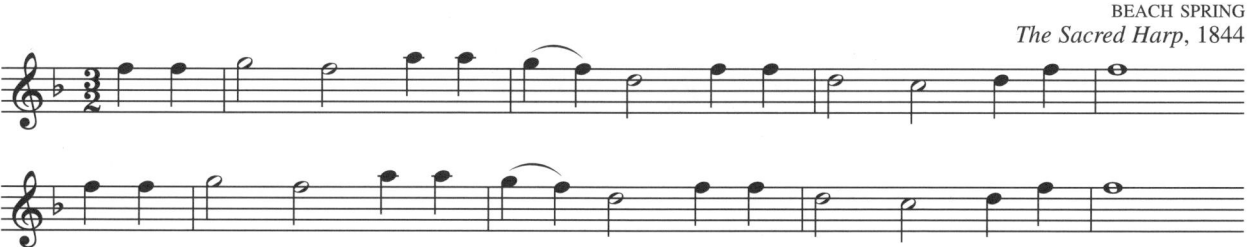

Track 1
a: Effect of Good Standing Posture on Intonation
"God of Day and God of Darkness" – mm. 1–4, flute and piano
b: Effect of Poor Standing Posture on Intonation
"God of Day and God of Darkness" – mm. 1–4, flute and piano

The difference is obvious. The first example on the CD demonstrates a beautiful sound, excellent intonation, and musical phrasing. The second example demonstrates a pinched tone that is flat in pitch and an inability to complete long phrases in one breath.

Similar comparisons can be made of proper and improper posture in the seated position.

Seated Position

For proper seated posture:

- Place both feet flat on the floor, sitting forward on the chair with your back away from the back of the chair.
- Your head and arms remain in the same placement as in the standing position.
- As with the standing position, place the music stand an arm's length away from you, with the top of the stand positioned about chin high.
- Be sure to allow enough room on your right to hold your flute properly. This is just as essential as the space a trombonist needs to extend the slide or a violinist needs to extend the bow. Never put yourself in a position in which you drape your right arm over the back of the chair or hold the flute too low.

PROPER SEATED POSTURE

POOR SEATED POSTURE

Play "God of Day and God of Darkness," first in proper standing position and then seated. Pay close attention to your posture, emulating the sound of the flute on the first part of Track 1 on the CD.

Breathing
a primary element for sustaining life
essence of quality musicianship for the flutist
a means to carry and convey a phrase

Flutists need an enormous amount of air to fill the flute and support the sound; thus, breath control is essential for good tone quality. It goes without saying that we must take care of our bodies to maximize our lung capacity. Good rest, proper nutrition, physical exercise, and avoiding smoking will enable you to get the greatest benefit from the following breathing exercises.

Practice these exercises without using the flute.

EXERCISE

1. Set the metronome to quarter = 60. Inhale through your mouth for 4 beats. For the purpose of this exercise, be sure the inhalation is audible.

2. Exhale through your mouth for 4 beats, again making sure the exhalation is audible.

3. Keeping the inhalation to 4 beats, increase the exhalation to 8 beats, and then 12. Be sure the intensity is the same on beat 12 as it was on beat 1. To check the intensity level, hold a small piece of tissue paper at arm's length from your mouth. Make sure the paper flutters with the same intensity during the entire exhalation process.

Now listen to the examples for Steps 1 and 2 of the above exercise on the CD (Track 2).

Track 2: Slow Inhalation and Sustained Exhalation
Metronome set at quarter = 60; voice command "Inhale" followed by sound of inhalation for 4 beats; voice command "Exhale" followed by sound of exhalation for 4 beats

EXHALATION

EXERCISE

Modify the exercise to quicken the speed of your inhalation. The object is to take in the greatest amount of air in the shortest amount of time. Think of what happens when someone surprises you. Your response is a gasp on the syllable "huh." Your lungs fill with air, expanding your rib cage, opening up your airway, and creating a large, open space inside your mouth. This is an ideal image for flutists.

1. Repeat the breathing exercises. Again, set the metronome at quarter = 60, but this time inhale quickly (only as a pick-up to the exhalation). Then sustain the exhalation for 4 beats.

2. Repeat the inhalation as in Step 1 above, now sustaining the exhalation for 8 beats, then 12.

Listen to the example for Step 1 of the above exercise on the CD (Track 3).

Track 3: Fast Inhalation and Sustained Exhalation
Metronome set at quarter = 60; voice command "Breathe" followed by sound of quick inhalation and 4-beat exhalation

Now modify your inhalation to mimic what happens when you play flute. That means you'll need to inhale through your mouth while forming your **embouchure.** The key is to inhale as silently as possible, keeping your throat open in the same fashion as a yawn. (This "silent" breath becomes especially important when playing directly in front of a microphone!) Use the exercise below to practice this technique with your flute. You may want to view yourself in a mirror while performing this exercise.

EXERCISE

1. Make the inhalation inaudible, and keep the exhalation steady and controlled, with the metronome set at quarter = 60.

2. Begin with a middle-octave B♭, first holding the note for 4 beats, then 8, and then 12.

3. Repeat the exercise on low-octave B♭.

4. Repeat the exercise again, this time on high-octave F.

5. You might also choose to repeat this exercise on other pitches.

Listen to the four-beat portion of this exercise on the CD (Track 4). Play with the CD, striving to match the tone quality demonstrated there.

Track 4: Breathing Exercises with the Flute
Metronome set at quarter = 60; flute alone, playing middle B♭, low B♭, and high F, each for 4 counts.

Intonation
centered
accuracy of pitch
aural perception of relationship

A discussion of breathing is incomplete without studying intonation. The two concepts are impossible to separate. Good intonation can only be achieved when proper posture and correct breathing habits are in place.

Intonation can be defined as the accuracy of the pitch—the flatness, sharpness, or correctness of the pitch of each note. The importance of good intonation cannot be emphasized enough. One flutist playing out of tune can make an entire assembly uncomfortable, even though they may not be able to pinpoint the reason for their discomfort. One flutist playing with good intonation can meld into the texture and take the assembly to new plateaus. Again, the assembly cannot articulate how this happens. Suffice it to say that good intonation plays an extremely important role for the liturgical flutist.

Standard pitch in the United States is designated as "A440." This means that the A above middle C on the piano will resonate at 440 cycles per second. As you ascend the scale, the pitches are produced with more cycles per second; as you descend the scale, it takes fewer cycles per second to produce the sound.

There are variances of this standard. The more you understand about this auditory realm, the easier it will be to adjust your own intonation. Some ensembles are currently tuning to A442—or even higher. Knowing the standard pitch of your group will enable you to hone your aural skills and adjust your own intonation more quickly and correctly. Ask your parish music director or the piano/organ technician for this information. For purposes of this discussion, A440 will be used.

Note: All wind instruments are manufactured to play in tune when the mouthpiece is pulled out slightly. On the flute, this means you should pull the **headjoint** out approximately 1/8 inch. This gives you room to push the mouthpiece in if you find yourself playing with other instruments that are tuned sharp.

It is easiest to practice intonation exercises with a tuner. The tuner will give you visual cues to an aural problem. It will indicate whether you are playing sharp, flat, or precisely in tune.

EXERCISE

1. Begin by calibrating the tuner to A440 (or A442, as applicable).

2. Try playing middle D with the headjoint pulled out approximately 1/8 inch. If the needle stays on zero, you are playing in tune. If the needle stays to the right of the zero, your pitch is sharp. Pull the headjoint out to adjust the sharp pitch. If the needle stays to the left of the zero, your pitch is flat. Push the headjoint in to adjust the flat pitch. Work with this note until you can consistently keep the needle on zero.

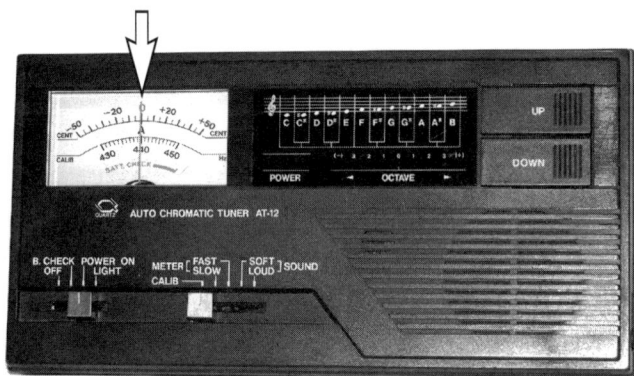

TUNER WITH NEEDLE ON ZERO INDICATING PROPER PITCH

3. When you are comfortable keeping middle D in tune, then move to middle A and check the position of the needle again. Make headjoint adjustments as needed.

4. Move on to low A and check the tuner once more.

These three notes are good yardsticks for measuring the overall pitch of your flute. Pull the headjoint out or push it in as needed to keep the needle on zero for these three notes.

Spend a great deal of time checking pitch on many different notes with the tuner so you get to know the peculiar tendencies of your flute. Train your ear to hear what the visual placement of the needle is indicating. This is the first step to being able to adjust pitch without the aid of a tuner, using your ears to determine whether or not you are playing in tune.

Each instrument will have unique tendencies. In general, however, the lowest notes of the flute range tend to be flat, while the extreme upper notes tend to be sharp. Here are some tips:

IF PITCH IS…	THEN…
consistently sharp…	pull the headjoint out a fraction of an inch.
consistently flat…	push the headjoint in.
sharp on only a few isolated notes…	adjust by aiming the airstream down (or rolling in) slightly on those notes to lower the pitch.
flat on only a few isolated notes…	tighten the corners of your embouchure, push your lower jaw forward, and aim the airstream up (or roll out) slightly on those notes to raise the pitch.

Note: If intonation becomes a problem that cannot be resolved even with good posture and proper breathing techniques, perhaps the cause is a poorly aligned **adjusting cork** in the headjoint of the flute. If you are uncomfortable moving this cork by yourself, seek the help of a qualified instrument repair technician.

Volume could also affect pitch. In general, passages played at very soft dynamic levels can tend to be flat, especially if the sound is unsupported. The opposite is also true. Passages played at very loud dynamic levels can tend to be sharp, especially if the player overblows. You must learn to adjust to compensate for these tendencies.

EXERCISE

Play several scales at different dynamic levels (see "Scales" later in this chapter). Use your tuner to check the effect different dynamic levels can have on your playing.

Another element that can affect intonation is the direction of the airstream. Some players blow down into the flute too much, thereby covering too much tonehole, usually a result of holding the head too low. When this occurs, the pitch is usually flat and has a very thin quality due to a constriction of the airway in the throat.

EXERCISE

Refer back to "God of Day and God of Darkness" in Example 1.

1. Play this piece once more, this time purposely covering too much tonehole.

2. Check your intonation on the tuner. It should be registering to the left of the middle, indicating a flat pitch.

Now listen to the CD (Track 5) to hear what happens when too much tonehole is covered. Compare this to Track 1, where the same piece is played with good intonation.

 **Track 5: Effect of Playing with Too Much Tonehole Covered**
"God of Day and God of Darkness" – mm. 1–4, flute only

FLUTIST COVERING TOO MUCH TONEHOLE

Occasionally players will aim their airstream too high, thus covering too little tonehole. This is often the result of playing with the head cocked back too far. The consequence is a sound that is too sharp in pitch and has an airy, unfocused quality.

EXERCISE

1. Play "God of Day and God of Darkness" once again, this time purposely covering too little tonehole.

2. Check your intonation on the tuner. It should be registering to the right of the middle, indicating a sharp pitch.

Now listen to the CD (Track 6) to hear what happens when too little tonehole is covered. Again, compare this to the intonation sounded on Track 1.

Track 6: Effect of Playing with Too Little Tonehole Covered
"God of Day and God of Darkness" – mm. 1–4, flute only

FLUTIST COVERING TOO LITTLE TONEHOLE

Your ultimate goal is to find someplace in the middle of these two. Even so, there still might be times when you need to adjust your pitch in one direction or the other based on the circumstances. Use your ears—and, if possible, your tuner—as your guide.

This leads us back to the discussion on posture and breathing. With good posture and correct breathing habits, your lungs are unrestricted, your airway is open, and your sound is rich and resonant at all dynamic levels and in every register of the flute. You are now working at your optimum and can control intonation with much greater ease. However, if any one of these elements is underdeveloped, you will experience problems that will only get worse with time. In other words, the hard work you put into these basic elements today will result in great payoffs tomorrow.

EXERCISE

Practice proper posture, deep breathing, and good intonation using the tune "Deep Within." Practice playing 4-measure phrases in one breath, especially checking to make sure your pitch stays supported to the ends of phrases.

EXAMPLE 2: EXCERPT FROM "DEEP WITHIN"

D. Haas

Track 7

a: Application of Good Posture, Breathing, and Intonation
"Deep Within" – piano introduction; refrain with flute and piano
b: Application of Good Posture, Breathing, and Intonation with Accompaniment Only
"Deep Within" – piano introduction; refrain with piano only

Now listen to the CD (Track 7). The first excerpt on Track 7 includes flute and keyboard accompaniment, while the second excerpt is accompaniment alone. Play along or just listen to the first excerpt with flute and accompaniment. In the second excerpt, you become the flute soloist by playing with the accompaniment alone. Think about your posture, breathing, and intonation. Paying close attention to these elements must become second nature, like brushing your teeth. Lack of attention to these elements will prevent even the most advanced technical player from being a good church musician.

Remember that controlling intonation is a never-ending process. You must **always** listen and adjust as necessary. Even after all adjustments and considerations are made, you might still hear sounds that are out of tune. Perhaps you are playing with other instrumentalists or vocalists who are not being attentive to their pitch, or you are playing with instruments that have fixed pitch (such as piano or organ) and are out of tune. Musicians who play these instruments cannot adjust their pitch on the spot, so you may have to make the adjustments to achieve the best sound for the entire ensemble. It serves no purpose for one person to play at A440 when others are not. Always remember to keep those for whom you're playing in mind and do the best you can given all of the variables in any particular situation.

Tonguing/Articulation
musical enunciation
key to definition
catalyst to giving color to the sound

All flutists are taught to tongue notes from their earliest days of instruction. The placement of the tongue behind the top teeth produces a "tu" sound, enabling flutists to begin notes clearly and distinctly. When studying standard flute solo and orchestral literature, it is important to tongue and *slur* as written on the printed page, paying close attention to these marks as the intent of the composer/arranger.

In contrast to the orchestral musician, oftentimes the liturgical flutist is reading from a part devoid of articulation markings. When this is the case, a casual glance might lead you to believe that every note should be tongued, but often this is not the composer's intent.

Take a look at "The Summons."

EXAMPLE 3: EXCERPT FROM "THE SUMMONS"

KELVINGROVE
Scottish traditional; arr. J. Bell

This arrangement is taken from a C Instrument book published by GIA and is written without slurs of any kind, as is quite typical of liturgical music. It is often the intent of the composer/arranger for the instrumentalist to add slurs that are appropriate to the style of the piece.

Example 4 provides some possible slurring patterns for this piece. The first *phrase* (the first 8 measures) uses one slur per measure. The second phrase changes the pattern to one slur for every 2 measures. The third phrase slurs every 4 measures, while the final phrase uses but one slur for the entire 8-measure phrase.

EXAMPLE 4: EXCERPT FROM "THE SUMMONS" (WITH SLURRING EXAMPLES)

KELVINGROVE
Scottish traditional; arr. J. Bell

EXERCISE

Play through "The Summons" several times using the slurring patterns indicated in Example 4.

Note that this variety of slurring examples is for demonstration purposes only. In liturgical settings, you should be much more consistent than this. Either of the first two choices—slurring 1 or 2 measures at a time—works well in liturgical settings. They both give some definition to the phrases because of the periodic tongued notes. At the same time, the slurs prevent the melody from sounding disconnected, which could happen if every note is tongued as written in Example 3. The slurring patterns found in measures 16–32 don't work well because they are too long; they almost cause the phrases to lose definition.

Pay special attention to the last 3 measures of the piece. In measure 30, there is a dotted half note F. Measure 31 also has a dotted half note F, this time tied to a quarter note F in measure 32. Of course, the *tie* indicates the need to hold the last two notes for a total of four counts. However, it is the beginning of that note that might be confusing. The long slur over the phrase might cause the player to think that all three of the last measures should be tied together (from measures 30–32). Closer study would show that the F in measure 31 needs to be lightly rearticulated because the F in measure 30 is not part of the tie. Remember that repeated pitches under a slur need to be gently re-tongued. They are only tied if there is an additional tie under the slur, as in measures 31–32 in Example 4.

Now look at a portion of "Joyful, Joyful, We Adore You." Although the original version has no articulation marks at all, Examples 5 through 7 will each explore a different style of articulation for demonstration purposes only.

EXERCISE

Play this portion of "Joyful, Joyful, We Adore You" in a **legato** style, observing the tenuto marks on each note in Example 5.

EXAMPLE 5: EXCERPT FROM "JOYFUL, JOYFUL, WE ADORE YOU" (WITH TENUTO MARKS)

HYMN TO JOY
L. van Beethoven

Listen to this example on the CD (Track 8) to hear this articulation.

Track 8: Legato Style
"Joyful, Joyful, We Adore You" – mm. 1–4, flute alone

EXERCISE

Play this section of "Joyful, Joyful, We Adore You" again, this time in a **marcato** style, observing the **accent** marks on each note of Example 6.

EXAMPLE 6: EXCERPT FROM "JOYFUL, JOYFUL, WE ADORE YOU" (WITH ACCENT MARKS)

HYMN TO JOY
L. van Beethoven

Now listen to the same phrase on the CD (Track 9) to hear this style.

Track 9: Marcato Style
"Joyful, Joyful, We Adore You" – mm. 1–4, flute alone

EXERCISE

Play "Joyful, Joyful, We Adore You" once more, using a style somewhere between legato and marcato. Add slurs as desired, using the slurs in Example 7 as a guide.

EXAMPLE 7: EXCERPT FROM "JOYFUL, JOYFUL, WE ADORE YOU"

HYMN TO JOY
L. van Beethoven

Now listen to the first phrase once again on the CD (Track 10) to hear this style.

Track 10: Slurring Patterns
"Joyful, Joyful, We Adore You" – mm. 1–4, flute alone

Your decision concerning the style of tonguing for this or any other piece will be determined by the piece itself, the era of history from which it comes, its placement within the liturgy, the type of prayer itself, the space, and acoustics. (These topics are addressed in later chapters.)

The adept liturgical flutist is able to adjust the style of articulation to suit the occasion. However, these decisions cannot be made in a vacuum. You need to discuss articulation choices with the music director and the other instrumentalists to come to a consensus. Initially there will be a degree of effort involved, but you will develop more of a "sixth sense" with experience.

Note: Many flutists are able to move beyond basic single-tonguing to use a technique called "double-tonguing" or even "triple-tonguing." With both of these skills, two different syllables are used for articulation, the "t" sound and the "k" sound—or in more legato passages, the "d" sound and the "g" sound. The use of these different syllables in alternation enables the flutist to tongue very rapidly. For the most part, there is very little need for these styles of tonguing when playing liturgical music. However, should the need arise (e.g., in the context of pastoral music), refer to the listing of reference books in Appendix II for resources on developing these skills.

Scales
key to flexibility and evenness of line
fundamental building blocks
foundation for recognition of key signatures

Scales are to music-making as the basement is to a skyscraper. Without this foundational element, everything else will topple. A working knowledge of scales and their key signatures is essential for all musicians.

Since the Baroque era (1600–1750), Western music has commonly used two different types of scales—major and minor—that are made up of various combinations of **half steps** and **whole steps**. (See Appendix I for more information on the Baroque era.)

Major Scales

Major scales are constructed by juxtaposing two **tetrachords**, each consisting of the pattern whole step–whole step–half step. There is also a whole step between the two tetrachords.

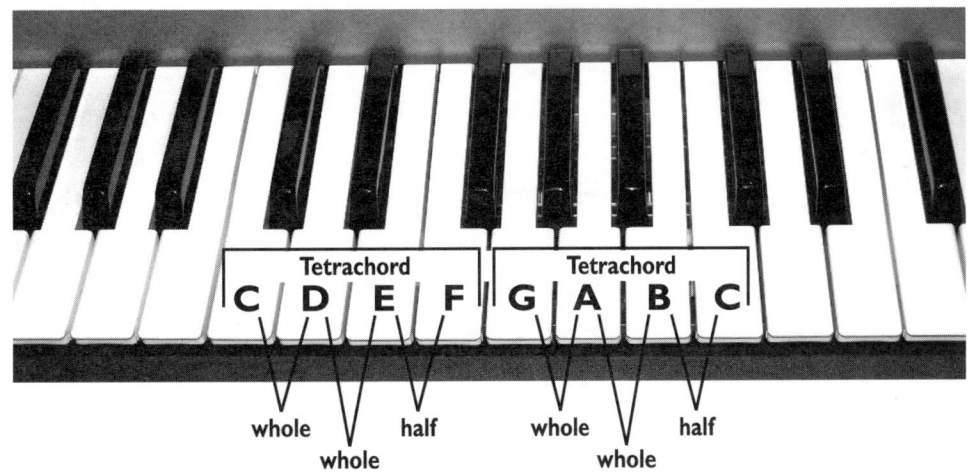

C MAJOR SCALE

A C major scale is shown above. The **interval** from C to D is a whole step (same as two half steps). The interval from D to E is also a whole step. The interval from E to F, however, is only a half step since there is no black key between these two white keys. The half step, therefore, is the smallest interval used in Western tonal music.

The next tetrachord begins with G. There is a whole step between G and A, another whole step between A and B, and then a half step between B and C.

Each scale degree is also given a name. (See Glossary for a description of each name.)

I	II	III	IV	V	VI	VII	VIII
Tonic	Supertonic	Mediant	Subdominant	Dominant	Submediant	Leading Tone	Tonic

For the C major scale, this translates to the following:

I	II	III	IV	V	VI	VII	VIII
Tonic	Supertonic	Mediant	Subdominant	Dominant	Submediant	Leading Tone	Tonic
C	D	E	F	G	A	B	C

Notice that scale degrees I and VIII have the same name. These notes are an **octave** apart and, hence, have the same letter name. Therefore, they are both "tonic" in the key of C.

The formula for building major scales can be repeated starting on any other pitch, resulting in twelve different major scales. The names of these scales can be found on the **Circle of Fifths**.

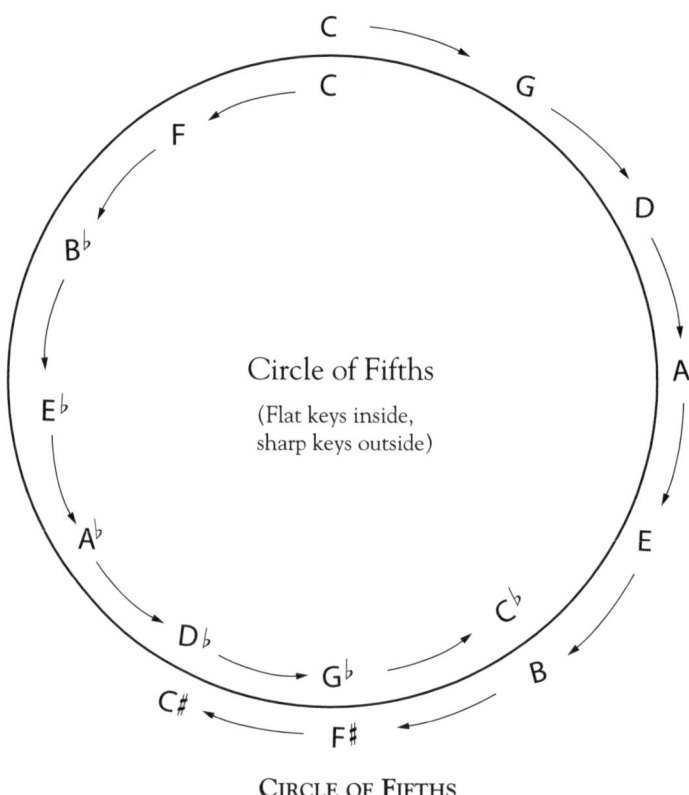

CIRCLE OF FIFTHS

The Circle of Fifths gets its name from the interval between the scale names. The tonic of each scale is five scale degrees away from the tonic of the scales before and after it. As you go around the circle clockwise from C, you need to add one sharp to each key signature. When you go counterclockwise from C, you need to add one flat to each successive key signature. The key of C major has no flats or sharps in the key signature; every note is natural.

Note: Since there are only seven different letter names that we use in music—A, B, C, D, E, F, G—there can only be seven or fewer sharps (or seven or fewer flats) in any given key signature. Sharps and flats are never mixed within the same key signature. The order of the sharps or flats in a key signature never varies. The sharps occur in the following order: F, C, G, D, A, E, and B. The flats occur in the reverse order: B, E, A, D, G, C, and F.

Notice there are several scales that have two different names: C♯ and D♭, F♯ and G♭, and B and C♭. The two scales in each of these pairs sound alike; however, they have different key signatures and, hence, different *enharmonic* spellings of each note of the scale.

The scales with sharp key signatures are shown in Example 8. They should all be committed to memory. Notice that the name of the scale is one half step higher than the last sharp of that key signature.

EXAMPLE 8: MAJOR SCALES (WITH SHARP KEY SIGNATURES)

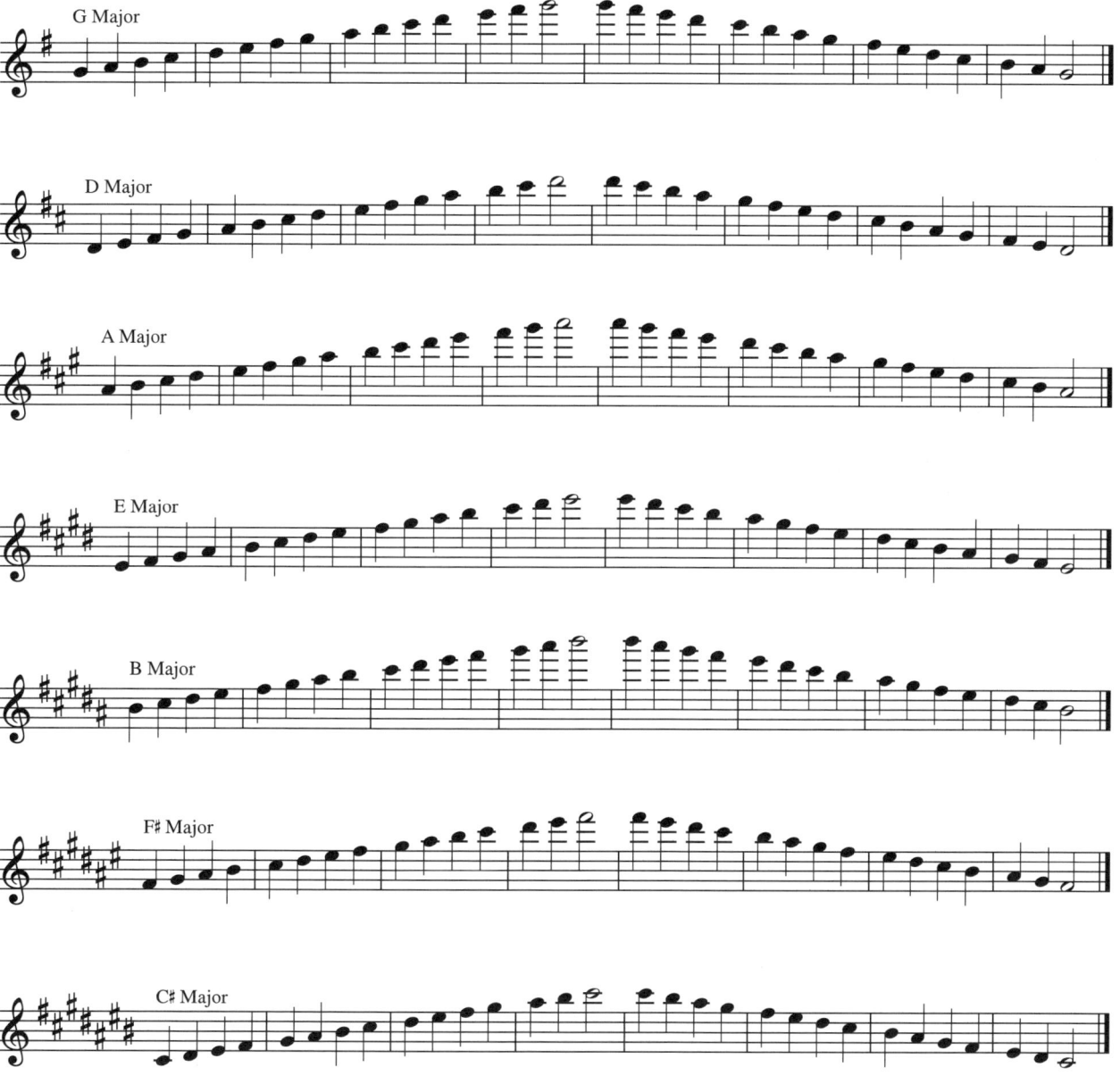

The scales with flat key signatures are shown in Example 9. They should also be committed to memory. Notice that the name of the scale is the same as the second to last flat in the key signature.

EXAMPLE 9: MAJOR SCALES (WITH FLAT KEY SIGNATURES)

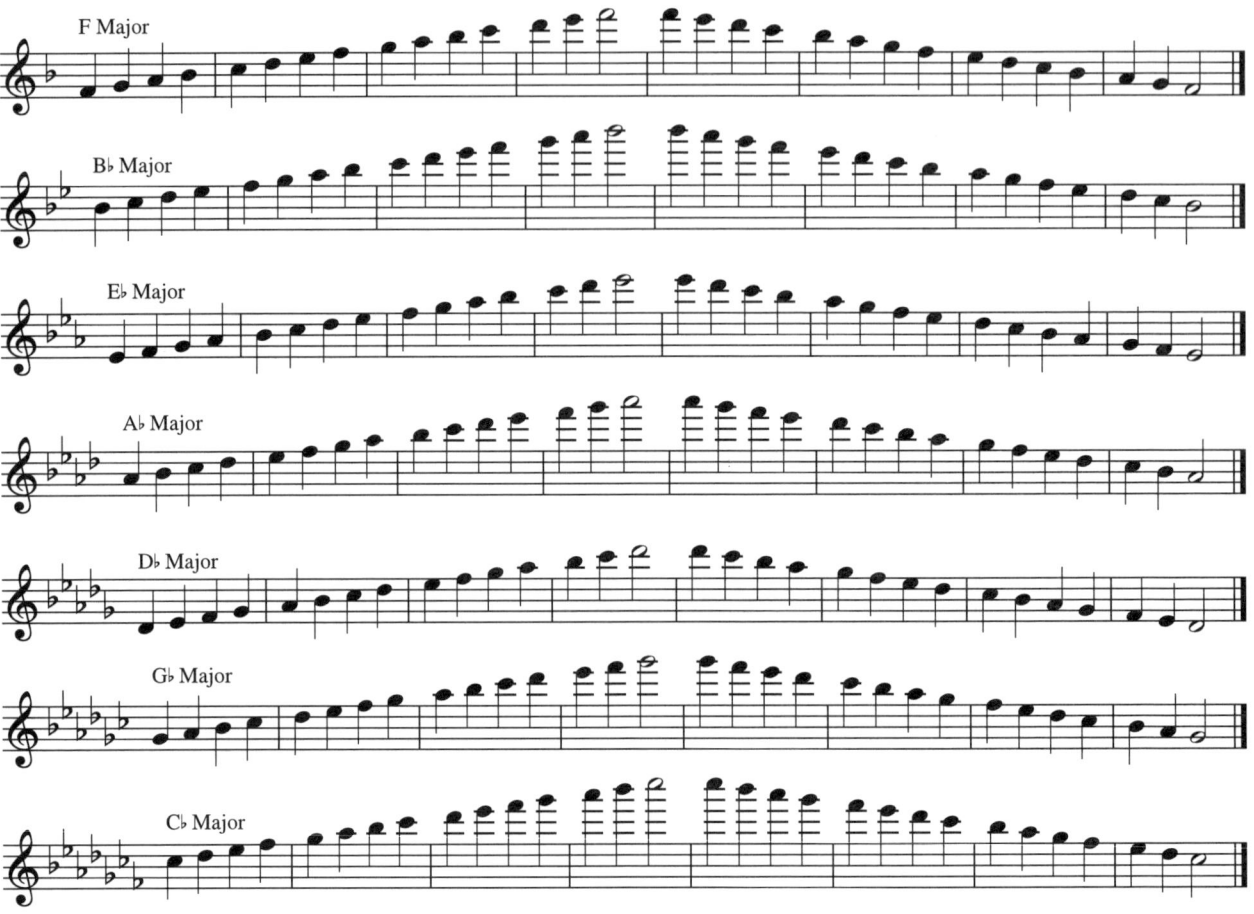

Last among the major scales, but certainly not least, is the one in which there are no sharps or flats—the key of C major. This scale should be learned as a three-octave scale (see Example 10), encompassing the entire range of the flute.

EXAMPLE 10: C MAJOR SCALE (3 OCTAVES)

There are many exercises you can use to increase your proficiency with these scales. A very effective pattern using the F major scale is given in Example 11, but you could also apply this exercise to all other major keys.

EXERCISE

1. Set the metronome to quarter = 60.

2. Play the F major scale as written in Example 11.

3. For the sake of proficiency and variety, practice the entire exercise using different tonguing and slurring patterns.

EXAMPLE 11: F MAJOR SCALE

As you progress through this book, references are often made to scales and their key signatures. It behooves you to be able to recognize key signatures and immediately associate the name of the scale with its key signature.

EXERCISE

Test yourself using this short quiz:

Name the key of each of the following examples. (The correct answers follow the quiz.)

EXAMPLE 12:

EXCERPT FROM "FOR THE BEAUTY OF THE EARTH"

DIX
C. Kocher

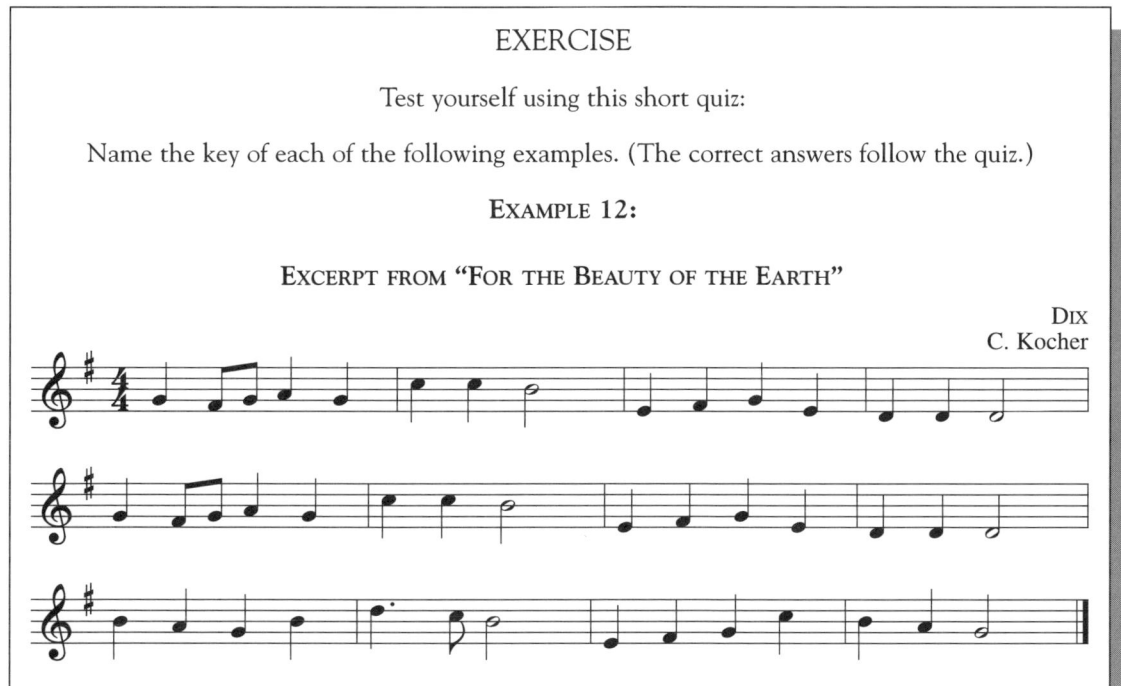

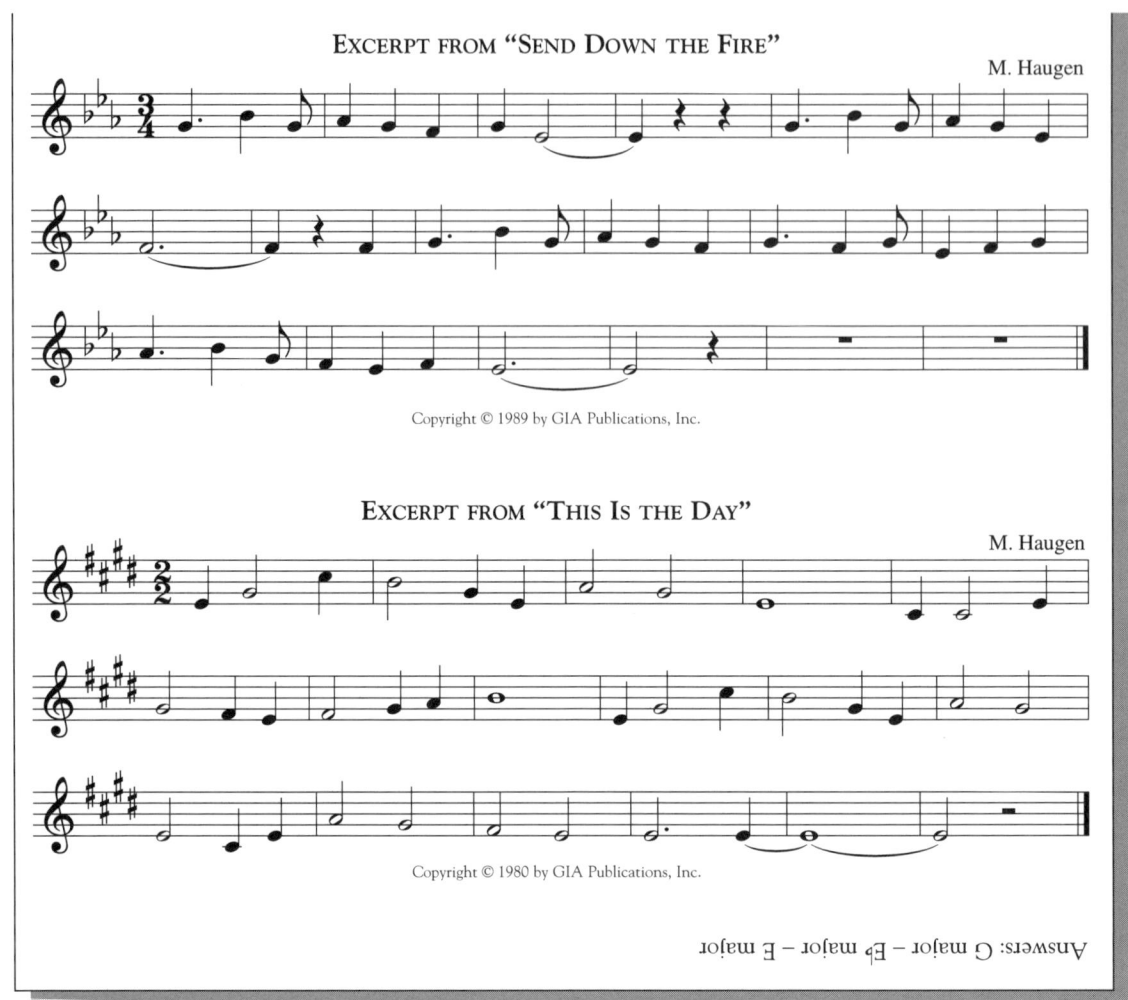

EXCERPT FROM "SEND DOWN THE FIRE"

M. Haugen

Copyright © 1989 by GIA Publications, Inc.

EXCERPT FROM "THIS IS THE DAY"

M. Haugen

Copyright © 1980 by GIA Publications, Inc.

Answers: G major – E♭ major – E major

Minor Scales

For every key signature, there is not only a major key but also a minor key that uses the same key signature. The name of the minor key is the same as the sixth note of the major scale. In other words, the submediant of the major scale becomes the tonic of its relative minor. Unlike the major scales, each **minor scale** has three forms: **natural minor**, **harmonic minor**, and **melodic minor**.

In Example 13, look at the first scale (C major scale), and compare it to the second scale (A minor scale in its natural form).

EXAMPLE 13: MAJOR SCALE; MINOR SCALE (NATURAL FORM)

24

You will notice that the A minor scale has the same key signature as C major, which is no sharps or flats. Both scales involve the same notes; the only difference is that the minor scale begins on the sixth note of the major scale. This changes the whole-step and half-step relationship, thus creating a scale of a very different sound. The natural minor scale is comprised of the following intervals: whole step, half step, whole step, whole step, half step, whole step, whole step (as shown below).

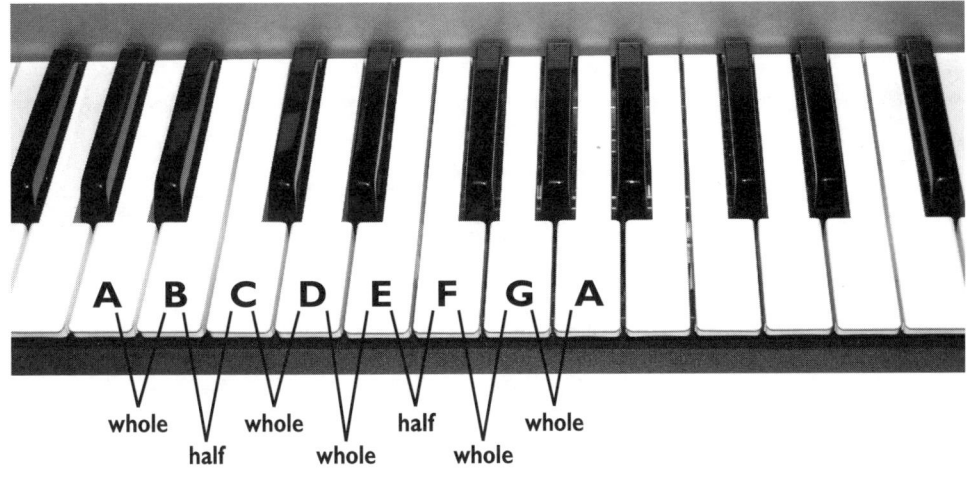

A MINOR SCALE (NATURAL FORM)

The second form of the minor scale is the harmonic minor form. It is similar to the natural minor scale except that the seventh degree (the leading tone) is raised by one half step, both in the ascending and descending forms of the scale, as shown in Example 14.

EXAMPLE 14: MINOR SCALE (HARMONIC FORM)

Notice that the seventh degree of the scale is now G# instead of G.

The third form of the minor scales is the melodic minor form. This form raises both the sixth and seventh degrees in the ascending scale, and cancels out these accidentals in the descending scale, as shown in Example 15.

EXAMPLE 15: MINOR SCALE (MELODIC FORM)

Notice that the sixth and seventh degrees are now F# and G# in the ascending scale, and G♮ and F♮ in the descending scale. The melodic minor is the most commonly used form of the minor scales because of the momentum toward the tonic, which is created by raising the sixth and seventh degrees in the ascending portion. Since there is no need to create this feeling of movement toward the tonic in the descending portion, the accidentals are cancelled.

The melodic minor forms of each scale are shown in Example 16; they are written in the appropriate range for the flute. Once again, these scales should be committed to memory.

EXAMPLE 16: MINOR SCALES (MELODIC FORM)

You may choose to practice these minor scales in the same manner as the major scales.

EXERCISE

Set the metronome to quarter = 60, and play the melodic minor scales in quarter notes, then eighths, and then sixteenths. (Refer to the rhythmic pattern in Example 11.)

Remember that you should be equally comfortable tonguing and slurring these scales.

It is important to be able to discern by ear whether a scale is major or minor. As an aid to developing your aural skills, listen to the CD (Track 11).

EXERCISE

You will hear five different scales on the CD (Track 11). Your task is to determine whether the scale is major or minor. (It is not important to know the letter name of each scale simply by listening to it. You only need to determine the **mode**—either major or minor.) If the scale is a minor scale, you will need to decide whether it is natural, harmonic, or melodic minor.

Answers: major – melodic minor – major – major – natural minor

---

Track 11: Listening Exercise for Major and Minor Scales
Various scales – 1 octave each (ascending and descending), flute alone
(Specific scale names can be found in the Listing of CD Tracks at the back of this book.)

Expanding upon this skill, let's now focus on using both aural and visual clues to determine whether a piece of music is in a major or a minor key. Listen to two sections of Marty Haugen's *Mass of Remembrance*, played on piano: "Gloria" (CD Track 12) and "Kyrie" (CD Track 13). Notice the difference in the sound of the "Gloria" (which is in a major key) as compared to the "Kyrie" (which is in a minor key).

Track 12: Listening for Major Key
"Gloria" from *Mass of Remembrance* – refrain, piano alone

Track 13: Listening for Minor Key
"Kyrie" from *Mass of Remembrance* – refrain, piano alone

Now let's look at these two pieces to determine their keys through a visual study (see Examples 17 and 18).

EXAMPLE 17: EXCERPT FROM "GLORIA" FROM MASS OF REMEMBRANCE

M. Haugen

EXAMPLE 18: EXCERPT FROM "KYRIE" FROM MASS OF REMEMBRANCE

M. Haugen

Both pieces have the same key signature: one sharp. This indicates the key of G major or E minor. It is usually the last note of the melody that determines which of these keys is correct. Look at the last melody note of the "Gloria." The note is G, which indicates you are in the key of G major.

Now look at the "Kyrie." Since the last melody note of the refrain is E, you can say with some degree of certainty that you are in the key of E minor. Another indicator is the D♯ in measures 2 and 6 of the accompaniment. The D♯ is the leading tone in the key of E minor and, therefore, propels the momentum toward the tonic of E. Putting this together, you can safely say that the "Kyrie" is in the key of E minor. This matches the information learned by listening to these two pieces. The "Gloria" is in G, while the "Kyrie" is in E minor.

EXERCISE

Continue to hone your aural skills at recognizing major and minor keys. Listen to the CD (Track 14). Determine the **modality** (either major or minor) of each piece.

Answers: minor – major – major – minor – minor

Track 14: Listening Exercise for Major and Minor Keys
"Let All Mortal Flesh Keep Silence" – mm. 7–19; "Alleluia! Sing to Jesus" – mm. 1–8 and 17–32; "Song of Farewell" – refrain; "Shepherd Me, O God" – refrain; "We Three Kings" – verse, flute alone

Now study each piece visually.

EXERCISE

Identify the key of each piece below. The answers can be found at the end of this exercise.

EXAMPLE 19:

EXCERPT FROM "LET ALL MORTAL FLESH KEEP SILENCE"

PICARDY
French carol

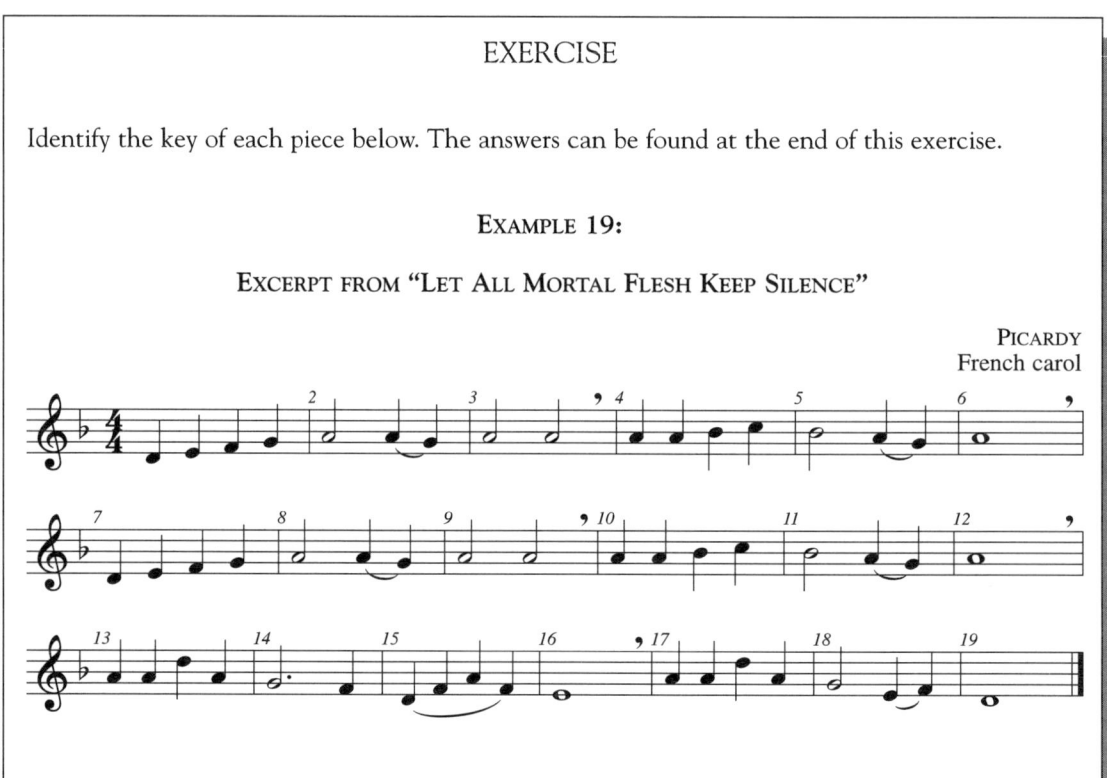

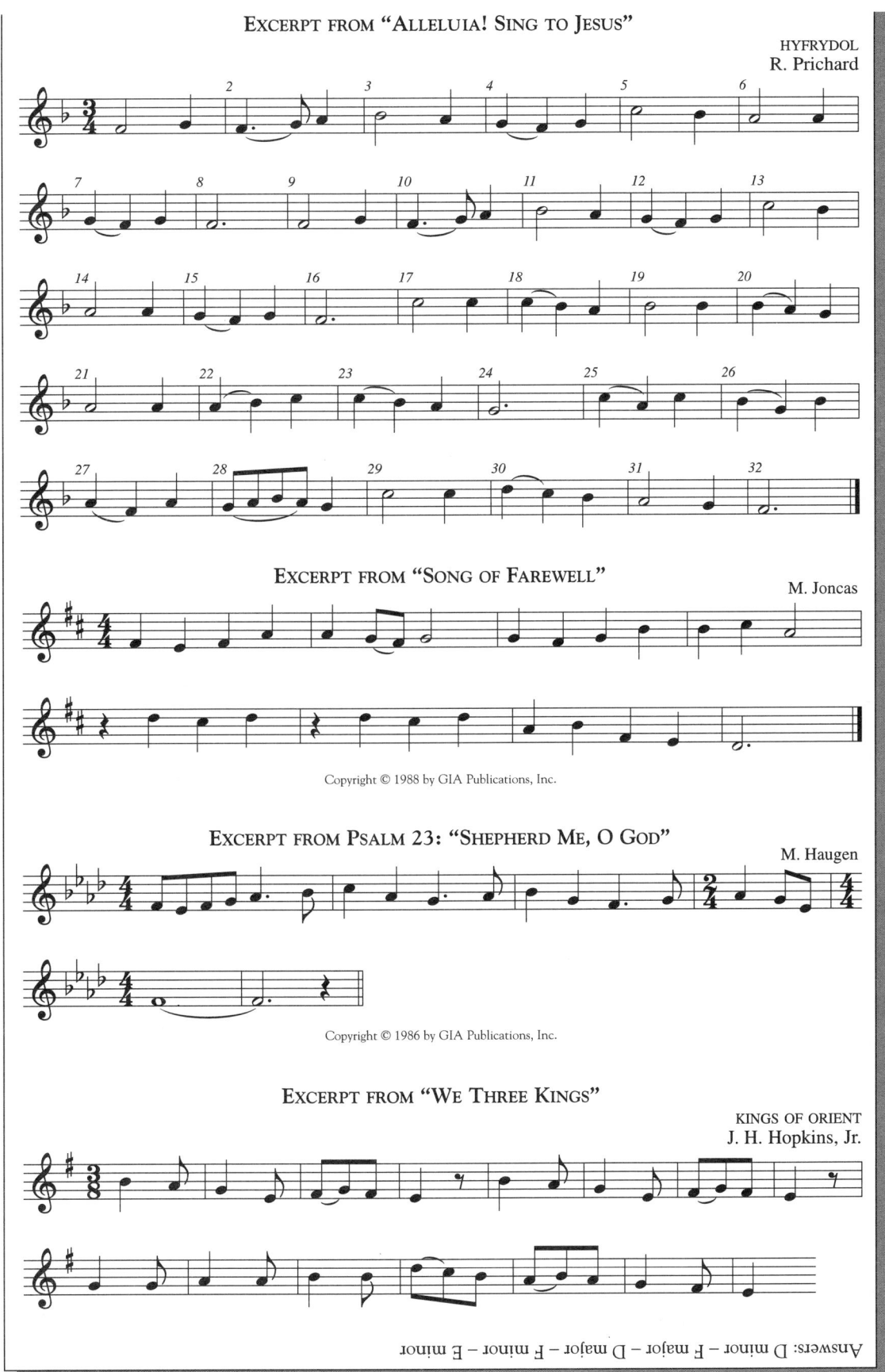

EXCERPT FROM "ALLELUIA! SING TO JESUS"

HYFRYDOL
R. Prichard

EXCERPT FROM "SONG OF FAREWELL"

M. Joncas

Copyright © 1988 by GIA Publications, Inc.

EXCERPT FROM PSALM 23: "SHEPHERD ME, O GOD"

M. Haugen

Copyright © 1986 by GIA Publications, Inc.

EXCERPT FROM "WE THREE KINGS"

KINGS OF ORIENT
J. H. Hopkins, Jr.

Answers: D minor – F major – D major – F minor – E minor

The importance of the development of these visual and aural skills cannot be emphasized enough. It is essential to be able to recognize keys and key signatures, and to be capable of aurally determining the modality of a piece. These skills will be invaluable in conquering the more advanced tasks of transposing and improvising, both of which will be addressed in later chapters.

Note: When writing the name of any major key and/or major scale, always use uppercase letters. The word "major" is not even needed; the capital letter alone is enough to indicate a major key. Hence, *Sonata in G* is the same as *Sonata in G Major*. Minor keys can be spelled with lowercase letters, eliminating the need for the word "minor." For example, a music director might write a memo on his/her liturgical planning sheet, indicating that next Sunday's Opening Song will be played in the key of *e*. The "e" indicates the key of *e* minor. Minor keys and minor scales can also be identified using uppercase letters, but the word "minor" must follow the letter name. In other words, the key of *e* is the same as the key of E minor. Whenever the name of the minor key is used as part of a title of a work, it must be written with a capital letter followed by the word "minor" (e.g., *Suite in A Minor*).

Chromatic Scale

Before leaving this discussion on scales, it is necessary to examine one more—the **chromatic scale**. The chromatic scale is made up entirely of half-step intervals; thus, all notes are equidistant from each other.

EXAMPLE 20: CHROMATIC SCALE (3 OCTAVES)

All scales—major, minor, and chromatic—should be committed to memory. They are among the basic building blocks for all musicians.

Chords
harmonious relationship
embodiment of the texture
accord

A basic **chord** is made up of three specific notes, sometimes referred to as a **triad**. On keyboard instruments, all three notes can be played simultaneously. Since this is not possible on wind instruments such as the flute, the pattern is often referred to as a broken chord (or **arpeggio**); in this case, the notes of the triad are played one after the other. For the purposes of this discussion, we will use the terms "chord" and "triad" interchangeably.

There are four different types of triads: **major**, **minor**, **diminished**, and **augmented**.

Major and Minor Triads

The major triad consists of the first, third, and fifth degrees of the major scale (see Example 21).

EXAMPLE 21: MAJOR TRIAD

Minor chords are formed by using the first, third, and fifth notes of the minor scale (see Example 22).

EXAMPLE 22: MINOR TRIAD

Notice that there is only one note that is different between the C major chord and the C minor chord. The third scale degree is an E♮ in the C major chord but an E♭ in the C minor chord.

These triads can also be thought of in terms of their component intervals. Major triads consist of a major third (an interval of four half steps) between the lower two notes and a minor third (an interval of three half steps) between the upper two notes. Minor triads consist of a minor third and then a major third.

EXAMPLE 23: COMPARISON OF MAJOR TRIAD TO MINOR TRIAD

The symbol for the major chord is an uppercase "M," whereas minor chords are identified by a lowercase "m." For example, a C major chord can be labeled "CM," which is typically shortened to simply C. The second chord, the C minor chord, is identified "Cm." This information is very useful when improvising flute parts from a guitar score. (See Chapter 4 for more on playing from a guitar score.)

EXERCISE

Quiz yourself on your ability to identify the triads in this exercise. Write the name of each chord on the line beneath the chord.

EXAMPLE 24: TRIADS

_____   _____   _____   _____   _____

Answers: G major (or G) – C minor (or Cm) – F minor (or Fm) – A♭ major (or A♭) – D minor (or Dm)

 **Track 15: Listening Exercise for Major and Minor Chords**
Various chords – piano alone
(Specific chord names can be found in the Listing of CD Tracks at the back of this book.)

Now listen to the sounds of these chords on the CD (Track 15) without looking at the chords or their answers in this book. See if you can identify each of the chords as being either major or minor by their sound alone. This is an effective way to develop your aural skills. Check your answers by looking at the names of the chords shown above. It is not important to be able to identify by ear the letter name of the chord but simply to discern whether the chord is major or minor.

Look at Chord Exercise I below. The chords are written in four-part harmony, the same style used in many keyboard accompaniments. Notice that this style utilizes both treble and bass clef. (Refer to Chapter 4 for more on reading bass clef pitches.) Even though there are four notes in each chord, one pitch is repeated, thus making them three-note chords (triads).

CHORD EXERCISE I

Listen to the CD (Track 16). Use your ear to determine whether each of the following chords is major or minor. Write your answer on the line on the left-hand side under each chord.

EXAMPLE 25

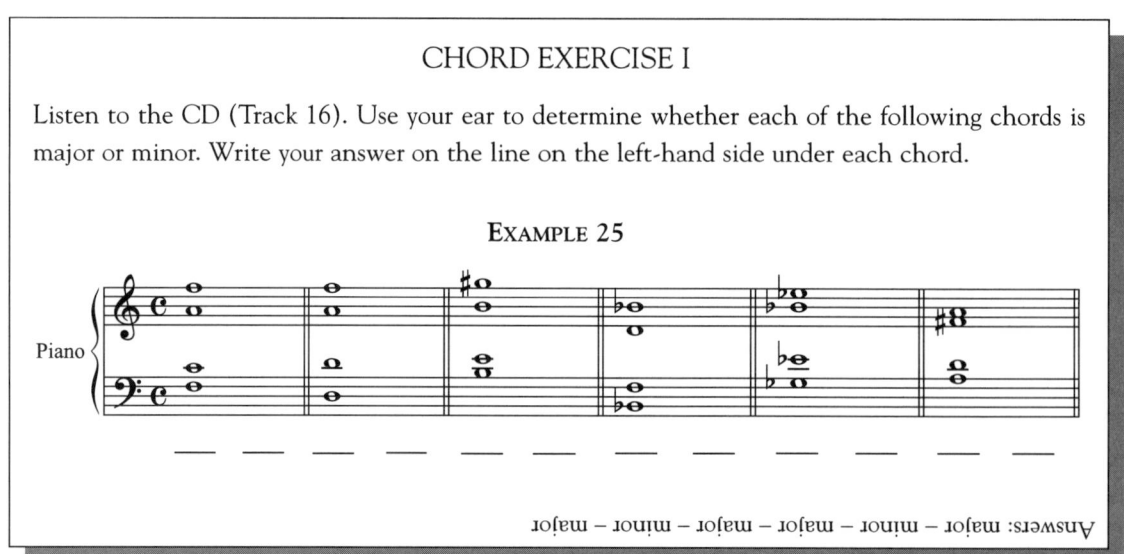

Answers: major – minor – major – major – minor – major

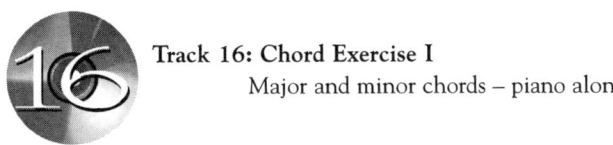

Track 16: Chord Exercise I
Major and minor chords – piano alone

Now let's do a visual study of these chords to figure out the name of each chord. First determine which note is the **root**, or the first degree of the chord. If you have chosen the correct note, the other two notes will line up as follows: If the root is on a space, the other two notes will be one space and two spaces higher, respectively. If the root is on a line, the other two notes will be one line and two lines higher, respectively.

Look at the first chord in Chord Exercise I. The lowest note is F. Going up from there, the next pitch is C, the next is A, and the highest note is F. It is obvious that F is the pitch that is doubled in this chord. By trial and error, determine which of the three notes—F, C, or A—is the root of the chord. To do this, write an F on the treble clef in the empty space to the right of this chord (as shown in Example 26).

EXAMPLE 26

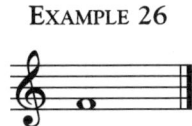

Next place the C and finally the A above the F (as shown in Example 27).

EXAMPLE 27

The three notes of the chord are now lined up on three successive spaces of the treble clef. Therefore, the chord is now in **root position**, meaning the root of the chord is the lowest note. By labeling the root of the chord as "F," you now know that this is some type of F chord. Now think of the key signature for F major (which is B♭). The three notes of the chord in question—F, A, C—are indeed the first, third, and fifth degrees of the F major scale. Therefore, this is an F major chord. Write this answer on the line on the right-hand side under this chord in Chord Exercise I (Example 25).

Let's try a similar analysis on the second chord. The lowest note of the chord is D, the next pitch is also D, the next is A, and the highest is F. The three notes of this chord are D, A, and F, with the D being doubled. Next, determine which note is the root of the chord. Use the empty space to the right of the chord in Chord Exercise I for your work. First, write a D on the staff. Then place the other two notes on the **staff** as close to the D as possible. If you have chosen to put your notes on the treble clef, they should look like one of the following chords (see Example 28).

EXAMPLE 28

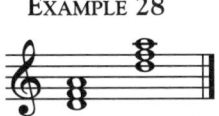

35

It doesn't matter which octave you have chosen. The result is the same. In each case, the notes are lining up on successive spaces or successive lines of the staff. This means the chord is in root position. Thus, you know that D is the root of the chord, so this is some type of D chord. Again, think of the key signature for the key of D (which is F♯ and C♯). The notes of the chord in question do not quite match the notes of the D major scale: the third degree in the D scale is F♯, while the third degree in this chord is F♮. You already know the third degree of the minor chord is one half step lower than the third degree of the major chord. Therefore, you can now determine that this is a D minor chord.

You can also analyze this same chord in the following way: Think of the key signature for a D minor scale (B♭). The notes of this chord are indeed the first, third, and fifth degrees of the D minor scale; hence, it is a D minor chord.

Yet another method identifies the chord by intervals. Count the number of half steps between the lower two notes of the chord. To do this, visualize a piano keyboard.

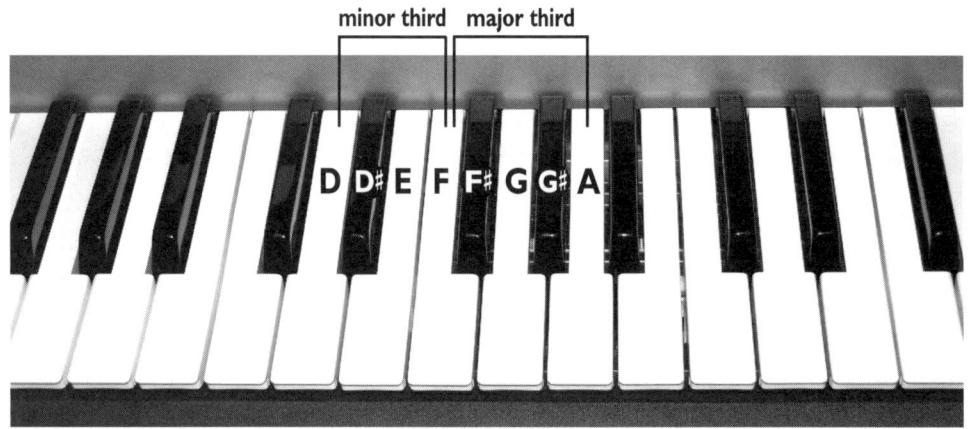

Going up from D, you first arrive at D♯, then E, and finally F. There are three half steps between D and F, the interval of a minor third. Next count the half steps between the upper two notes. Starting with F, the next half step is F♯, then G, then G♯, and finally A. So the upper interval is a major third (four half steps). As previously stated, these are the intervals that comprise a minor chord. All of these methods lead to the same answer: a D minor chord. Write this answer on the right-hand line under this chord (in Example 25).

Note: You could also determine the intervals by playing the notes of a chromatic scale on your flute, using the same directions as given in the keyboard example above. Choose whatever method works for you.

Let's now analyze the third chord in Chord Exercise I. This time the notes are B, E, and G♯, with the B being doubled. Place these notes on the staff until they line up space, space, space or line, line, line. With the B on the bottom, the notes look like this.

EXAMPLE 29

In this configuration, the B is on a line, but the other two notes are on spaces. Therefore, the B cannot be the root of the chord.

Next, try E on the bottom. The chord should look like this.

EXAMPLE 30

Now the notes occur on successive lines of the staff, so you know that the chord is in root position, with E being the chord's root. Therefore, this is some type of E chord. Again, think of the key signature for E major (four sharps). The three notes of this chord are indeed the first, third, and fifth degrees of the E major scale. Hence, this is an E major chord. Write this answer on the right-hand line under this chord.

Using the same methods, identify the remaining three chords in Chord Exercise I. Use the blank space to the right of each chord for your work. If you need more room, use the blank manuscript paper at the back of this book. Write your answers on the right-hand line under each chord. The answers for both parts of this exercise appear in Example 31; complete the exercise for yourself before looking at the answers. The first answer is for the ear training portion (CD Track 16, Example 25), while the second answer is for the visual study of the same chords. You will also see each chord written in root position on the treble clef to the right of the chord.

CHORD EXERCISE I
(with answers)
EXAMPLE 31

Of the four-note chords in Chord Exercise I, the first, second, and fourth are written in root position. (The root of the chord is the lowest note.) The fifth example is in *first inversion* because the third degree of the chord is the lowest note. The third and sixth examples are both *second inversion* chords because the fifth degree of both chords is the lowest note.

In Chord Exercise II, the notes of the chords are spelled out one after the other. These are broken chords, otherwise knows as arpeggios. Study and then play this exercise.

Now take another look at this example. Analyze and identify each of the chords before looking at the answers in Example 33. You can use the blank manuscript paper at the back of this book for your work.

Hint: There is only one chord per measure.

Diminished Triads

Diminished triads are similar to minor triads, except the fifth degree is lowered one half step. The diminished chord consists of a minor third (three half steps between its two lower notes) and another minor third (three half steps between its two upper notes). The symbol for the diminished chord is "dim" or "°."

EXAMPLE 34: C DIMINISHED CHORD

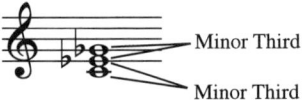

Notice that the fifth scale degree has now been lowered to G♭.

38

Augmented Triads

Augmented triads are similar to major triads, except the fifth degree is raised one half step. The augmented chord consists of a major third (four half steps between its two lower notes) and another major third (four more half steps between its two upper notes). Augmented chords are identified by "aug" or "+."

EXAMPLE 35: C AUGMENTED CHORD

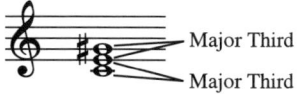

Listen to the sound of diminished and augmented chords on the CD (Track 17). Each is played first as a block chord, with all three notes sounding simultaneously. Then the same chord is repeated as a broken chord, sounding one note after the other. Aim to get the sound of these chords in your ear. The first three chords are diminished; the last three are augmented (see Example 36).

EXAMPLE 36

DIMINISHED CHORDS   AUGMENTED CHORDS

 **Track 17: Chord Exercise II**
Diminished and augmented chords in block and broken forms – piano alone

Now let's combine all four types of triads: major, minor, diminished, and augmented.

Chord Exercise III contains various chords written in four-part harmony. Listen to them on the CD (Track 18). Identify each chord by ear as either major, minor, diminished, or augmented. Write your answers on the line on the left-hand side under each chord.

CHORD EXERCISE III
EXAMPLE 37

 **Track 18: Chord Exercise III**
Four-part harmony of major, minor, diminished, and augmented chords – piano alone

Spend some time doing a visual study of these chords to determine their letter name and to confirm the type of chord. You may use the blank space to the right of each chord or the blank manuscript paper at the back of this book for your work. Using the same techniques that were discussed previously in this section, find the root of the chord. Then write the chord in root position. Finally determine whether each chord is major, minor, diminished, or augmented. Your answers from the ear training portion of this exercise should match the responses from your visual study of these chords. The correct answers are shown below.

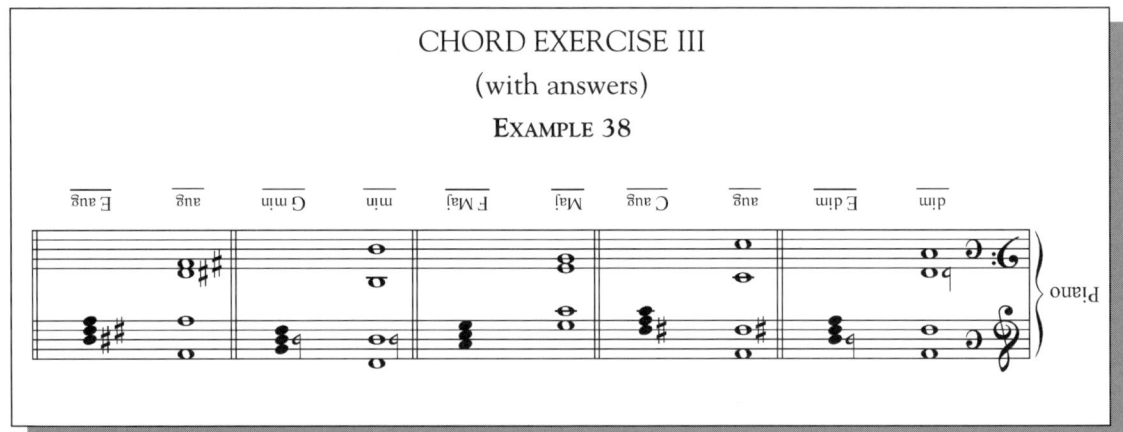

Now study Chord Exercise IV.

Track 19: Chord Exercise IV
Broken chords – flute alone

These are broken chords, since only one note is sounded at a time. Play through this exercise several times on your flute until you have developed a comfort level with these chords. Then close your eyes and listen to this progression on the CD (Track 19). Use your ear to identify each chord as either major, minor, diminished, or augmented. Write your answers on the line beneath the music. (There is no need to write a letter name for the aural portion of this exercise.) The answers can be found in Example 40.

Beware: Some measures may have more than one chord.

Next visually identify each chord and write its letter name and type of chord above the notes in Chord Exercise IV. The type of chord should match in both sets of answers. If you need extra room for your work, use the blank manuscript paper at the back of this book. (Answers are shown in Example 40.)

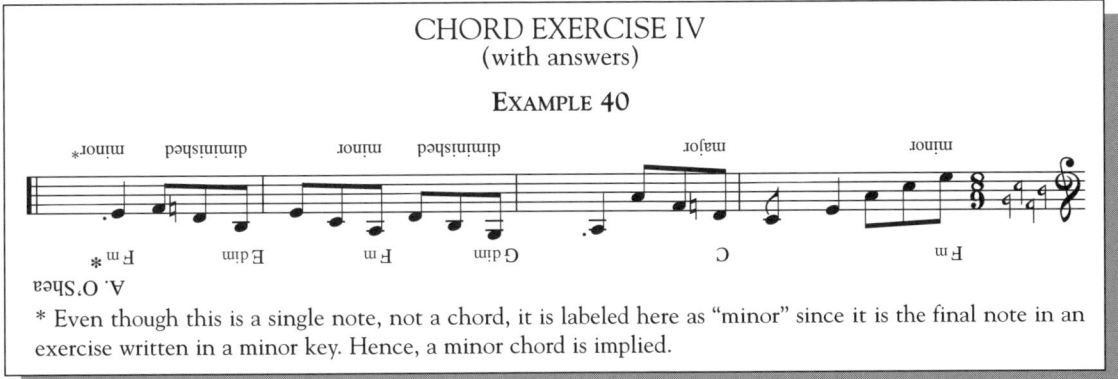

CHORD EXERCISE IV
(with answers)

EXAMPLE 40

* Even though this is a single note, not a chord, it is labeled here as "minor" since it is the final note in an exercise written in a minor key. Hence, a minor chord is implied.

By now it should be obvious to you that a thorough knowledge of chords is essential for all musicians. You have already committed your scales to memory. You should also memorize the following chord exercises. As you play through them, associate the sound of each chord with its type: major, minor, diminished, or augmented.

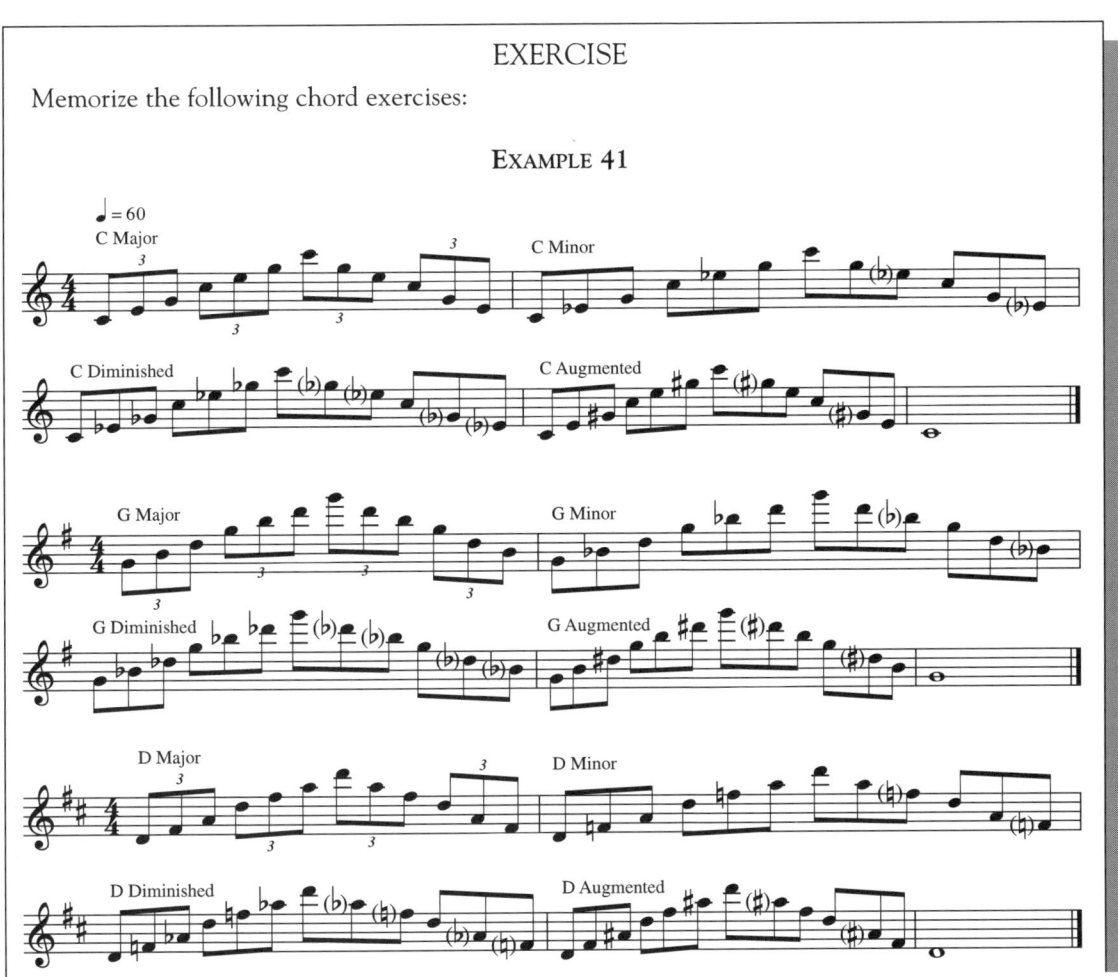

EXERCISE

Memorize the following chord exercises:

EXAMPLE 41

Vibrato
conveys expression
identifies the unique character of each flutist's sound
provides the means to effect a better blend with other instruments

Vibrato gives life to the sound. Simply put, vibrato is the pulsation that occurs in the airstream. These pulsations happen as a result of the controlled movement of the diaphragm. The following exercise will assist you in developing a good vibrato.

EXERCISE

You will not need your flute for the first portions of this exercise.

1. Visualize a lighted candle affixed to the top of your music stand. Try to repeatedly blow out the imaginary candle while standing (or sitting) at your usual distance from the music stand. The flame keeps flickering, but it won't go out.

2. Now try the same exercise again, still without your flute in hand. Form your flute embouchure and then "blow out the candle." With the metronome set at quarter = 60, first practice 1 pulse per beat, then 2, then 3, and finally 4.

3. After you are comfortable doing this exercise without your flute, then repeat Step 2 with your flute while playing a two-octave F major scale, holding each note for 4 beats. (If necessary, refer back to the F major scale in the "Scales" section earlier in this chapter.) With the metronome set at quarter = 60, play the scale with each 4-beat note receiving 1 pulse per beat. Repeat the scale with 2 pulses per beat, then 3, and finally 4.

Track 20: Vibrato Exercise on F Scale
  Metronome set at quarter = 60; first four notes of scale played in following patterns:
  1 vibrato pulse per beat, then 2, then 3, and then 4; flute alone

Now listen to the first four notes of this scale played on the CD (Track 20).

Even the most beautiful vibrato can sound monotonous if played at the same speed and in the same manner for each and every piece of music. The ability to control vibrato provides one essential ingredient for conveying various emotions with the flute. Does the piece, or the occasion, or the place during the liturgy call for a lot of vibrato, no vibrato, or something in between? The sensitive flutist must be able to vary the speed and amount of vibrato at will.

EXERCISE

Practice vibrato using the tune "I Know That My Redeemer Lives" (see Example 42).

1. Set the metronome at quarter = 120. Use 1 vibrato pulse per count at first. Listen to the first phrase as demonstrated on the CD (Track 21).

2. Now play the same piece again, still keeping the metronome set at quarter = 120, this time with 2 pulses per beat. Listen to the first phrase on the CD (Track 22).

3. Play the same piece again, this time using 3 pulses per beat, with the metronome at quarter = 104. Listen to this version of the first phrase on the CD (Track 23).

4. Reset the metronome to quarter = 88 and repeat the exercise using 4 pulses per beat. Listen to the first phrase on the CD (Track 24).

5. Next play with no vibrato at all. Listen to this same phrase on the CD (Track 25).

6. Now play the entire piece once more with the CD, varying the vibrato as one would do for a Sunday liturgy. To simulate Sunday liturgy, accompaniment has been added for the entire verse on the CD (Track 26). Listen carefully to the flute part. The changes in vibrato speed are subtle.

7. Finally, go back and play the piece again, this time without the sound of another flute against your own sound. Use the accompaniment track on the CD (Track 27) so you are now the soloist.

EXAMPLE 42: EXCERPT FROM "I KNOW THAT MY REDEEMER LIVES"

DUKE STREET
J. Hatton

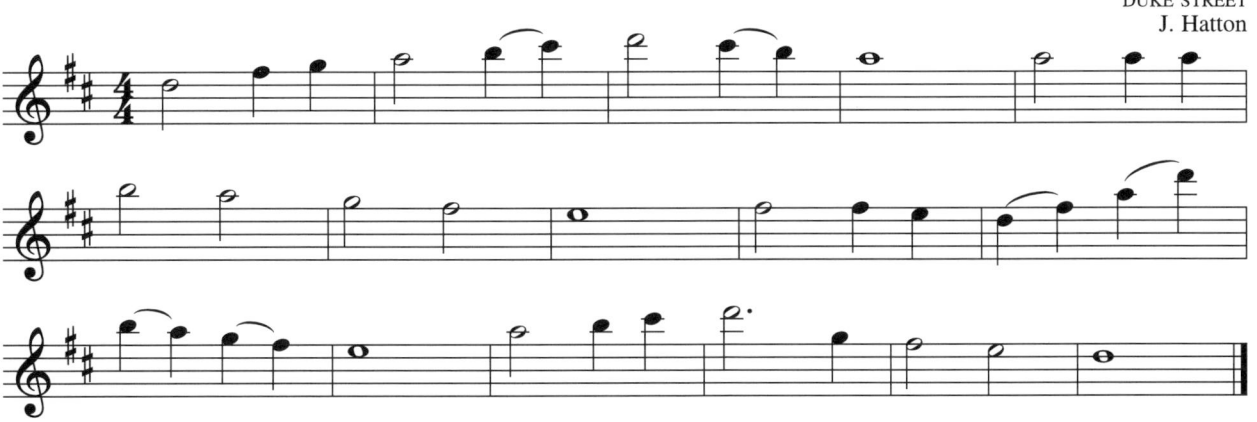

Track 21: Vibrato Exercise I on a Tune
"I Know That My Redeemer Lives" – metronome set at quarter = 120; first phrase; 1 vibrato pulse per beat; flute alone

Track 22: Vibrato Exercise II on a Tune
"I Know That My Redeemer Lives" – metronome set at quarter = 120; first phrase; 2 vibrato pulses per beat; flute alone

Track 23: Vibrato Exercise III on a Tune
"I Know That My Redeemer Lives" – metronome set at quarter = 104; first phrase; 3 vibrato pulses per beat; flute alone

Track 24: Vibrato Exercise IV on a Tune
"I Know That My Redeemer Lives" – metronome set at quarter = 88; first phrase; 4 vibrato pulses per beat; flute alone

Track 25: Exercise Using No Vibrato
"I Know That My Redeemer Lives" – first phrase; no vibrato; flute alone

Track 26: Varying Vibrato Speeds
"I Know That My Redeemer Lives" – piano introduction and one verse; flute and piano

Track 27: Focus on Vibrato with Accompaniment Only
"I Know That My Redeemer Lives" – piano introduction and one verse; piano only

It takes many months of practice to develop vibrato to the point where it becomes an automatic part of your playing, and many more months to become comfortable varying your vibrato speed. Take your time with these steps. It will be worth your perseverance in the long run.

Tone
voice of the flute
means for expressing color and beauty
conveyor of pitch control

Your tone is as individualistic as your voice. Just as your friends can identify you on the telephone by the sound of your voice even though they can't see you, each and every flutist can be identified by the sound of his/her tone.

By now it should go without saying that posture and breath support greatly affect tone quality. Tone quality, in turn, affects vibrato and intonation. Everything is intertwined.

The color of your flute tone can be varied according to the needs of the occasion. To create a dark, warm tone quality, aim your airstream downward just a bit, thus covering more tonehole. Increase the size of the opening between your lips—your *aperture*—by relaxing the muscles around the corners of your mouth. Also open your throat, imagining that you are yawning. Increase the intensity of your vibrato by widening the breadth of the pulses.

EXAMPLE OF LARGER APERTURE, DOWNWARD AIRSTREAM, RELAXED CHEEK AND
MOUTH MUSCLES, AND COVERING MORE TONEHOLE TO PRODUCE A DARKER SOUND

The opposite approach is used for creating a lighter, more delicate sound. Make your vibrato pulses more shallow and aim your airstream upwards, thus covering less tonehole. Also decrease the size of your aperture and firm the muscles around the corners of your mouth, creating a more focused and faster airstream. (See Chapter 8 for more on tone color.)

EXAMPLE OF SMALLER APERTURE, UPWARD AIRSTREAM, FIRM CHEEK AND
MOUTH MUSCLES, AND COVERING LESS TONEHOLE TO PRODUCE A LIGHTER SOUND

Although the differences in these two photos are subtle, they provide visual examples of the ways that changes in the aperture can affect tone quality. Even when applying these techniques, you will need to listen and make adjustments to maintain good intonation on individual notes. (Refer to the "Intonation" section earlier in this chapter.) Because of the uniqueness of each flute and the individuality of each flute player, these adjustments will be different for everyone.

Reminder: A tuner is a helpful companion for maintaining good intonation while you develop and shape your tone.

Practice tone quality by playing scales in long tones. Experiment with different dynamic levels, vibrato speeds, and tone colors, always maintaining control of pitch.

EXERCISE

Set your metronome to quarter = 72. Play a two-octave G major scale in whole notes. (If necessary, refer back to the G major scale in the "Scales" section earlier in this chapter.) Vary the tone color, vibrato speed, and dynamic level.

Track 28: Scale Exercise for Tone Color, Vibrato Speed, and Dynamic Level
G scale – metronome set at quarter = 72; one octave (ascending only); flute alone

Listen to one octave of this exercise on the CD (Track 28) for ideas. Now try these techniques on a piece of music from the solo flute repertoire.

EXERCISE

Practice tone quality techniques while playing the following excerpt from Bach's "Sinfonia" from *Cantata No.156.* Vary tone color, vibrato speed, and dynamics to create a pleasing result. Listen to the CD (Track 29) for the subtle changes in tone color demonstrated there.

EXAMPLE 43: EXCERPT FROM "SINFONIA" FROM
ICH STEH MIT EINEM FUß IM GRABE (CANTATA NO. 156)

Track 29: Solo Exercise for Tone Color, Vibrato Speed, and Dynamic Level
"Sinfonia" from *Cantata No. 156* by J. S. Bach – mm. 1–13, flute alone

Warm-ups at a Glance

Whatever time you put into upgrading your skills during practice at home, you should do at least a minimum amount of warming up before playing at any liturgy. The following outline should become routine:

- Physical warm-ups
- Musical warm-ups
- Tuning
- Quiet reflection

Physical Warm-ups

Physical warm-ups involve movements that loosen and stretch your muscles, preparing them for the task at hand. It is good to start with exercises for the larger muscle groups, moving gradually to the smaller, more delicate muscles, which are of vital importance to the flutist.

1. Begin with shoulder circles, both forward and backward.
2. Lean your head to one side, holding that stretch for several seconds. Then go to the other side.
3. Next give your arms and hands a gentle shake, stimulating blood flow all the way to your fingertips.
4. Open and close your fists to warm up the small muscles in your hands and fingers.
5. Massage your facial muscles, beginning with your cheek and jaw, and then moving to the muscles around your mouth.

This list is certainly not exhaustive, but it will give you an idea of various ways to prepare your body for the task it is about to undertake. These exercises can be done in the privacy of your own home before any practice session, rehearsal, liturgy, concert, etc.

Musical Warm-ups

On those days when you will be serving as a music minister for liturgy, be sure to arrive at church early enough to play some musical warm-up exercises. Below are several simple examples that will only take about five minutes (see Example 44). (It is rare that circumstances would not allow an instrumentalist to take this small amount of time to prepare to play, but if it does, you can play these exercises at home before going to church.)

EXAMPLE 44: WARM-UP EXERCISES

As you go through these exercises:

- Listen carefully for good tone quality and intonation. As needed, make adjustments in pitch.
- Pay attention to your breathing, making sure it is deep and even.
- Play a smooth, legato line. The octave exercise is especially helpful in addressing the problem of breaks in the flow of sound. This is a fairly common problem on certain pitches. Make adjustments in the placement of the flute on your lips to correct any break in the sound.
- Adapt the octave exercise to play different intervals—thirds, fourths, fifths, sixths, etc.

Perhaps you have other simple warm-ups that you prefer to use. If so, use these as an occasional substitute for the sake of variety.

Tuning

Now that you have done exercises to warm up your body and your instrument, you are ready to tune your flute to the piano, organ, guitar, and/or other instruments of your ensemble, as the case may be.

Quiet Reflection

With all of the energy you expend doing "warm-ups" for your body and your instrument, you would be remiss if you did not also attend to your spirit. We are so much more than our body or our musical gifts. So just as we pay attention to nourishing the body and just as we know we must play our instrument regularly to nurture our musical gift, a belief that our deepest self is spirit calls us to nourish that "spirit" as well. Here are some suggestions:

- One way to do this, of course, is by fully entering into prayer at any of the worship services for which we play.
- Another way is simply by living life in a spirit of gratitude and thanksgiving, continually being open to life's many blessings even with its many difficulties.
- There are spiritual exercises, too, such as meditation or centering prayer. Some musicians make it a practice to attend **Taizé Prayer** once a month as a way of feeding their souls, so to speak.
- Another "spiritual warm-up" might be reading the Scriptures ahead of time for the Sunday Eucharist at which you will play and then reflecting on those readings in connection with your own life situation.
- Reading a bit of poetry or any inspirational text is another form of spiritual warm-up.
- One simple and very helpful exercise is to allow time for even just 5 minutes of quiet before going to play. Try to let go of everything—any thoughts about the past or the future—and just empty yourself in readiness to give and receive in the present. At the end of the quiet time, use your imagination to think of all those to whom you will minister at the worship service and who will minister to you, and then give thanks for their presence in your life. Stay in this mindfulness of community, of our interdependence with one another and all of creation.

Conclusion

This chapter has covered the foundational skills of flute playing in whatever context the musician chooses. However, since the focus of this resource is THE LITURGICAL FLUTIST, these basic principles represent the flutist's preparation for the ministry of prayer at community worship.

The next chapter will explore the various rites of Sunday Eucharist so your music-making can be better integrated into this particular prayer setting.

Chapter 2
The Sunday Eucharist: An Overview

Source and Summit of Christian Life
Word and Table
Prayer of the Assembly

Prayer is communication with God. It is relational. The Scriptures tell us to pray always and without ceasing—in other words, to be always in "communion" with God, whose desire is to pour out abundant love for us. Much as with human love relationships, the more we are "in relation" with God, the more we are able to receive this love. It is important, then, to pray/communicate with all the variety of our human potential: in spoken and sung word, in action and deed, in silence and contemplation, in all and everything, and in every way. It is just as vital to listen for God's communication to us with open heart, mind, and soul. The Sunday Eucharist is at the core of the identity of Catholic-Christians. It is an opportunity both publicly and collectively as community to communicate with God and listen for God's communication with us.

Yet we communicate best when we "know the language," its rhythms and cadences. What a difference in communication, for instance, between those who have immersed themselves in a culture and learned its language from "the inside out" and those who have studied a language for one year in the more sterile environment of a classroom!

The same is true for pastoral flutists. One way to pray at the Eucharist is to play your instrument. We communicate/pray best when we have an "inside-out" understanding of the flow and contour of the Eucharist, its different parts, and their relationship to the whole. Whether or not you are already familiar with the Mass, there is always the potential for an ever-deepening integration of its prayer form—hence, the reason for this chapter of the book, which includes the flow of the Mass as well as consideration of the liturgical seasons and liturgical year. The invitation is to respond to this overview from a heart place as well as a head place.

We are what we repeatedly do. Excellence, then, is not an act, but a habit.

—**Aristotle, 4th c. BCE**

THE ORDER OF MASS

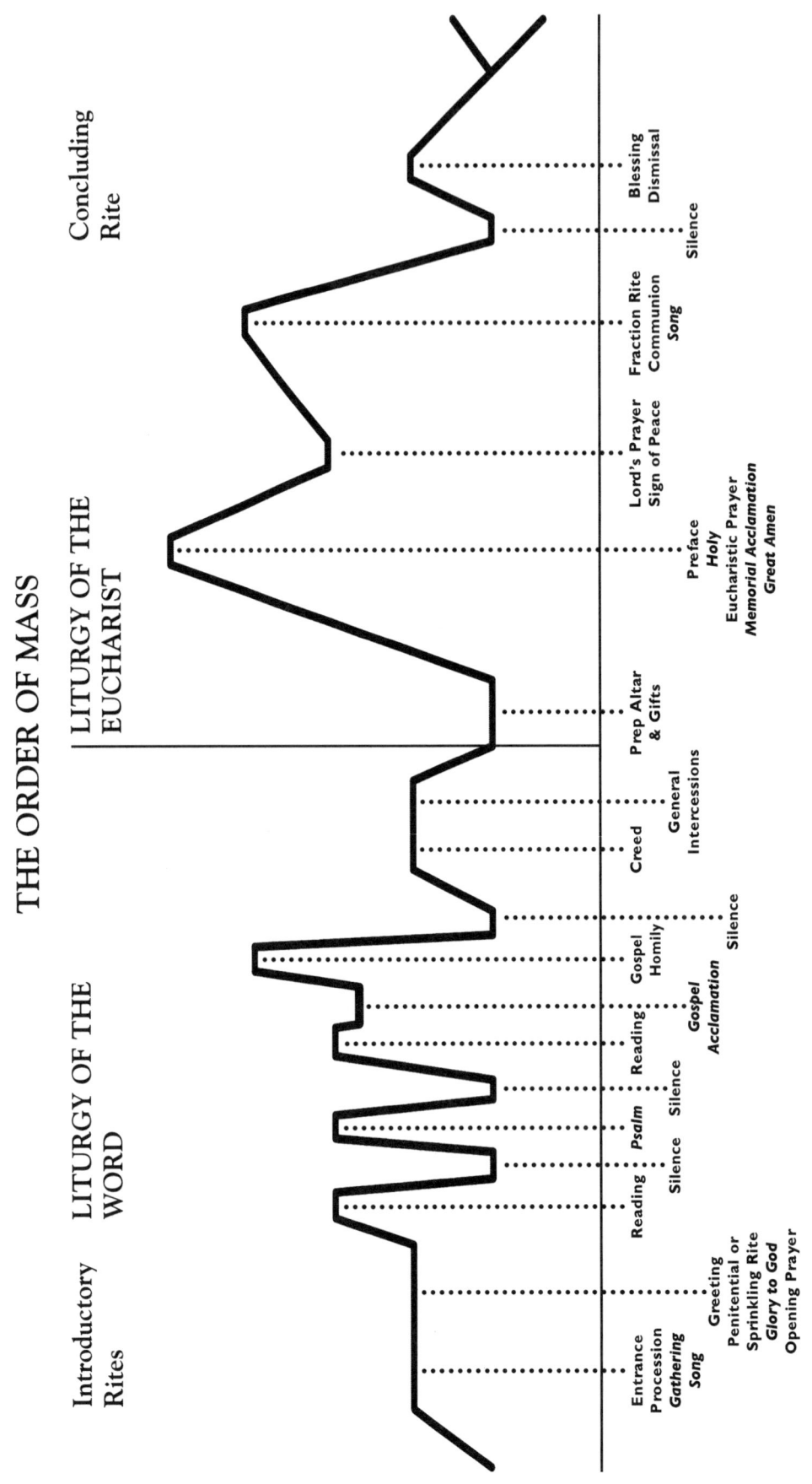

Introductory Rites

LITURGY OF THE WORD

LITURGY OF THE EUCHARIST

Concluding Rite

Entrance
Procession
Gathering Song
Greeting
Penitential or Sprinkling Rite
Glory to God
Opening Prayer

Reading
Silence
Psalm
Silence
Reading
Gospel Acclamation
Gospel
Homily
Silence

Creed
General Intercessions

Prep Altar & Gifts
Preface
Holy
Eucharistic Prayer
Memorial Acclamation
Great Amen
Lord's Prayer
Sign of Peace
Fraction Rite
Communion *Song*
Silence
Blessing
Dismissal

italics = assembly song

Prepared by Vivian E. Williams

Flow of the Mass

In looking at the Order of Mass on the previous page, note the high and low points. Also note the times of silence and how they help to prepare you for what comes next or allow you to "be with" what has just taken place.

Basically, the Mass is divided into two main sections:

- Liturgy of the Word
- Liturgy of the Eucharist

The introductory rites are intended to gather us and ready us to receive the Word of God in the Old and New Testaments; they should not overshadow the Word. The silence between the readings is vital; it gives us a few moments to take in what we have just heard proclaimed in word or song. The general intercessions end the Liturgy of the Word. Having heard the Word of God, we are moved to pray for the needs of the church, the world, our community, the sick, and the dying.

As the introductory rites open us to better receive God's Word, so the Liturgy of the Word draws us to the table. The preparation of the altar and preparation of our community gifts transition us from the table of the Word to the table of the Eucharist. The Eucharistic Prayer is the community's prayer, prayed in our name by the priest-presider and punctuated with sung acclamations by the assembly. It is the core of the Mass—its very heart. It is a prayer of praise and blessing, thanksgiving and remembering. It carries us into our community meal, our communion. Our "Amen" to the body and blood of Christ means we choose to become as Christ in the world. The concluding rites dismiss and bless us to go forth and be life for the world until we return to be nourished once again at the community worship of the Mass. Stated most simply…

> we gather;
> we listen to God's Word;
> we pray for ourselves and others;
> we praise, bless, give thanks, and remember;
> we eat and drink Christ's body and blood;
> we go forth.

Keep in mind that each Sunday Eucharist is prayed in the context of a liturgical season, which is part of an entire liturgical year. Just as Sunday Eucharist connects us to the broader Church—the Body of Christ—so, too, does the liturgical year. The particular time in the liturgical year affects not only

During the course of the year, the different mysteries of redemption are celebrated at Mass so that in some way they are made present. Each feast and season has its own spirit and its own music.

—Music in Catholic Worship, #19

the dynamics of the worship celebration but also the musical selections. For example, community prayer is different during the Lenten season (with an emphasis on penitence) than during the Easter season (when we celebrate the Resurrection of Christ). Therefore, it would not be appropriate to use "Jesus Christ Is Risen Today" during Lent or "Again We Keep This Solemn Fast" during the Easter season.

Flow of the Liturgical Year

In looking at a general overview of the liturgical year, we see God's presence in all the cycles of our lives:

- The four weeks of Advent remind us that we are a "waiting" people.
- The Christmas/Epiphany season, which lasts through the Baptism of the Lord, focuses us on how Christ is continually born anew in our lives.
- During the forty days of Lent, we revitalize ourselves (through prayer, fasting, and almsgiving) as people of God and prepare ourselves to welcome new members into the community at the Easter Vigil.

Within the cycle of a year, moreover, the Church unfolds the whole mystery of Christ, from his incarnation and birth until his ascension, the day of Pentecost, and the expectation of blessed hope and of the Lord's return. Recalling thus the mysteries of redemption, the Church opens to the faithful the riches of the Lord's powers and merits so that these are in some way made present in every age, in order that the faithful may lay hold on them and be filled with saving grace.

—Constitution on the Sacred Liturgy, #102

- The three days of the Triduum (Holy Thursday, Good Friday, and Holy Saturday) followed by the Easter Vigil unfold the Paschal Mystery for us. Christ has died. Christ is risen. Christ will come again.
- The great celebration of the fifty days between Easter Sunday and Pentecost impresses upon us the mysteries of the Resurrection.
- The weeks of Ordinary Time (which vary in number depending on the particular year's church calendar) remind us of how the "ordered" day in and day out of our lives is holy.

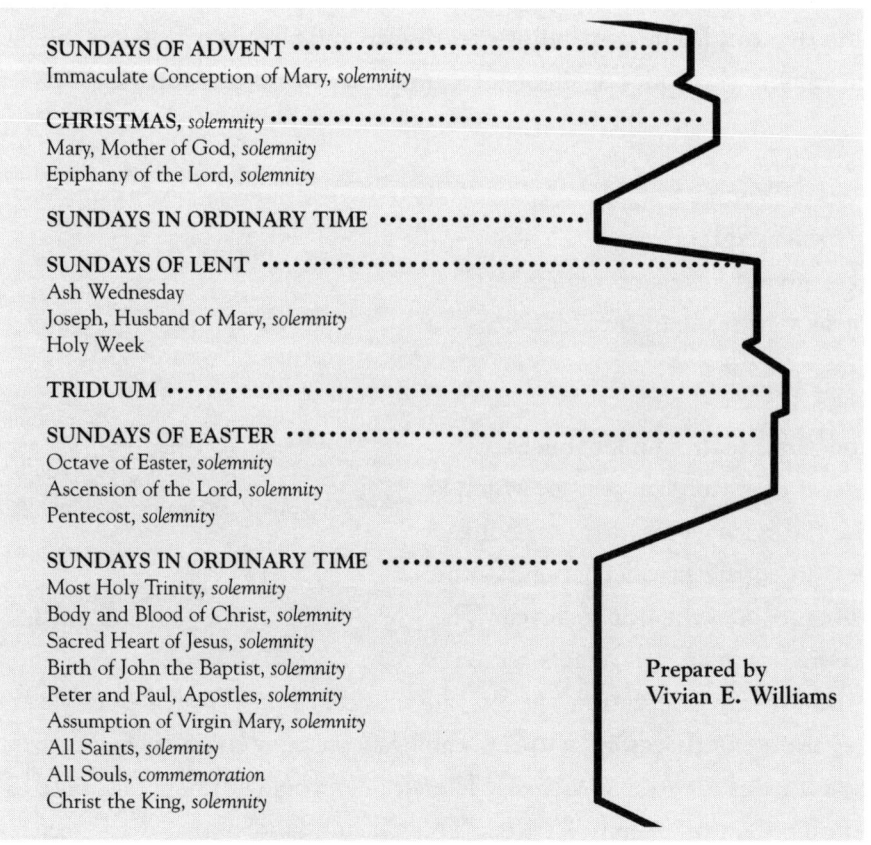

SUNDAYS OF ADVENT ·····················
Immaculate Conception of Mary, *solemnity*

CHRISTMAS, *solemnity* ···························
Mary, Mother of God, *solemnity*
Epiphany of the Lord, *solemnity*

SUNDAYS IN ORDINARY TIME ·················

SUNDAYS OF LENT ·····················
Ash Wednesday
Joseph, Husband of Mary, *solemnity*
Holy Week

TRIDUUM ································

SUNDAYS OF EASTER ···················
Octave of Easter, *solemnity*
Ascension of the Lord, *solemnity*
Pentecost, *solemnity*

SUNDAYS IN ORDINARY TIME ·················
Most Holy Trinity, *solemnity*
Body and Blood of Christ, *solemnity*
Sacred Heart of Jesus, *solemnity*
Birth of John the Baptist, *solemnity*
Peter and Paul, Apostles, *solemnity*
Assumption of Virgin Mary, *solemnity*
All Saints, *solemnity*
All Souls, *commemoration*
Christ the King, *solemnity*

**Prepared by
Vivian E. Williams**

RHYTHMS OF THE LITURGICAL YEAR

As musicians, it is helpful to approach an understanding of the Eucharist from another perspective as well. The primary minister at Mass is the assembly. All who pray the Eucharist are a part of the assembly. Those who have a further role within the Mass—a liturgical ministry—are servants to the assembly. Since the responsibility of the assembly is to participate fully, consciously, and actively, your relationship to the assembly as a liturgical minister demands that you use your gifts and talents to foster and support this level of participation by the community, and also participate fully, consciously, and actively in the entire prayer. For example, the assembly is expected to sing the entrance song, the Glory to God, the Psalm scripture, the Gospel Acclamation, the Eucharistic Prayer responses, and the communion song. Depending on specific

A liturgical celebration can have no more solemn or pleasing feature than the whole assembly's expressing its faith and devotion in song.

—Sacred Music, #16

choices for a particular Eucharist, the assembly often also sings the Kyrie, the Lamb of God, and the song at the sprinkling rite or other litanies, as well as sometimes singing the general intercessory response, the song at the preparation of the altar, the Lord's Prayer, the communion meditation, and the recessional.

The instrumentalist at the Eucharist serves the assembly song, joins his/her instrumental sound with the sound of the assembly, and adds the prayer of his/her instrumental music to the assembly's sung prayer. Your primary consideration should be the assembly and how using your gifts at a liturgical service could help the community find its voice and further grow into that voice. You help the assembly, then, when you play in relationship to the flow of the liturgy, soaring majestically at the high points of the liturgy and playing more reflectively during more quiet and meditative moments. The way in which the Eucharist engages us in prayer is complex, and thus, your playing must respond to the rise and fall of its rhythms—the flow of the Mass.

Conclusion

Now that we have taken a more general look at the Sunday Eucharist and the liturgical year, we are ready to consider the specific musical elements of the Sunday Eucharist.

Chapter 3
The Musical Elements of the Sunday Eucharist

Musical Leadership and Teamwork
Supporting Prayer and Being Prayer
Versatility and Flexibility

For most liturgical flutists, the musical elements of the Sunday Eucharist are decided by the liturgical music director. On one hand, this can be a great relief, for it frees up the instrumentalist to focus more on playing the music than

> *Music, chosen with care, can serve as a bridge to faith as well as an expression of it.*
> —**Music in Catholic Worship**
> (Pastoral Planning for Celebration, par. 16)

selecting the music—one less thing to think about! On the other hand, it is an exercise in trust. When we put ourselves in the hands of another pastoral musician, we hope that individual will not only honor our gifts in the moment but also encourage continual improvement and growth, and that he/she will be a sign of art as prayer as well as a support to us in our own deepening prayer life within the music.

Understand that there will be times when you have to let go of your own way of doing things to best serve the moment: perhaps, for example, a tempo that is taken faster or slower than you would have chosen, or a particular part you would like to play that is given to another instrumentalist or is left out altogether. As liturgical musicians, we "die to ourselves" for the sake of the community's prayer and for the sake of unity. How important it is, then, that we trust the judgment and discernment of the director! However, there will also be times within an established relationship when the director will trust you to make decisions as to where and when to play, or perhaps even what to play when considering a reflective piece. All the more, it is important to understand the flow of the liturgy and how to make particular choices. As a result, both director and instrumentalist experience servanthood in the course of doing liturgical ministry. Besides trust, then, music ministry also fosters humility.

Let us be careful to seek the inner meaning of liturgical actions and strive to perceive, in signs accessible to people of flesh and blood, an invisible reality pertaining to the kingdom.
—**The Rule of Taizé**

In the years since **Vatican II**, the music composed for Catholic worship has diversified and multiplied immensely. Having so much music from which to choose is certainly an advantage, yet at times this can be overwhelming. Even if you are not making the musical choices, you should have an understanding of how those decisions are made.

The Musical Moments of the Mass

Music in Catholic Worship, one of the documents from Vatican II, sets forth guidelines for making liturgical music choices. According to *Music in Catholic Worship*, there are three judgments to consider regarding any musical element of ritual:

1. **Pastoral judgment** – a sensitivity to the needs of the particular assembly (for example, parish history, present cultural make-up, familiarity with the rites, the reason for gathering, etc.)
2. **Liturgical judgment** – knowledge of the text, ritual, and movement, as well as all other elements relating to the worship
3. **Musical judgment** – selecting music that has long-lasting value based on its quality—in other words, music that will stand the test of time—and is also accessible to the assembly

With musical judgment, you are servant to the art and to the assembly; with pastoral and liturgical judgments, you are servant to the community/assembly as well as the larger church community. Each must be kept in balance with the others. One way to keep this balance is to recognize the need for variety, not only in musical styles but also in musical forms, which include **chant, through-composed, call-and-response, acclamations, litanies,** and **hymnody,** to name some. While there are many different forms of music to use, there are certain forms that serve the liturgy better at some moments than others.

- In general, the sung Mass parts (i.e., the penitential rite, glory to God, gospel acclamation, Eucharistic prayer responses, Lamb of God) are best supported by music in acclamation, call-and-response, litany, or chant form so the assembly can learn them by heart or easily respond to the cantor and not be tied to a printed sheet.
- The Psalm refrain is almost always sung in response to the cantor.
- Hymnody or through-composed forms of music are best used during the processions—entrance, preparation of gifts, communion, sending forth—although even then a shorter **mantra** or simple refrain better frees the worshippers to move in procession, with less need to carry a hymnal or worship aid.

Note that, depending on cultural considerations, the period in which the melody was written, the text of the piece, or the music's position in the liturgy, the potential for versatility in interpretation exists even within each of these forms.

The flute lends itself very well to all of this. First, being one of the most ancient instruments, the flute has been used in every culture and within every musical period. Second, it blends well with voices and other instruments:

- Cantor and/or choir
- Accompaniment instruments – organ, piano, harpsichord, harp, guitar
- Other treble instruments – another flute, oboe, recorder, violin, soprano or alto saxophone, trumpet, clarinet
- Bass clef instruments – cello, string bass, bassoon

Third, it is portable; it can be carried easily. It is flexible and can adapt its playing style to be part of the Eucharist in just about every setting: church, small chapel, home, park, church or school hall, retreat center, etc. Depending on the space, and especially if played in the middle and upper *registers*, the flute can usually be heard well without any amplification.

The Flutist's Role within the Musical Prayer

While it is certainly possible for the flute to be a part of all of the musical moments of the liturgy, the question is whether it should be. The answer: Although there is a wide berth for variation depending on one's particular situation, it is neither necessary nor desirable to have the flute (or any other instrument) play all the time. The following synopsis gives an overview of a "typical" flute playing experience at a Sunday Eucharist. (Subsequent chapters of this book will discuss these issues in greater detail.)

Gathering Song

The gathering song is almost always sung. Often the flutist will join the keyboardist or guitarist in playing the hymn or song as an introduction. The flutist can support the assembly by playing the melody for the first verse of the hymn (or for the *refrain*, as the case may be); other harmonic lines can be used for the rest of the hymn, or perhaps the flutist will play only on the first and third verses, or the first, second, and

We are celebrating when we involve ourselves meaningfully in the thoughts, words, songs, and gestures of the worshiping community— when everything we do is wholehearted and authentic for us—when we mean the words and want to do what is done.
—**Music in Catholic Worship (par. 3)**

fourth. The flutist might play interludes or a coda. To the degree that it can be accomplished, you should join the assembly in singing whenever you are not playing. (Remember, your first ministry is that of being part of the assembly.) Whenever you do sing, take caution when there are microphones present so your voice is not heard above everyone else. Be sure to step away from any microphone when singing.

Glory to God

Most often the singing of the Glory to God is shared by the assembly, cantor, and/or choir. Many arrangements of the Glory to God have parts already written for flute. If not, the flutist could simply support the assembly by playing the melody of the refrain or perhaps a *descant* created from a harmony line.

Psalm

Often the flutist intones the refrain of the psalm, either alone or along with the piano, guitar, or organ. The flutist usually drops out as the cantor sings the refrain once, and then re-enters when the assembly repeats the refrain. There is often a part written for flute to add color to the sung verses and/or to subsequent refrains. If not, you might consider adding a harmony line. (Refer to Chapter 4 for basic information on playing without the benefit of a written flute part.)

Gospel Acclamation

Much the same approach applies here as with the psalm. However, if there is a trumpeter or oboist or violinist, then there is an opportunity for contrast: the flutist could play on the psalm and the other instrumentalist on the acclamation, or vice versa.

Other Music at the Eucharist

The other songs or hymns used at Mass (e.g., at the preparation of the gifts, at communion, or at the recessional) are approached much like the gathering song. The acclamations of the Eucharistic Prayer (Holy, Holy; Memorial Acclamation; Great Amen)—whichever arrangement is used—either have written parts for C instrument or can be referenced in the hymnal and played in unison with the assembly. In fact, when litanies like the Lamb of God, the Kyrie, or the intercessions are prayed in song, most often the flute doubles the assembly part, although sometimes there are written parts for C instrument.

Meditation Music

There are several times within the Sunday Eucharist when meditative music might be appropriate: prelude, homily reflection, preparation of the gifts, communion meditation, or postlude. Of course, it is not advisable to play during all of these moments in any one liturgy. Rather, vary the choices from week to week, or from season to season. While the music director usually makes the choices, you might occasionally inquire about playing a piece. Often this requires extra rehearsals with the accompanist so everyone is properly prepared for worship.

Music from the Baroque or Classical era is especially lovely for meditation. There is also a wealth of contemporary music well suited to these liturgical moments. (Refer to Appendix I for more information about music history and Appendix II for repertoire suggestions.)

> *Beauty is an effective—even sacramental—sign of God's presence and action in the world. The beautiful expresses the joy and delight which prefigure the glory of the liturgy of the heavenly Jerusalem.*
>
> —Snowbird Statement
> on Catholic Liturgical Music

Before moving on, there are a few more considerations in your formation as a liturgical musician. The very way you execute your music will help the assembly to learn its own role in the "ensemble." For example, the flutist often helps to give greater clarity to the melody line, which aids the assembly in taking ownership of the song or acclamation. Once the music is firmly rooted, the flutist can embellish with lovely descants and harmonizations, adding delightful contrasts to the assembly song. The flutist can join other instrumentalists in giving strong cues to the assembly in dynamics, tempos, and rhythms—all of which help to bring life and zest to the music.

Presence, good listening, focus, prayer—all are essential elements within the music ministry. Your music is a way of making God's presence felt. It melds the human and the divine.

As a music minister, you must be able to envision yourself as a prayer. It is important not only to join in the song of the assembly whenever possible but also to participate in all of the gestures and postures of the

> *Liturgical music must be like John the Baptist: always pointing to Christ, never calling attention to itself.*
> —Brother Roger of Taizé

assembly: standing, kneeling, bowing, greeting, extending peace, etc. Your actions communicate to others. As a minister, you must communicate where the focus is; you are a sign and reminder for the assembly that the focus is the entire prayer of the Eucharist. Nothing you do should be a distraction from this, such as talking to another musician, shuffling through music, moving from one spot to another, or having a detached, passive attitude when not playing. This takes planning—to have all music in order, to have all questions about introductions and endings and tempos asked ahead of time, to have tuned well, to have thought through at what points you will move into playing position. Of course, sometimes communication between musician and director during the Mass cannot be avoided; still, it should take place as discreetly as possible and only when absolutely necessary.

Note: One part of the Mass that requires special attention is Communion. Discuss in advance the procedure for the musicians to receive Communion.

It takes discipline and desire to enter into the prayer, to enter into the silent moments, to enter into the sacraments, to resist setting ourselves apart from the ritual action. As with the ongoing process of musical preparation, your spiritual preparation is a continual process as well. It is never finished. It is what makes you a liturgical musician rather than strictly a performing musician.

Conclusion

Having discussed a basic understanding of the flow of the Eucharist and having reflected on what it takes to be both musically and spiritually prepared for music ministry, we are ready to consider the basics of playing at the Sunday Eucharist.

Chapter 4
The Basics of Playing at the Sunday Eucharist

Ministry of Presence
Enabling of Prayer
Source of Melodic Creativity

As part of the process of growing and maturing, we allow our life experiences and our education to broaden for us the meaning of ideas, concepts, or even individual words. Such is the case with the idea of "discipline." For instance, when we were young, we may have focused on the word only as a set of consequences for something we did that was inappropriate. Now as musicians, there is the consideration of discipline from the standpoint of day-in and day-out musical practice, which can help us achieve the beautiful, graceful, and melodic line that is the nature of the flute. However, there is also the art of spiritual disciplines that, if nurtured, can help us deepen our prayer and communion with God.

While there are many more "layers" to our relationship with the word "discipline," another important one is found in the discipline of approaching a task in such a way as to see it in its fullness instead of only one-dimensionally. For example, the task of approaching a musical score with this type of discipline means it will not be rushed or minimized. Rather, it will be seen as an opportunity to heighten your awareness of the parts that make up a whole and to open your eyes beyond first impressions. For instance, rather than simply seeing a line of notes to play, you can broaden your reference to the score by taking the time to look at dynamics and articulations, tempo changes, and phrasing. This is much like the difference between only seeing the road ahead as you drive in the country or noticing the trees, wheat fields, clouds, and wildflowers. You can enhance your musicianship simply by considering whether to play the melody line or to embellish it by playing a harmony line—much like the difference between having broiled chicken every day or having it one day baked, another prepared in a casserole, stir-fried, or country fried. Our lives are enhanced by perceiving or experiencing something in a new way, but this requires openness to "something more." What a joy that all this happens within the context of preparing to play at the Sunday Eucharist! Music-making is such a gift in our lives—and also one source of our spiritual growth.

At the thought of God [my] heart leapt for joy, and [I] could not help [my] music's doing the same.
—Joseph Haydn, 18th c.

Previous chapters of this book have presented many foundational principles for the liturgical flutist, among them:

- The basic elements of music theory with related warm-up exercises
- An understanding of the Sunday Eucharist and its musical elements

This chapter focuses on the actual playing at the Eucharist. It covers in detail the variety of resources available from which to play and gives guidance in approaching the following:

- Keyboard accompaniment
    - melody line
    - alto, tenor, and bass lines
- Standard instrumental part
- Guitar part
- B♭ instrument part

Playing from a Keyboard Score

Reading Treble Clef Parts

The flute is a concert pitched instrument, which means that a C sounded on the flute is the same pitch as a C played on the piano. Therefore, a flutist can play directly from a keyboard score without needing to transpose the notes.

EXERCISE

Play the melody line (printed in full-sized notation) of "Good Christian Friends, Rejoice" from the keyboard score shown in Example 45. Be sure to use a tuner to check your intonation.

EXAMPLE 45: "GOOD CHRISTIAN FRIENDS, REJOICE"

(WITH MELODY IN FULL-SIZED NOTATION)

IN DULCI JUBILO
Harm. R. L. Pearsall

Track 30: Playing the Melody as Written
"Good Christian Friends, Rejoice" – piano introduction; mm. 1–8, flute and piano

Often, as shown in Example 45, the melody as written in the keyboard score will fall in the lowest register of the flute. Listen to the first phrase of this piece played on the CD (Track 30) with flute and keyboard, much like Sunday Eucharist. This range typically does not project well on the flute. This is also the register that doubles the singing range of the human voice, so it rarely cuts through the texture of the Sunday assembly. There may be times when a flutist can effectively use this octave because the conscious decision will be to surround the assembly with sound in its own range. However, most of the time a flutist will choose not to play in this octave because the sound will be covered by the assembly and the keyboard.

Instead, it is usually wise to play the melody an octave higher. In this way, the sound of the flute becomes a melodic support for the voice of the assembly.

EXERCISE

Play Example 45 once more, but this time play the melody one octave higher (*8va*). If you feel the need to write out the part first, use the blank manuscript paper at the back of this book. It is important for the liturgical flutist to be able to transpose an octave higher on sight. Practice this skill until you can comfortably eliminate the written step.

Check your work by studying Example 78 at the end of this chapter.

Be cautious of your fingerings when playing any part *8va*. While many fingerings will be the same as the octave in which the music is written, some will be different. For example, make sure all high Ds (such as the last note in measure 3) are fingered correctly for the upper octave. (When in doubt about any fingering, refer to the Fingering Chart at the back of this book.)

WRITTEN PITCH   **SOUNDING PITCH**

Play along with the CD (Track 31), which demonstrates the first phrase of the melody *8va*. Listen to how well the flute projects in this octave. As always, check your intonation with a tuner.

Track 31: Playing the Melody *8va*
"Good Christian Friends, Rejoice" – piano introduction; mm. 1–8, flute and piano

For variety, now try playing one of the other lines from the keyboard score.

EXERCISE

Play the alto line (the bottom line on the treble clef), as shown in full-sized notation in Example 46.

EXAMPLE 46: "GOOD CHRISTIAN FRIENDS, REJOICE"
(WITH ALTO IN FULL-SIZED NOTATION)

IN DULCI JUBILO
Harm. R. L. Pearsall

Track 32: Playing the Alto Line 8va
"Good Christian Friends, Rejoice" – piano introduction; mm. 1–8, flute and piano

69

As you can tell, these low notes will not project well when played with a singing assembly. However, the same line played *8va* could be a very nice descant. Try playing this part *8va*. (Again, be sure the fingerings are correct for the octave you are sounding, not for the octave you are reading. The second note, D, is a good example. Be

WRITTEN PITCH   **SOUNDING PITCH**

sure to lift the index finger of your left hand for this note.) The first phrase of this example is demonstrated on the CD (Track 32). Play along while reading from the complete score as written in Example 46. You can check your work by studying Example 79 at the end of this chapter, where the alto line is printed *8va*.

Many melodies and alto lines include notes written below the staff. Hence, you should be comfortable reading these notes (as shown in Example 47). Although these pitches may sometimes go below the range of the flute, remember that you will be playing them *8va*.

EXAMPLE 47: LOW PITCHES ON THE TREBLE STAFF

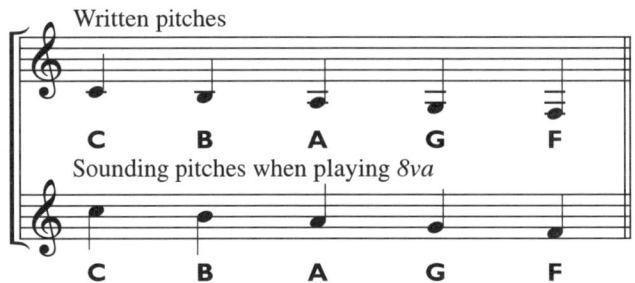

Reading Bass Clef Parts

All flutists are familiar with the notes of the **treble clef**. Those flutists who can also read **bass clef** pitches (and play them in the appropriate range for the flute) greatly increase their variety of choices on any given piece.

EXAMPLE 48: PLACEMENT OF BASS CLEF SYMBOL

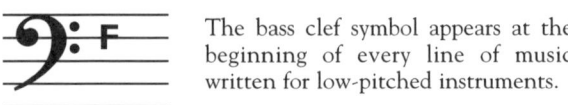

The bass clef symbol appears at the beginning of every line of music written for low-pitched instruments.

The bass clef is nicknamed the F clef because the two dots of the clef sign surround the line for F (see Example 48). You can determine the names of all other notes from here. Use this piece of information as well as the mnemonic devices shown in Example 49 to remember the names of bass clef notes.

EXAMPLE 49: BASS CLEF

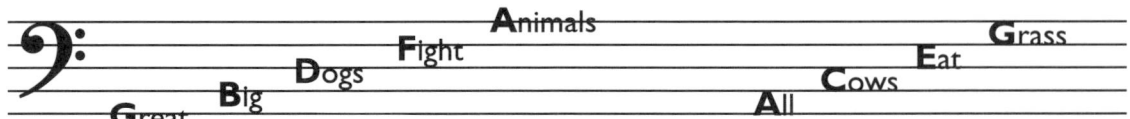

Now let's again consider "Good Christian Friends, Rejoice." Look at the tenor line, the upper notes of the bass clef in full-sized notation in Example 50.

EXAMPLE 50: "GOOD CHRISTIAN FRIENDS, REJOICE"
(WITH TENOR IN FULL-SIZED NOTATION)

IN DULCI JUBILO
Harm. R. L. Pearsall

71

Track 33: Playing the Tenor Line *8va*
    "Good Christian Friends, Rejoice" – piano introduction; mm. 1–8, flute and piano

---

EXERCISE

Play the tenor line of "Good Christian Friends, Rejoice" one octave higher than written. If needed, write out the part using the blank manuscript paper at the back of this book. The correct pitches are printed in Example 80, which appears at the end of this chapter. Listen to the CD (Track 33), on which the first phrase of the tenor line is played *8va*.

This part falls in the lowest register of the flute; therefore, it may not project well when played with a singing assembly.

EXERCISE

Play the tenor line again, this time two octaves higher than written in Example 50. The correct pitches are shown in Example 81 at the end of this chapter.

This is a more resonant part of the flute range. Listen to the first phrase played on the CD (Track 34) to hear how well the flute projects in this register.

Track 34: Playing the Tenor Line Two Octaves Higher
    "Good Christian Friends, Rejoice" – piano introduction; mm. 1–8, flute and piano

The same can be done with the bass line (the lower line of the bass clef), as shown in full-sized notation in Example 51. This part will only be effective on the flute when played two octaves higher than written. Even though this line is admittedly simplistic when played alone, it does provide another musical option when rendered in the context of the Sunday Eucharist.

EXAMPLE 51: "GOOD CHRISTIAN FRIENDS, REJOICE"
(WITH BASS IN FULL-SIZED NOTATION)

IN DULCI JUBILO
Harm. R. L. Pearsall

Track 35: Playing the Bass Line Two Octaves Higher
"Good Christian Friends, Rejoice" – piano introduction; mm. 1–8, flute and piano

---

EXERCISE

Play along with the CD (Track 35), on which the first phrase of the bass line is played 2 octaves higher. If needed, write out the part first, as shown in Example 82, found at the end of this chapter.

When you become comfortable reading the notes of the bass clef without rewriting them as treble clef notes, you will have greatly expanded your tonal possibilities.

The following exercise combines the skills learned in the previous examples.

EXERCISE

Look back to Example 45.

Play "Good Christian Friends, Rejoice" once more, this time playing the alto line on verse 1, the tenor line on verse 2, and the bass line on verse 3. Be sure to use octaves that are appropriate for the range of the flute.

Here is another suggestion: Play the melody *8va* on verse 1, lay out on verse 2, and play the tenor line two octaves higher on verse 3. These are just a few of the ways to vary your playing when reading from a keyboard score. As you can see, the possibilities become endless!

Playing from Printed Instrumental Parts

Many pieces of music currently used in Roman Catholic liturgy already have very good parts written for C instruments. The instrumental parts are often included within an **octavo** edition, although sometimes they must be purchased separately. Some publishers have compiled collections of instrumental parts as a supplement to their hymnals. For example, the instrumental editions of GIA's various hymnals include melody lines (often written in two different octaves), with harmony and descant parts for most pieces. To inquire about particular instrumental parts, check with your music director or call the music publisher directly. (For information on contacting publishers of Catholic resources, see Appendix II: Repertoire/Resource List.)

Let's take one more look at "Good Christian Friends, Rejoice," this time from the C Instrument edition of *Gather Comprehensive* (see Example 52). There are two **staves**, the top being the melody and the bottom being a harmony line. Keep in mind that these parts are written for all concert pitch instruments (i.e., violin, recorder, oboe, and flute). Although other C instruments project well in this printed range, the sound of most flutists will be covered up if they play these parts as written. Therefore, practice playing the parts one octave higher (using correct fingerings, of course!).

EXAMPLE 52: EXCERPT FROM "GOOD CHRISTIAN FRIENDS, REJOICE"

IN DULCI JUBILO
Descant S. S. Withrow

You might consider playing different parts on different verses, similar to the previous exercise.

EXERCISE

1. Play "Good Christian Friends, Rejoice" from Example 52 as follows: play the top staff on verse 1, **tacet** (don't play) on verse 2, and play the bottom staff on verse 3.

2. Next try a different approach: tacet on verse 1, play the top staff *8va* on verse 2, and play the bottom staff *8va* on verse 3. Play along with the portion of this example that is demonstrated on the CD (Track 36). The keyboard accompaniment begins with the last phrase of verse 1. (You are tacet at this point.) Play along on verses 2 and 3.

Track 36: Playing from Written Instrumental Parts
   "Good Christian Friends, Rejoice" – verse 1, mm. 25–32, piano alone; verse 2, flute on melody *8va* with piano; verse 3, flute on descant *8va* with piano

To be an effective liturgical flutist, you must be aware of much more than the printed page. The text, for example, is very important. It can determine breath marks, articulation, and style. Examine "Good Christian Friends, Rejoice," as shown in Example 53, where the text is included with the music. The first phrase of the text ends in measure 8, which is a good place for a breath, whether playing the melody or another part. The remainder of the piece also falls into 8-measure phrases. You may wish to mark these in your part (as shown in Example 53).

EXAMPLE 53: "GOOD CHRISTIAN FRIENDS, REJOICE"
(WITH TEXT AND BREATH MARKS)

IN DULCI JUBILO
Descant S. S. Withrow

J. M. Neale, alt.

Good Christ - ian friends, re - joice_____ With heart and soul and

voice;_____
1. O give heed to what we say: Je - sus
2. Now you hear of end - less bliss: Je - sus
3. Now ye need not fear the grave: Je - sus

Now look at the style of this piece. Its lilting nature lends itself to a light character and delicate articulation. To tongue all the notes as written would not necessarily fit the occasion. Experiment by adding slurs until you find a pattern that works for you. If necessary, refer back to the section on "Tonguing/Articulation" in Chapter 1 of this book. Example 54 shows some suggestions for adjusting the articulation on the melody of "Good Christian Friends, Rejoice." You might experiment with adding your own slurs to the harmony line.

EXAMPLE 54: EXCERPT FROM "GOOD CHRISTIAN FRIENDS, REJOICE"
(WITH SLURS)

IN DULCI JUBILO
Descant S. S. Withrow

Descant © 1980 by GIA Publications, Inc.

This is where liturgical music differs from solo and symphonic literature. For the classically trained orchestral musician, the printed page is strictly observed, complete with all articulation marks. As mentioned in Chapter 1, the liturgical musician has more leeway to adjust articulation unless clearly specified.

Note: Always remember that these and any other musical decisions need to be made in collaboration with the music director and/or other musicians.

Now let's look at a different piece, "Song of the Lord's Supper." The C Instrument part is shown in Example 55.

EXAMPLE 55: EXCERPT FROM "SONG OF THE LORD'S SUPPER"

M. Joncas

The top staff includes the melody in two different octaves. The middle and bottom staves contain descant parts, countermelodies, often written in a higher range than the melody line. A visual study of these lines will show that the middle staff is written in a wonderful range for flute. The bottom staff could be played as written but would probably project better if played *8va*.

Now you have choices to make. You could play the upper part of the melody line on verse 1, tacet on verse 2, and play the middle or bottom part on verse 3. Another possibility is to rest for the first half of any verse and re-enter on the second phrase. On the middle staff, that would mean resting till measure 10. On the lowest staff, you would re-enter in the middle of measure 9 (see Example 56).

EXAMPLE 56: EXCERPT FROM "SONG OF THE LORD'S SUPPER"
(WITH ARROWS TO INDICATE ENTRANCES)

M. Joncas

Yet another possibility is to play the bottom staff for the first phrase and switch to the middle staff for the second phrase (see Example 57).

EXAMPLE 57: EXCERPT FROM "SONG OF THE LORD'S SUPPER"
(WITH ARROWS TO INDICATE MOVEMENT BETWEEN STAVES)

M. Joncas

If your ensemble includes more than one C instrument player, you and your fellow instrumentalists could play the bottom two staves at the same time, or play all three staves together as an instrumental interlude. Again, be sure to make your musical decisions as a team, coming to a consensus with the music director and the other ensemble players.

Further visual study of this piece will show that the bottom two staves are already well articulated for flutists, so no adjustments are needed there. However, you might add slurs to the melody part (as shown in Example 58).

EXAMPLE 58: EXCERPT FROM "SONG OF THE LORD'S SUPPER"
(WITH SLURS)

M. Joncas

Copyright © 1988 by GIA Publications, Inc.

Let your imagination evoke more possibilities as you play these and other pieces from instrumental editions.

Playing from a Guitar Score/Lead Sheet

We have already discussed ways to interpret keyboard scores and C instrument parts. Flutists can also read directly from a guitar part, sometimes referred to as a "lead sheet," which includes the melody line and chord symbols. If choosing to play the melody line, you could either play it as written or *8va*.

To interpret chord symbols, a basic knowledge of theory is necessary. (Refer to the section on "Chords" in Chapter 1 for a discussion of major, minor, diminished, and augmented chords.)

Let's take a look at the guitar score from the refrain for "We Are Many Parts" (see Example 59).

EXAMPLE 59: GUITAR SCORE FOR "WE ARE MANY PARTS"

M. Haugen

Note the appearance of two sets of guitar chords. The top set is preceded by "Capo 3," and its chords are written in parentheses. You should ignore this line since these chords are written in a different key. The guitarist is able to play these chords only with the use of a capo (a bar-like device that clamps onto a specific fret of the neck of a guitar, thus transposing the chords the desired number of half steps). The lower set of chords is written in concert pitch, the same pitch as the piano part. This is the set of chords you should follow.

Notice that the first two chords in the lower line are F and B♭6/D. This pattern continues to alternate throughout most of the refrain. Let's examine the first chord—the F major chord. The notes involved in this chord are F–A–C. To improvise a flute descant, choose any one of these notes whenever the guitarist is playing an F chord. The other chord is B♭6/D. The notes of the B♭ chord are B♭–D–F. The "6" indicates an added note 6 steps higher than B♭, which is the root of the chord. That makes the added sixth a G (as shown in Example 60).

EXAMPLE 60: INTERVAL OF A SIXTH

The "D" after the slash mark indicates that the guitarist's bass note, or lowest sounding pitch, is a D. This means you could play either B♭, D, F, or G while the guitarist is playing this chord.

You will notice that several of the chords have the number 7 after the letter name. This indicates a **seventh chord**, which is a four-note chord that adds the note seven steps higher than the root of the chord. For example, the C7 chord in measure 10 would include the notes C, E, G, and B♭. The B♭ is 7 steps higher than C, the chord's root.

EXAMPLE 61: C7 CHORD

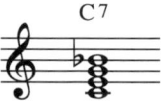

Seventh chords often occur on the dominant (fifth) degree of the scale, which is the case with this chord. Remember that the key is F major; therefore, its fifth degree is C and its **dominant seventh chord** is C7. The dominant seventh chord creates a strong pull toward its tonic; in this case, the C7 chord leads to an F chord. (See the guitar chords in measures 10–11 of Example 59.)

Note: A quick way to find the notes for any dominant seventh chord is to think in intervals. Starting at the root, go up a major third, then up a minor third, and finally up another minor third.

It is important to note that the "7" of the seventh chord usually resolves down to the next scale note. Thus, the B♭ of the C7 chord would resolve downward to the A of the F chord in the next measure. Two examples of this progression are shown in Example 62. Listen to them on the CD (Track 37).

EXAMPLE 62: RESOLUTION OF THE SEVENTH CHORD

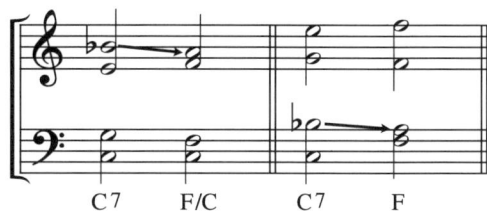

C7   F/C   C7   F

Track 37: Chord Resolution
Two examples of the following chords: C⁷ to F, piano alone

Note that in the second example, the F chord is incomplete. The fifth degree—the C—is missing. This is a rather common occurrence. The fifth degree of the chord is sometimes omitted because of the voice leading of the other notes. It is still an F major chord even though it only has two different notes: F and A.

Now take a look at the F⁷ chords in measures 8 and 12 of Example 59. In each case, the chord is followed by a B♭ chord. This is another example of a dominant seventh chord, but in this case it is called a "secondary dominant." To bring clarity to this concept, consider for a moment the tonality of B♭ major (see Example 63).

EXAMPLE 63: TONALITY OF B♭ MAJOR

Dominant

Notice that the dominant tone (fifth degree) of the B♭ scale is F. Hence, an F⁷ chord is the dominant seventh chord for the key of B♭, and would be so called here if we were permanently in the key of B♭. However, since we are in the key of F, the tonality of B♭ is only temporary. Therefore, the F⁷ chord is called a "secondary dominant." Its notes are F–A–C–E♭, even though there is no E♭ in the key signature. The chord follows the interval pattern indicated above for dominant seventh chords: root, a major third higher, a minor third higher than that, and finally another minor third higher. Again, the "7" of the seventh chord usually resolves down to the next lower note in the following chord. In Example 64, the E♭ of the F⁷ chord is followed by the D of the B♭ chord.

EXAMPLE 64: CHORD RESOLUTION

F7   B♭

In measures 16 and 20 of Example 59, the word "tacet" indicates a time during which the guitarist should remain silent. In each case, the guitarist plays on the downbeat and then rests for the remainder of the measure. During these "tacet" beats, the flutist would choose between playing without guitar accompaniment or remaining tacet with the guitarist. The latter choice is probably the more prudent one.

The chord in measure 17 is E♭add9. This symbol indicates another four-note chord, this time adding a note 9 steps higher than the root tone of E♭. Thus, the added ninth is F; hence, the E♭add9 chord is E♭–G–B♭–F (as shown in Example 65).

EXAMPLE 65: ADDED NINTH CHORD

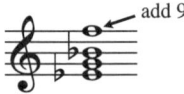

Take another look at measure 20. The chord symbol on beat 1 is Csus4. The "sus" is an abbreviation for the word **suspension.** The "4" indicates the note four steps higher than the root note C. This note is F. Hence, the F, even though it is a **non-chordal note** for a C chord, is played as a part of the Csus4 chord, resolving to a chordal note in the next chord. "Sus4" also implies that the third degree of the chord is omitted. (See Example 66.)

EXAMPLE 66: SUSPENDED CHORD

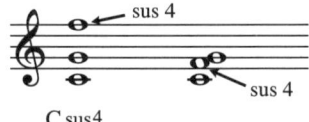

C sus4

**Notice the omission of the third scale degree;
there are no Es in these Csus4 chords.**

The "sus4" usually resolves downward to the third degree of the next chord. That is not the case here because this particular Csus4 chord is followed by tacet. So for the next 3 beats, you would probably choose to remain silent along with the guitarist.

Now that you have acquired a basic understanding of chords, let's compose a flute descant for this piece.

You can never go wrong playing the note indicated by the first letter of the guitar chord. This creates a very adequate improvised flute part, as shown in Example 67. As you can see, the descant moves in the same rhythm as the chord changes, even when the melody note sustains a tie. Listen to the CD (Track 38) to hear this flute descant played with cantor and guitar accompaniment. This is a simple example of **improvisation**. (More techniques for improvisation and descant writing will follow in later chapters.)

EXAMPLE 67: DESCANT #1 (GOOD) FOR "WE ARE MANY PARTS"

M. Haugen

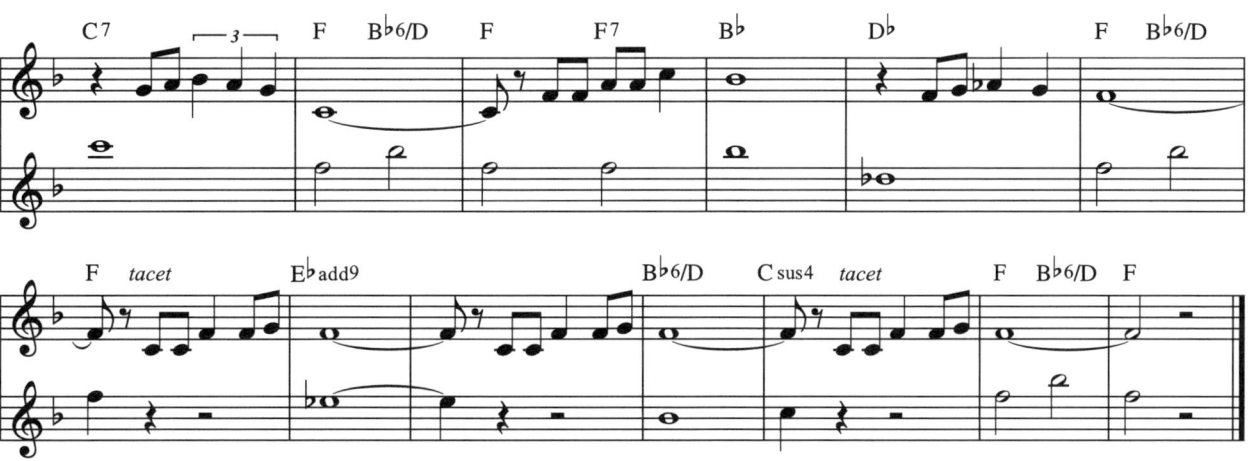

Track 38: Playing from Guitar Score: Descant #1
   "We Are Many Parts" – guitar introduction; refrain with flute descant, cantor, and guitar

This descant lacks rhythmic interest and variety, and is admittedly very simplistic in nature.

You might do well to add more melodic interest to your flute descant (see Example 68).

EXAMPLE 68: DESCANT #2 (BETTER) FOR "WE ARE MANY PARTS"

M. Haugen

87

Track 39: Playing from Guitar Score: Descant #2
"We Are Many Parts" – guitar introduction; refrain with flute descant, cantor, and guitar

Even a quick glance reveals that Descant #2 is more involved than Descant #1. The flute part now includes notes other than the chord root. Notice, too, that when the melody line is sustaining a long note, the flute descant has a moving line, thus adding rhythmic variety as well as melodic interest. Listen to this example played on the CD (Track 39) with flute, cantor, and guitar.

Descant #3 (shown in Example 69) is even more complex.

EXAMPLE 69: DESCANT #3 (BEST) FOR "WE ARE MANY PARTS"

M. Haugen

Track 40: Playing from Guitar Score: Descant #3
"We Are Many Parts" – guitar introduction; refrain with flute descant, cantor, and guitar

Listen to this example played on the CD (Track 40). The descant has now gained more independence from the melody. Not only does it begin one measure later than the melody, but it also uses more interesting rhythmic lines while the melody sustains long notes, thereby connecting one phrase to the next. Non-chordal notes are also used in this descant. For example, the C in measure 4 does not belong to the B♭6/D chord. It is a ***passing tone***, a non-chordal note that passes between one chordal note and another.

You have now had a small taste of the type of work involved in writing a descant. We will explore these techniques in much greater detail in Section III. Suffice it to say at this point that the ability to read a guitar part is a very important step on the road to improvisation.

Transposition

In your ministry as a liturgical flutist, there may be times when the music director will ask you to transpose your part to a different key. Perhaps the cantor's range would necessitate this, or maybe the piece is out of the range of the assembly. Or further still, maybe there is a great B♭ trumpet part you would like to be able to play. You could, if you understand the basics of transposition.

Back in Chapter 1, you memorized scales and their key signatures. This information is invaluable when it comes to transposing music.

> SCENARIO 1:
> The music director tells you the cantor has requested that the psalm be lowered one half step. For many keyboardists today, that simply means turning the dial on the transposer to the needed setting, but it's not quite that simple for the flutist.

Let's look at Marty Haugen's setting of Psalm 25: "To You, O Lord" (see Example 70).

EXAMPLE 70: REFRAIN FOR PSALM 25: "TO YOU, O LORD"

M. Haugen

To lower your part one half step, you must first know the name of the original key—in this case, E♭. One half step lower is the key of D. Your knowledge of scales and key signatures tells you there are 2 sharps in the key of D: F♯ and C♯.

EXERCISE

Transpose the melody (the top staff) of Psalm 25: "To You, O Lord" to the key of D.

In Example 70, the first note of the melody is E♭. You would need to go down one half step to D, which becomes the first note in the new key. Simply apply the key signature of D and play the melody one half step lower. In other words, if the printed melody note were written on a line, the transposed note would occur on the next space lower. If the printed melody note were written on a space, the transposed note would occur on the next line lower. Write out your transposition using the blank manuscript paper at the back of this book. Check your work by turning to Example 83 at the end of this chapter. The upper octave of the melody of "To You, O Lord" is written there in the key of D.

EXERCISE

Now that you have had experience writing your transposition, try the next step: transposing on sight.

Play the refrain melody for Psalm 25: "To You, O Lord" in the key of D while reading from the E♭ version, as written in Example 70.

When you feel comfortable with the melody line, try transposing the harmony line on the middle staff of Example 70. Next, try the upper part of the lowest staff. Finally, try the lower part of this staff. Listen to all four parts played together in the key of D on the CD (Track 41). Play your transposed parts with the CD while reading from Example 70. Check your transpositions by studying Example 84, shown at the end of this chapter.

Track 41: Transposing Melody, Harmony, and Descant Lines One Half Step Lower
"To You, O Lord" (key of D) – refrain with four flutes

SCENARIO 2:
The music director has decided that this assembly will participate more enthusiastically if today's communion song is sung one half step higher.

Let's look at Marty Haugen's setting of Psalm 34: "Taste and See" (see Example 71).

EXAMPLE 71: EXCERPT FROM REFRAIN FOR PSALM 34: "TASTE AND SEE"

M. Haugen

Copyright © 1980 by GIA Publications, Inc.

Your first step is to identify the original key—E major. One half step higher puts you in the key of F, with one flat (B♭) in the key signature. You would now need to play everything one half step higher than printed, thus starting the melody on C instead of the printed B. In other words, if the printed note were on a line, the transposed note would be on the next space higher. If the printed note were on a space, the transposed note would be on the next line higher.

Transpose the melody into the key of F. If you feel it is necessary, you may wish to write out the transposition first. There is blank manuscript paper at the back of this book for this purpose. Check your work by looking at Example 85, found at the end of this chapter. The upper octave of the melody of Psalm 34: "Taste and See" is written there in the key of F.

EXERCISE

Play the refrain melody for Psalm 34: "Taste and See" in the key of F while reading from the E version (see Example 71). Play along with the CD (Track 42) to make sure all of the notes are correct.

Track 42: Transposing Melody Line One Half Step Higher
"Taste and See" (key of F) – mm. 1–7 of refrain, flute alone

Now look at the lower staff of Example 71. There are a few accidentals in measure 5. These need special consideration when transposing. In the upper part of this measure, the third note is written as G♮. Remember that you are transposing up one half step. When you play this note in the new key, it would be A♭. In the same measure, the lower part begins with a written D♮. In the key of F, this note becomes E♭. Listen to all three parts (the melody in the upper octave, and the upper and lower parts of the bottom staff) played simultaneously on the CD (Track 43) in the key of F. Play along with the CD while reading from Example 71 in E. Check your transpositions in the key of F by studying Example 86, found at the end of this chapter.

Track 43: Transposing All Parts One Half Step Higher
"Taste and See" (key of F) – mm. 1–7 of refrain, three flutes

SCENARIO 3:
Sunday's Gathering Song is "All People That on Earth Do Dwell," and the music director hands you the B♭ trumpet descant part.

The B♭ trumpet is a transposing instrument (as is the B♭ clarinet), which means that when a trumpeter or clarinetist plays a C, it sounds like a B♭ on the piano. Therefore, parts for these instruments are written one whole step higher than they sound. (See "Playing from Parts Written for Other Instruments" later in this chapter.)

Take a look at the B♭ trumpet part for "All People That on Earth Do Dwell" (see Example 72).

EXAMPLE 72: EXCERPT FROM TRUMPET PART FOR "ALL PEOPLE THAT ON EARTH DO DWELL"

OLD HUNDREDTH
Genevan Psalter, 1551
Arr. Robert J. Powell

Tune

Stanzas 1–2 tacet
Stanza 3

This part is written in the key of A major, which when played on B♭ trumpet sounds in the key of G. The flutist would need to transpose down one whole step to be able to play this part in the same concert key with the other members of your ensemble.

The melody in the trumpet part begins on a written A♮. Playing one whole step down is the equivalent of two half steps. To go down two half steps, just imagine you are playing a chromatic scale starting on A. (Refer back to Chapter 1, "Chromatic Scale.") You would first arrive at A♭ and then at G, which is the note you would need to play at the beginning of this piece. Continue the same method of transposition throughout the piece. In other words, any note written on a space would be played on the next line lower. A note written on a line would be played on the next space lower. Remember to apply the correct key signature for the key of G (F♯). Watch the accidental in measure 10 of *stanza* 3—the written D♯ becomes a sounding C♯.

Notice that music written for trumpet often lies in the low register for flute. Thus, it would be more effective to play these parts one octave higher than written.

EXERCISE

1. Read any of the parts from Example 72 written in A while playing in G.

2. Play along with the CD (Track 44), where flutists are playing the melody and both descant parts in concert pitch, 1 octave higher than shown.

3. Check your transposition by studying Example 87, shown at the end of this chapter.

Track 44: Transposing from a Trumpet Part
"All People That on Earth Do Dwell" (key of G) – piano introduction; one verse, three flutes *8va* with piano

SCENARIO 4:
The music director has decided that the key for "Canticle of the Sun" (see Example 73) is too high for the 7:30 a.m. assembly.

EXAMPLE 73: EXCERPT FROM "CANTICLE OF THE SUN"

M. Haugen

Copyright © 1980 by GIA Publications, Inc.

The music director tells you he/she will be transposing the accompaniment to the key of F. Your first step is to determine the key of the printed part. Three sharps in the key signature, in a major key, indicates the key of A major.

Knowing the new key is F, you must determine the interval of the transposition. Going down from A to F is the interval of a major third (four half steps.) So to play in the key of F, you would need to transpose everything down a major third. Remember that the new key signature would have one flat—which is B♭.

This is a relatively simple transposition. If the printed note is on a line, the new note would also be on a line, but one line lower than the printed note. For example, the first note of the melody is a printed E. The next line lower than E is C. So the first melody note in the new key is C. Similarly, if the printed note is on a space, the transposed note would also be on a space, but one space lower than the printed note. For example, in the first full measure of the melody, the second note is a printed A. The transposed note would be F, one space lower than A. Continue in this same manner for the entire piece. Check your transposition by turning to Example 88 at the end of this chapter. "Canticle of the Sun" is printed there in the key of F.

Again, notice that the range of this melody lies in the lowest register of the flute, so it would be more effective to play this part one octave higher than written.

Note: Transposition a third higher would involve the opposite method, with the transposed part being one line or one space higher than the printed notes.

SCENARIO 5:

The Eucharistic Prayer for the day's liturgy will be sung in the key of A♭. The music director has decided to transpose the song at the Preparation of Gifts, "You Are the Voice," to A♭ so there will be a continuous tonality, facilitating a flow from the Preparation of Gifts into the Eucharistic Prayer. The refrain for "You Are the Voice," written in the key of A, is shown in Example 74.

94

EXAMPLE 74: EXCERPT FROM "YOU ARE THE VOICE"
(IN KEY OF A)

D. Haas

To play this piece in the key of A♭, you would need to transpose everything down one half step. You know that the key signature for A♭ has four flats: B♭, E♭, A♭, and D♭. All you would need to do for this transposition would be to play the music as written, simply using the new key signature. A quick visual glance reveals that there are no accidentals in any of the parts for this piece. If there were, you would need to remember to simply go down one half step, applying the appropriate accidental for the new key.

This is the kind of transposition you would likely do most often. It is visually less difficult than the other transpositions and would not need any separate notation. For practice sake, you may want to transpose the melody and each of the descants printed in Example 74.

Listen to the CD (Track 45) to hear all of these parts transposed to the key of A♭. Practice your transposition skills by playing in A♭ with the CD while looking at the music written in A in Example 74. Check your work by studying Example 89, written in the key of A♭, which is found at the end of this chapter.

Track 45: Transposing Instrumental Parts One Half Step Lower
"You Are the Voice" (key of A♭) – five flutes

You can use these same skills with other half-step transpositions. Consider a situation in which a piece written in the key of E♭ needs to be played in the key of E, or one written in D needs to be played in D♭. Just replace the old key signature with the new and play the music as written. Always be alert to the use of accidentals in the original score. Simply remember that you are moving just one half step, and be mindful of whether you are transposing up or down.

Playing from Parts Written for Other Instruments

As a liturgical flutist, you might be called upon to play a part originally written for a different instrument, especially another C instrument such as violin, oboe, or soprano recorder. Like the flute, these are concert pitched instruments, which means they play the same notes as the piano with no transposition needed. Depending on the range of a particular piece, you might decide to play the part an octave higher than written, but no additional transposition would be needed.

Sometimes you might find yourself being handed a part written for a non-concert pitched instrument (such as B♭ trumpet), whose written notes sound different than those same notes played on a piano. B♭ instruments, such as trumpet and clarinet, read one step higher than they sound. Their written C would sound a B♭. (Refer to Scenario 3 under "Transposition" in this chapter for more about playing from a B♭ part.)

You might occasionally run across a part written for E♭ alto saxophone or E♭ soprano flute. For these instruments, their written C will sound an E♭. To play from these parts, you would need to go up a minor third (three half steps). For example, if the part is written in the key of G, you would need to play in the key of B♭. Apply this new key signature, and read one staff line (or one staff space) higher than written, as shown in Example 75.

EXAMPLE 75: EXCERPT FROM "MY SHEPHERD WILL SUPPLY MY NEED"
(WRITTEN PITCHES FOR E♭ INSTRUMENTS)

RESIGNATION
Southern Harmony, 1835

EXCERPT FROM "MY SHEPHERD WILL SUPPLY MY NEED"
(SOUNDING PITCHES FOR C INSTRUMENTS)

RESIGNATION
Southern Harmony, 1835

In rare instances, you might need to read from a part written for French horn in F (which reads a fifth higher than concert pitch) or alto flute in G (which reads a fourth higher than concert pitch). To play from these parts, the same principles of transposition would apply, but with the appropriate intervals. A French horn part written in the key of C would be played in the concert key of F (as shown in Example 76).

EXAMPLE 76: EXCERPT FROM "PEACE WITH THE FATHER"
(WRITTEN PITCHES FOR F INSTRUMENTS)

O. Gibbons

EXCERPT FROM "PEACE WITH THE FATHER"
(SOUNDING PITCHES FOR C INSTRUMENTS)

O. Gibbons

Notice that the transposed line lies in a low range for the flute. As indicated in similar examples, it would probably be better to play this part an octave higher than written.

An alto flute part written in the key of C would be played in the concert key of G (as shown in Example 77).

EXAMPLE 77: EXCERPT FROM "AMAZING GRACE"
(WRITTEN PITCHES FOR G INSTRUMENTS)

NEW BRITAIN
Virginia Harmony, 1831

EXCERPT FROM "AMAZING GRACE"
(SOUNDING PITCHES FOR C INSTRUMENTS)

NEW BRITAIN
Virginia Harmony, 1831

Notice once again that the transposed part lies in the lowest register of the flute range. Again, it would probably be better to play this part an octave higher than written.

Note: When transposing music written either for horn in F or alto flute in G, it is advisable to write out the concert pitch part in advance rather than do the transposition on sight because the intervals are so wide.

It is also possible for flutists to play from a part written for bass clef instruments, such as trombone or cello. These are concert-pitched instruments (as are all bass clef instruments). Therefore, you would follow the rules for reading from a bass clef part discussed earlier in this chapter, making the necessary octave transpositions.

Conclusion

At this point, you should start to feel comfortable putting some variety into your playing.

- You have learned to play melody lines in different octaves, both for the sake of variety as well as for balance and projection.
- You have read from a keyboard score and played its alto line an octave higher, thus turning it into a descant part.
- You have learned to read bass clef and have played tenor and bass parts in appropriate ranges for flute.
- You have studied instrumental parts and have freed yourself from the printed page by playing in different octaves, adding slurs, entering on phrases other than the first, and switching staves between phrases.
- You have continued to move away from printed parts by using chord symbols as a basis for improvising your own flute part.
- You have learned to transpose.

The more you exercise these skills, the more they will become second nature.

Take a look at other examples of liturgical music and practice your new skills on these pieces. We will explore more of these techniques in the next section.

It should be clear to you by now that the application of these basic principles to your ministry as a liturgical flutist will be an ongoing process. Allow yourself the space to be really rooted in these skills before moving on to the next chapters. Be respectful of your own uniqueness and aware that you must move through this process at your own pace. In other words, do not shortchange the process!

Musical Examples Referenced in Chapter 4

EXAMPLE 78: MELODY FROM "GOOD CHRISTIAN FRIENDS, REJOICE" (1 OCTAVE HIGHER)

IN DULCI JUBILO
German carol, 14th c.

EXAMPLE 79: ALTO LINE FROM "GOOD CHRISTIAN FRIENDS, REJOICE" (1 OCTAVE HIGHER)

IN DULCI JUBILO
Harm. R. L. Pearsall

EXAMPLE 80: TENOR LINE FROM "GOOD CHRISTIAN FRIENDS, REJOICE" (1 OCTAVE HIGHER)

IN DULCI JUBILO
Harm. R. L. Pearsall

EXAMPLE 81: TENOR LINE FROM "GOOD CHRISTIAN FRIENDS, REJOICE" (2 OCTAVES HIGHER)

IN DULCI JUBILO
Harm. R. L. Pearsall

EXAMPLE 82: BASS LINE FROM "GOOD CHRISTIAN FRIENDS, REJOICE" (2 OCTAVES HIGHER)

IN DULCI JUBILO
Harm. R. L. Pearsall

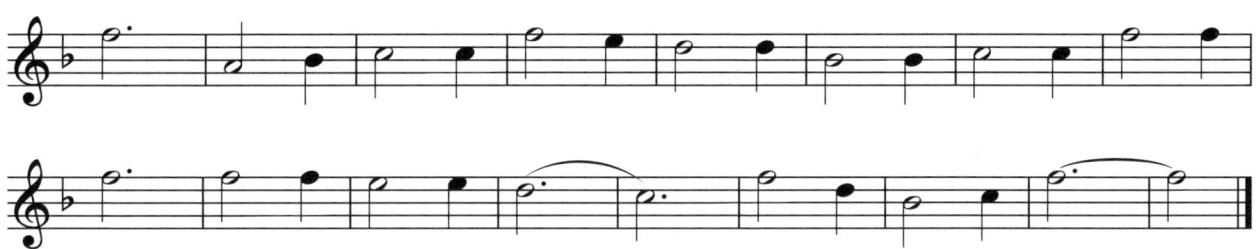

EXAMPLE 83: REFRAIN FOR PSALM 25: "TO YOU, O LORD"
(MELODY IN KEY OF D)

M. Haugen

EXAMPLE 84: REFRAIN FOR PSALM 25: "TO YOU, O LORD"
(MELODY AND DESCANTS IN KEY OF D)

M. Haugen

EXAMPLE 85: EXCERPT FROM REFRAIN FOR PSALM 34: "TASTE AND SEE"
(MELODY IN KEY OF F)

M. Haugen

EXAMPLE 86: EXCERPT FROM REFRAIN FOR PSALM 34: "TASTE AND SEE"
(BOTH STAVES IN KEY OF F)

M. Haugen

EXAMPLE 87: EXCERPT FROM TRUMPET PART FOR "ALL PEOPLE THAT ON EARTH DO DWELL"
(IN KEY OF G)

OLD HUNDREDTH
Genevan Psalter, 1551
Arr. Robert J. Powell

EXAMPLE 88: EXCERPT FROM "CANTICLE OF THE SUN"
(IN KEY OF F)

M. Haugen

EXAMPLE 89: EXCERPT FROM "YOU ARE THE VOICE"
(IN KEY OF A♭)

D. Haas

Section II

The Experienced Liturgical Flutist:
Exploring the Possibilities

Chapter 5
Versatility of the Flute as an Instrument for Music Ministry

Group Dynamics
Relational Skills
Expanded Ministry

A phrase in the popular culture that connotes a peak experience is, "It doesn't get any better than this." In the Christian tradition, there is the story of the transfiguration of Jesus on the mountain. (Matthew 17:1–9; Mark 9:2–10; Luke 9:28–36) It certainly was a peak experience for the three disciples who witnessed it—so much so they wanted to set up tents and stay there, but Jesus rejected the idea. It is every bit as impossible for us to stay in the moment of those experiences that have delighted us or that have been fulfilling or uplifting, even though we may want to at times. Yet it is just as well, for there is always more—always.

Each time you think, "It doesn't get any better than this," you are coming from a limited frame of reference. Remind yourself over and over of this, as it is so compelling to stay with what you know and what is comfortable for you—especially when it seems so rich and satisfying. Be willing to both enjoy the moment and then let it go. If you try to duplicate those moments or keep things as they are, you will never open yourself to what more there is.

Reflect for a moment on some of your best musical experiences as a flutist. At what age did you have a first peak experience as a musician? What was the circumstance? What was the music? How much have you evolved since then? How many more experiences of similar impact have you had? As you answer these questions, you can probably see that only through change and a willingness to respond to new and different situations did you develop. How open are you to continuing to grow and stretch as a liturgical musician?

The chapters that follow present a myriad of possibilities for a liturgical flutist to consider. And the simple blessing is that the flute itself, by its very nature, provides the potential for the fruition of these ideas. Not every instrumentalist is given such an innate gift.

We cannot be whole without music. Music is not a decoration applied to the liturgy, like icing on a cake. Music is not an ornament on a liturgy that is substantially intact without it. Music is an integral part of liturgical celebration because it is an integral part of a whole human communication, of a full, rich, human celebration.
—Robert Hovda (from "There's Nothing like a Professional Musician"
by Robert Hovda in Worship, September 1996)

The flute is one of the most versatile of all instruments. It has a history that spans approximately four thousand years! It has enjoyed the honor of calling our Jewish ancestors to prayer and of entertaining kings and queens in the courts of European royalty. It is also an often-featured instrument in jazz ensembles and rock bands today.

In Western music, the flute has enjoyed equal opportunities in chamber ensembles as well as full symphony orchestras. It is also an instrument that complements the human voice very well, which makes it a wonderful tool for praise and worship, whether with a single cantor or a full choir.

This chapter will explore various avenues for the flutist as a liturgical musician. We will look at many different types of ensemble situations, namely:

- Flute and cantor
- Flute and choir
- Flute and another melodic instrument
- Flute choir
- Flute in a folk ensemble

We will also consider different situations for solo playing:

- Solo flute with accompaniment
- Solo flute without accompaniment

Let this chapter be a springboard from which you explore new possibilities. Let go of any stereotypical images you may have of the demure, small sound of the flute. Be open to the new opportunities and exciting challenges that lie ahead. Let go of your inhibitions and just praise God!

Different Ensemble Situations

Flute and Cantor

An experienced and well-trained cantor and a flutist can be a very effective ensemble for music ministry, supporting the assembly even without the use of a keyboard instrument.

When this is the situation, the flutist needs to think like an accompanist. Prepare in advance the phrases you will play for an introduction. Be sure to give a strong, steady pulse with a clear indication of the assembly's entrance, and also make sure the assembly can easily discern their starting pitch.

It is wise to play the assembly's line (usually *8va*) for the first **verse** or at least the first portion of the first verse, and then you would need to make an on-the-spot decision whether or not to stray from the melody. If you sense the assembly might fall apart if they hear you playing a different line, then you would probably do well to stay with the melody. If the assembly sounds sure of its part and you sense they will stay with the tune even if you play a different part, then feel free to move away from the melody.

The above techniques also apply if there is no cantor and you, the flutist, are supporting the assembly alone. In either case, there is one very important distinction that must be made when ministering without keyboard or another accompaniment instrument. Without an accompaniment instrument, you are the musical leader. You must listen for the verbal cues of the presider to know when to begin introductions. You are also responsible for setting tempos and leading the assembly with a solid pulse and steady beat. This is very different than reacting to the lead of a keyboardist or music director, following their *tempos*, entrances, etc. As the sole instrumentalist, you become the assembly's musical guide.

Listen to "The Summons" on the CD (Tracks 46a and 46b) while studying Example 90, taken from the C Instrument book. Track 46a demonstrates the sound of the flutist and cantor alone. Notice that the flute part follows the printed page some of the time but also improvises some of the time. Track 46b gives the flute introduction, but then just the cantor's voice remains. This gives you the chance to experiment with your own flute part, using your liturgical and musical creativity. Don't be afraid to move away from the melody line by switching to one of the descant parts or creating a new line of your own. (See Section III for more on improvisation.)

Track 46a: Flute and Cantor on a Song
 "The Summons" – flute introduction; one verse with flute and cantor
Track 46b: Flute and *A Capella* Cantor
 "The Summons" – flute introduction; one verse, cantor alone

EXAMPLE 90: EXCERPT FROM "THE SUMMONS"

KELVINGROVE
Scottish Traditional
Arr. J. Bell

As you can see some pieces of music (e.g., "The Summons") lend themselves very well to the combination of flute and cantor. "My Shepherd Is the Lord," by Joseph Gelineau, is another excellent example (see Example 91).

EXAMPLE 91: EXCERPT FROM PSALM 23: "MY SHEPHERD IS THE LORD"

Psalm 23; The Grail

J. Gelineau

My shep - herd is the Lord, noth - ing in - deed shall I want.

In this piece, the flutist could intone the melody of the refrain as an introduction, followed by the cantor singing the refrain alone. When the cantor invites the assembly to join on the repetition of the refrain, you could support the assembly by playing the melody. On the verses, a beautiful melodic line is created if you play the top notes of the accompaniment; this makes a lovely duet with the cantor. In measures 13–14 of the verse, the upper voice of the accompaniment line rests; you may wish to switch to the lower voice of the treble clef (*8va*) for these measures.

Notice that the text of verses 1 and 2 is longer than the text of the other verses. Therefore, in verses 3–5, it is necessary to skip measures 12–18. Listen for this on the CD (Track 47) as verses 1 and 4 are demonstrated for you. They are played on the CD without keyboard accompaniment; however, if a keyboardist is available, he/she may choose to play on the refrain but lay out on the verses. (See Chapter 6, "Baptism," for more on this psalm setting.)

Track 47: Flute and Cantor on a Psalm
Psalm 23: "My Shepherd Is the Lord" – refrain; verses 1 and 4, flute and cantor

Flute and Choir

Many flutists minister regularly with parish choirs. If the choir is comprised of adults, the flutist can often be free to improvise. (See Section III for more on improvisation.)

If the ensemble is a children's choir, then the flutist may need to adjust to the situation. For example, if it is a small group, you may need to reduce your volume to allow the children's voices to be heard. Depending on their level of experience, you may need to stay on the melody line more often so as not to confuse the children.

The music director is usually a good judge of how much improvising can be done in this situation. Note, however, that children are less likely to be confused if they know in advance that someone will be playing something other than what they are singing. For example, in the *Mass of Creation* setting for the Eucharistic Prayer for Children, there are additional acclamations with instrumental parts. The flutist, in conversation with the music director, can make the decision whether to play the instrumental part or double the vocal line.

Flute and Another Melodic Instrument

The lyrical tone quality of the flute enables the instrument to blend well with many other instruments. It goes without saying that the sound of the flute blends well with another flute. Therefore, let's discuss its relationship with other instruments.

Flute and oboe is a lovely combination that is often used in liturgical music today. The oboe is a concert pitched instrument that reads in basically the same range as the flute. The main difference is that the oboe can project very well in its lowest octave, contrary to the *tessitura* of the flute in this range. For this reason, when a flutist and an oboist are playing together, it is usually best for the flutist to play the upper part of a two-part version, or the upper octave of a two-octave version. Look back to the instrumental parts for "The Summons" (see Example 90). On the top staff (the melody line), the flutist can take the upper part while the oboist stays on the bottom. For the middle staff, the flutist can once again stay on the upper part, with the oboist taking the bottom, adjusting the octave as necessary. (The same scenario would hold true if a flutist is working with a violinist or recorder player, i.e., it is generally best for the flutist to take the top part and the other instrumentalist to take the bottom part.)

Flute and clarinet is another common pairing. These instruments can easily play together using, for example, the *Gather Comprehensive* C Instrument book for the flutist and the B♭ Instrument book for the clarinetist (both published by GIA Publications, Inc.). These instrumental volumes coordinate with GIA's various hymnals. The B♭ Instrument edition has exactly the same parts as the C Instrument edition, with the only difference being the transposition. This makes it very easy for C and B♭ instrumentalists to work together. Once again, it is usually best for the flutist to take the upper part and the clarinetist to take the lower part, but this can vary depending on the piece of music.

Another effective combination is **flute and trumpet**. Although the *timbres* of the two instruments are very different, their effect together is quite pleasing. Trumpet in B♭ is a transposing instrument, so the trumpeter could easily read from the B♭ Instrument book. The main difference between playing with a clarinetist and playing with a trumpeter is that the tone quality of the trumpet is much brighter than the clarinet. Thus, it is usually more effective for the trumpeter to stay on the melody while the flutist plays a descant or harmony line. If there are two harmony lines, the trumpeter can play the top and the flutist the bottom (usually *8va*).

When working with another instrumentalist, you may wish to vary the instrumentation by splitting the parts according to the verses. Take another look at "The Summons" (see Example 90). Variety can be achieved by simply alternating verses, with the flute playing on verses 2 and 4, and the other instrument playing on verses 1, 3, and 5. Another possibility would be to have both instruments play together on the melody on verse 1, then flute descant on verse 2, the other instrument on verse 3, both instruments tacet on verse 4, and both playing together on the middle staff on verse 5.

> *All musical elements have as their one purpose the celebration of divine worship...they must not be a hindrance to an intense participation of the assembly but must direct the mind's attention and the heart's sentiments toward the rites.... Instruments...should be limited in number and suited to the region and to community culture; they should prompt devotion and not be too loud.*
>
> —Liturgicae instaurationes, September 5, 1970, **"The Third Instruction on the orderly carrying out of the Constitution on the Liturgy"**

Notice that the instrumental books do not include the text. As an instrumentalist, you must look in the assembly book or ask the music director about the number of verses. Keep in mind that although there may be five verses listed in the assembly book, the music director may decide not to sing all of them. You must be alert to the situation and ready to follow the director's lead.

When there are more than two musicians, the same guidelines would still apply. Just use your imagination coupled with your common sense! Although there is no "liturgical law" that prohibits instrumentalists from playing the same part on every verse, boredom can quickly set in for both the players and the assembly. Remember, too, that everyone doesn't have to be playing all the time. Variety will help to engage the assembly and foster their participation.

Flute Choir

The proliferation of flutists today has brought about the creation of another type of ensemble: the flute choir. Even just one generation ago, flute choirs were virtually unheard of, but now they are quite popular.

Flute choirs consist of any number of flutists, from three players to thirty (and upwards). They may or may not include auxiliary instruments, such as piccolo, alto flute, and bass flute.

There are a number of good flute choir arrangements of standard hymn tunes and sacred pieces that work very well in liturgical settings. If your parish ensemble includes a number of flutists, consider having them play a lovely flute choir piece during the Preparation Rite or Communion Meditation. A portion of a setting of the hymn tune SLANE as arranged for three C flutes is shown in Example 92; it is titled "Be Thou My Vision."

EXAMPLE 92: EXCERPT FROM "BE THOU MY VISION"

SLANE
Arr. G. Schuster

FLUTE CHOIR

If your ensemble includes four flutists, there are many quartets you might try. Look at Example 93, Psalm 19: "The Lord Is Kind and Full of Mercy" (Proulx), scored for four C flutes, choir, and organ.

EXAMPLE 93: EXCERPT FROM PSALM 19: "THE LORD IS KIND AND FULL OF MERCY"

R. Proulx

Copyright © 1991 by GIA Publications, Inc.

Some quartets, such as this one, are arranged for four C flutes; others provide an option for using alto and/or bass flute. The Mozart *Quartet in C Major* (see Example 94) utilizes these auxiliary instruments. This piece was originally written for flute, violin, viola, and cello, but it has been arranged here for two C flutes, alto flute, and bass flute. Don't dismiss the opportunity of using these auxiliary flutes if you don't own them; explore the possibility of borrowing or renting them from a local college, university, or music dealer. Listen to this beautiful combination of instruments as played on the CD (Track 48).

Track 48: Flute Choir
Mozart's *Quartet in C Major* – mm. 1–24, two C flutes, alto flute, and bass flute

EXAMPLE 94: EXCERPT FROM QUARTET IN C MAJOR

W. A. Mozart
Arr. V. Jicha

In looking at the score, notice that the alto flute part is written in a different key than the other three parts. This is because the alto flute is a transposing instrument pitched in G; it sounds a fourth lower than printed, but the flutist reads, fingers, and plays the same notes as if playing a C flute. Since alto flute transposes down the interval of a fourth, the key signature will always have one more flat or one less sharp than that of the C flute. (See Chapter 4, "Transposition," for more on the alto flute.)

Bass flute is pitched in C but sounds one octave lower than C flute. Once again, the flutist reads, fingers, and plays the exact same notes as if playing a C flute. The instrument transposes down one octave. This is the opposite of the piccolo, which is also pitched in C but sounds one octave higher than written (i.e., one octave higher than the C flute).

It is a delight to play in an ensemble with several other flutists. If this is the situation in your parish, look into purchasing a few arrangements for flute trio or flute quartet. If you have access to an alto flute and/or a bass flute, consider purchasing some flute choir arrangements. Both your music ministers and your assembly will be blessed.

Flute in a Folk Ensemble

Folk ensembles, sometimes called "contemporary ensembles," began as an outgrowth of the reforms of Vatican II. Folk groups were formed with the intent of being more contemporary in nature than traditional choirs. These types of ensembles often include "folk" instruments (such as guitar, bass, piano, synthesizer, and/or percussion), as well as wind instruments and several singers. Quite often these musicians are amplified through the use of microphones. (See Appendix III: Sound Amplification for the Flutist for further discussion on the use of amplification.)

Just as in most other settings, the flutist in a folk ensemble could play various roles. A flutist could serve as a soloist accompanied by the ensemble, or as a support to the assembly by playing the melodic line. A flutist could also add interest and color to the ensemble by playing a descant.

The previously mentioned techniques concerning what line to play, playing 8va, how to read from a guitar score, etc., also apply when playing with a folk ensemble. Be careful, however, if you are playing from a keyboard score and the only accompanying instrument is a guitar. Sometimes the chords written in the guitar score do not match up with the keyboard accompaniment, so it is very important to rehearse ahead of time to see if the chord structures work together. Another potential problem exists when the organist or pianist chooses to use a different accompaniment because he/she likes the arrangement better. The chords might clash with the part you would be reading from, whether it is a standard instrumental part or a keyboard score. Keyboardists will usually let the instrumentalists know if they plan to play from a different arrangement, but it is always best to check.

Different Solo Situations

Solo Flute with Accompaniment

Due to its lyrical nature, the flute is a lovely instrument for solo work in liturgical celebrations. Whether with accompaniment or without, the flutist's solo repertoire can range from meditative music for prelude or Preparation of the Gifts, to majestic marches such as are common for the recessional of a wedding.

A diverse, broad repertoire is the key to success here. The well-rounded flutist knows the literature and is able to select a solo that would evoke the appropriate emotion or mood for the particular celebration. Your favorite piece may be very appropriate for a wedding but may do nothing to enable the prayer experience of a funeral assembly. Always remember the three judgments—musical, liturgical, and pastoral—discussed at the beginning of Chapter 3. Knowledge of the ritual and a familiarity with the music literature are also necessary ingredients for success, which we will explore further in the next chapter.

Find one or two books of appropriate solos to have on hand at all times. You may want to start with *Sacred Solos for the Flute, Volumes I and II*, published by Cathedral Music Press. The pieces are accessible for both flutist and accompanist, and also pleasing for the assembly. Another excellent collection is *Liturgical Meditations: Fourteen Pieces for Flute and Organ* by Jacques Berthier, published by GIA Publications. In addition, the slow movement of almost any Baroque or Classical sonata works very well for liturgical use.

Solo Flute without Accompaniment

There may be times when you will be called upon to play an unaccompanied flute solo. It may be for a liturgy in which you are the only music minister or in which there is an entire choir. No matter the circumstance, the sound of a single flute can be very effective in providing the necessary atmosphere for the occasion.

Imagine how effective it would be for a flutist to greet the mourners for a funeral liturgy and lead them into the **narthex** of the church with the haunting strains of "Amazing Grace." Just picture an unaccompanied flute solo as soothing background music during the laying on of hands for the Communal Anointing of the Sick. A jubilant flute solo can also conclude a Sunday liturgy or wedding celebration. (These ideas are further developed in the next chapter.)

In all of these instances, the flutist needs an instant repertoire of suitable music. An excellent resource is *Hymn Variations for Solo Flute* and *More Hymns for Solo Flute*, both by Victoria Jicha, published by Music Makers/Alry Publications. These books include common hymn tunes, each with two or three variations. Use these as a springboard for your own variations or as a model on which to base variations for other appropriate tunes.

There are also many standard pieces from the flute repertoire that were written for unaccompanied flute. *Unaccompanied Meditations* by Richard Proulx (published by GIA Publications), *Twelve Fantasies* by Telemann, and *Sonata in A Minor for Solo Flute* by J. S. Bach are but a few.

Conclusion

The ideas presented in this chapter are intended to expand your horizons and encourage you to think outside of your comfort zone. More ideas will be explored in the next chapter when we delve into the use of the flute for sacramental celebrations and other rites. Don't be afraid to use your imagination to touch the hearts of God's people. Fresh ideas and effective new sounds can aid in enabling the prayer of your assembly.

Chapter 6
Where, When, and What to Play Beyond the Sunday Eucharist

Spiritual Connectedness
Music as Expression of Life Situations
Gift and Challenge

Do you remember the first time you were invited to play your flute within the context of prayer? Did you say "yes" without hesitation? Did you have reservations? What encouraged you to say "yes"? How many times when we say "yes" to a situation do we understand all that it will demand of us?

If you remain open to being stretched as a liturgical musician, you might find yourself stopping from time to time and saying to yourself, "I didn't think saying 'yes' would mean *this!*" ("This" might mean more demands on your time, your presence, your need to practice, or a deepening of your spirituality, or perhaps even a questioning of things you used to take for granted.)

The reality is that a genuine, open, and freely given "yes" can take you places you could never imagine for yourself. Yet there is both blessing and responsibility in this. It is a blessing, for example, to share special moments in people's lives, such as marriage and baptism and death. As a liturgical musician, this privilege is open to you. To be present as embodied prayer, however, demands that you have a rich prayer life of your own, enter into a spiritual relationship with others, understand the power of music, be willing to be changed. We cannot take lightly any invitation to enter into people's lives with our music—even if it is ever so briefly. Music deepens the connection to one another and can continue communication even when words find their limit.

Do not forget that the value and interest of life is not so much to do conspicuous things (although we must have this ambition) as to do ordinary things with the perception of their enormous value.

—Teilhard de Chardin (from "Meditations with Teilhard de Chardin" by Blanche Gallagher, Bear & Co., Santa Fe, New Mexico)

In previous chapters, we discussed the use of the flute in the context of the Sunday Eucharist. To consider the use of the flute within other liturgical occasions is to imply the need for even greater versatility. In a variety of situations that are not as familiar as the Sunday Eucharist, you must consider

> *While music has traditionally been part of the celebration of weddings, funerals, and confirmation, the communal celebration of baptism, anointing, and penance has only recently been restored. The renewed rituals, following the Constitution on the Sacred Liturgy, provide for and encourage communal celebrations which, according to the capability of the congregation, should involve song.*
> —Music in Catholic Worship, #79

the context of the occasion, the setting, the flow of the ritual, and the appropriateness of the musical choices. How best can the flute be used in the many situations to which you might be called? This chapter will explore some of the various occasions and the possibilities of where, when, and what to play.

The Liturgical Use of the Flute for Various Sacramental Celebrations

There are seven sacraments of the Roman Catholic Church:

- Baptism
- Confirmation
- First Eucharist
- Reconciliation
- Anointing of the Sick
- Matrimony
- Ordination

Except for Reconciliation, all of the sacraments could be and often are celebrated within the context of Mass. In fact, the Liturgical Documents encourage the participation of the entire assembly. Hence, the sacraments take on a deeper meaning if they are shared with the larger community.

In each instance (except for First Communion), the sacrament comes as a

> *Liturgical services are not private functions, but are celebrations belonging to the Church, which is the "sacrament of unity," namely, the holy people united and ordered under their bishops.*
> —26. Cyprian, On the Unity of the Catholic Church 7; see Letter 66, n.8,3.
>
> *Therefore, liturgical services involve the whole Body of the Church; they manifest it and have effects upon it; but they also concern the individual members of the Church in different ways, according to their different orders, offices, and actual participation.*
> *Whenever rites, according to their specific nature, make provisions for communal celebration involving the presence and active participation of the faithful, it is to be stressed that this way of celebrating them is to be preferred, as far as possible, to a celebration that is individual and, so to speak, private.*
> *This applies with special force to the celebration of Mass and the administration of the sacraments, even though every Mass has of itself a public and social character.*
> —Constitution on the Sacred Liturgy, #26 and #27

response to the Liturgy of the Word. It directly follows the homily. It is our response to God's call. It is both a personal and communal moment. The individuals involved in the particular sacrament being celebrated are enriched by the presence and participation of the assembly, and the assembly is enriched by the individuals' witness to God's love.

When any sacrament is experienced within the Mass, you can generally apply the same guidelines used for the Sunday Eucharist. The focus of this chapter is to consider the specific rituals of each sacrament. Baptism, Reconciliation, Marriage, and Anointing of the Sick will be addressed in detail. The remaining sacraments—Confirmation, First Eucharist, and Ordination—will be addressed briefly later in this chapter.

We will present a basic outline for each sacrament's ritual, followed by an exploration of how the flute might be used to enhance the prayer within each sacramental moment. Let the ideas that follow be a catalyst for your own imagination, taking into consideration that each situation is unique.

Note: The Liturgical Documents allow for variations based on circumstances, such as whether or not the sacrament is celebrated within the Eucharist, the number and/or ages of the recipients, etc.

Baptism

Baptism is ideally celebrated at the Easter Vigil in the context of the Rite of Christian Initiation of Adults. The next preference for celebrating Baptism would be at the Sunday Eucharist in the presence of the community. However, children (particularly infants and toddlers) are often baptized outside of the Eucharist. Often this situation points out the unfortunate circumstance of public prayer without the normative inclusion of music. Herein lies an opportunity for a flutist and a single cantor to provide a meaningful service to the community. Consider taking the initiative to consult with the music director and those who preside at this sacrament to see if you might be of service in this ministry. To be of service, you would need to be familiar with the ritual.

OUTLINE OF THE RITE OF BAPTISM

Reception of the Candidate(s)

Liturgy of the Word
- Readings and Homily
- Intercessions
- Prayer of Exorcism and Anointing before Baptism

Celebration of the Sacrament
- Blessing and Invocation of God over Baptismal Water
- Renunciation of Sin and Profession of Faith
- Baptism

Explanatory Rites
- Anointing after Baptism
- Clothing with White Garment
- Lighted Candle
- Prayer over Ears and Mouth

Conclusion of the Rite
- The Lord's Prayer
- Blessing and Dismissal

The rite itself suggests moments where music is appropriate. The ritual often begins with the Questions of Consent being asked in the gathering space during the Reception of the Candidate(s). This is followed by the procession of those assembled into the church to hear the Word of God. One possibility is to play soft music as people assemble, quieting or stopping the music during the Rite of Reception, and supporting the Opening Song to be sung by all as the flutist and cantor lead the procession. The potential for assembly participation is enhanced by the use of short, repeated refrains or **mantras**; or consider any familiar, accessible music commonly used in your parish that might lend itself for use in processions. You might also consider using the same piece of music again for the Closing Song.

In this setting, both you and the cantor could walk in procession, leading the assembly. This assumes you are able to play the Opening/Closing Song from memory and are comfortable improvising without music. If not, perhaps the cantor could process while you play from a nearby stationary location, using music and a music stand.

An example of a processional mantra is "There Is One Lord" by Jacques Berthier (see Example 95).

EXAMPLE 95: EXCERPT FROM "THERE IS ONE LORD" OSTINATO RESPONSE FROM MUSIC FROM TAIZÉ, VOL. II

Copyright © 1982, 1983, 1984, Les Presses de Taizé, Taizé Community, France, published by GIA Publications, Inc., by exclusive agreement

You could play this melody line one octave higher as an introduction and then continue to play this line as support to the assembly. Once the assembly becomes comfortable with the refrain, feel free to improvise or enhance the music with harmonizations, such as those provided in the alto, tenor, or bass lines (in the appropriate octave for flute). You could also choose to play one of the descants provided in the C Instrument book (see Example 96) while the cantor continues to lead the assembly. Remember that even the part that is labeled "Oboe" can be played by flute, either as written or an octave higher.

EXAMPLE 96: EXCERPT FROM "THERE IS ONE LORD" FROM *MUSIC FROM TAIZÉ, VOL. II*
(INSTRUMENTAL DESCANTS)

J. Berthier

If a psalm is used during the Liturgy of the Word, it is best to have it sung. An example of an appropriate psalm setting is "Psalm 23: My Shepherd Is the Lord." Joseph Gelineau's arrangement of this psalm is excellent (see Example 97). This musical example is also referenced in Chapter 5 (see Example 91).

EXAMPLE 97: EXCERPT FROM PSALM 23: "MY SHEPHERD IS THE LORD"

As stated in Chapter 5, the flutist could intone the refrain, lay out while the cantor sings the refrain alone, and then support the song of the entire assembly by playing the melody as the refrain is repeated. The accompaniment for the verses provides fairly easy yet interesting flute lines against which the cantor could sing the verses. One such possibility is shown in full-sized notation in Example 98, starting on the following page.

EXAMPLE 98: EXCERPT FROM PSALM 23: "MY SHEPHERD IS THE LORD"

Gelineau Tone

1. Lord, you are my shepherd;
2. You guide me along the right path;
3. You have prepared a banquet for me
4. Surely goodness and kindness shall follow me
5. To the Father and Son give glory,

1. there is nothing I shall want.
2. You are true to your name. If I should
3. in the sight of my foes. My
4. all the days of my life. In the
5. give glory to the Spirit. To God who

1. Fresh and green are the pastures where you
2. walk in the valley of darkness no
3. head you have a-nointed with oil, [——
4. Lord's own house shall I dwell [——
5. is, who was, and who will be [——

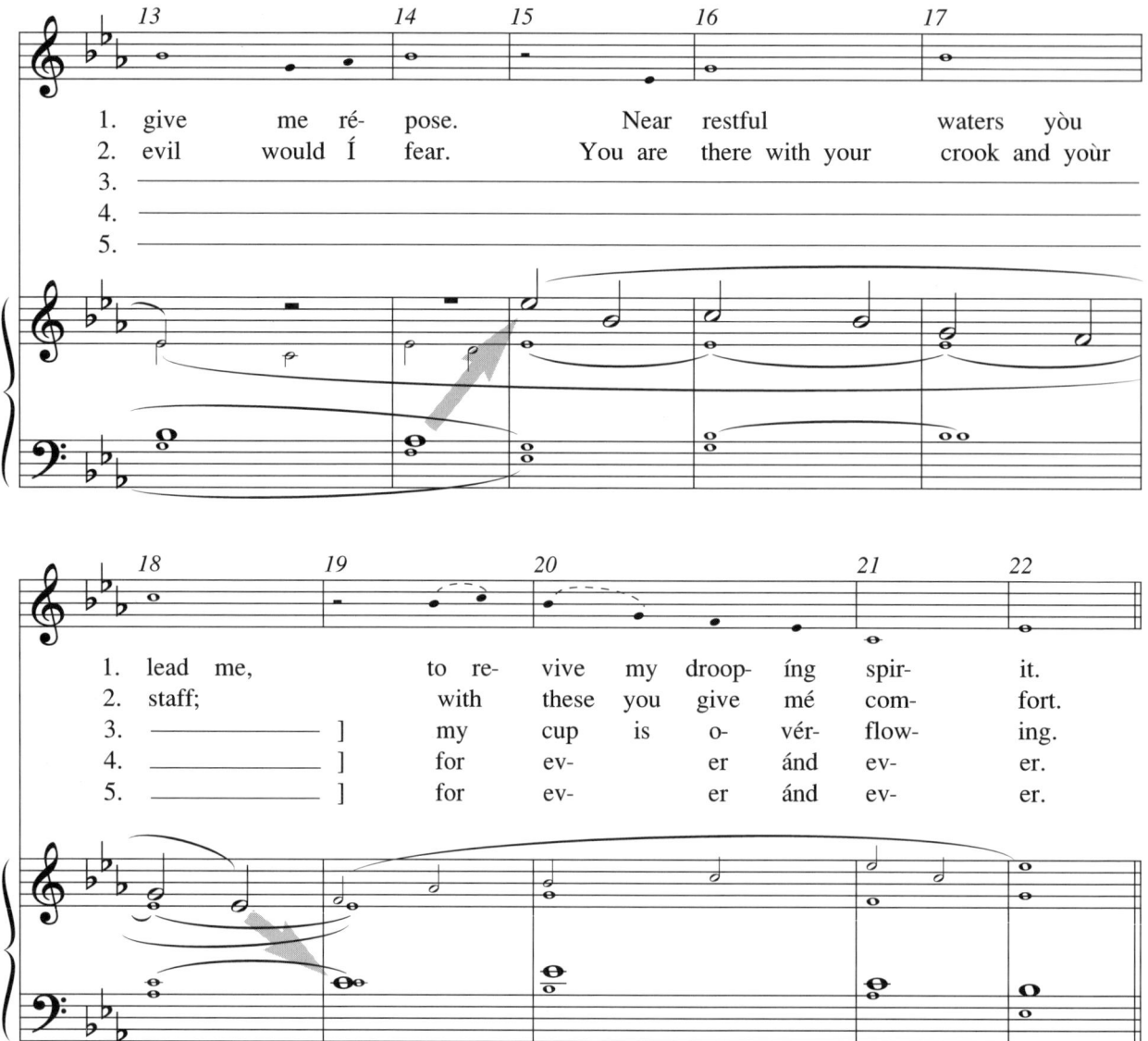

In measures 9–14 and 19–22, if you can read bass clef, you could play the upper voice of that line *8va* (see the part shown in full-sized notation in Example 98).

Assuming Baptisms will only be celebrated outside of the season of Lent, the Gospel Acclamation would be an Alleluia. One possible choice is the Gregorian chant "Alleluia" (see Example 99). Just as done previously in the psalm, the flutist could intone the refrain as an introduction. The cantor would then sing the refrain alone, followed by the entire assembly repeating the refrain supported by the flute. The verse could be sung *a cappella* or, if necessary, be spoken. On the repetition of the refrain, the flutist might choose to add some harmony against the assembly's vocal line. Listen to the example on the CD (Track 49).

EXAMPLE 99: EXCERPT FROM GREGORIAN CHANT "ALLELUIA," ALONG WITH A BAPTISM VERSE

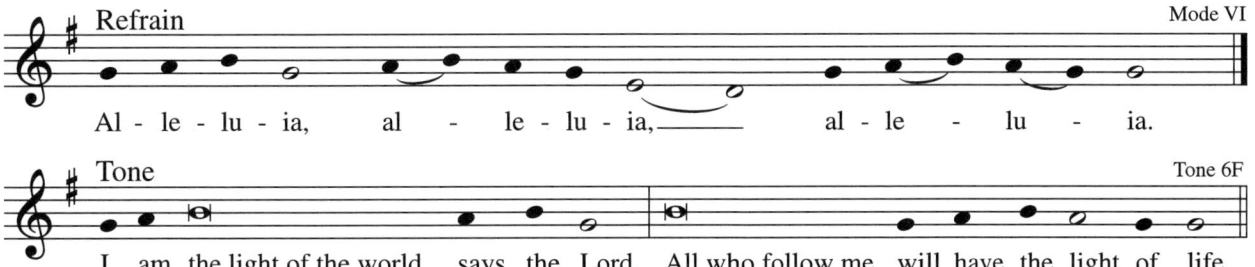

Refrain — Mode VI

Al - le - lu - ia,   al - le - lu - ia,_____ al - le - lu - ia.

Tone — Tone 6F

I am the light of the world   says the Lord.   All who follow me   will have the light of   life.

Track 49: Flute and Cantor on Gospel Acclamation
Gregorian chant "Alleluia" – flute introduction; refrain and verse, flute, cantor, and assembly

The ritual assumes the various parts of the celebration will take place at different stations in the church. A song or acclamation could be sung, or solo flute music could be played as needed to accompany any processional movement from one station to another (e.g., from the pews to the font, or from the font to the altar). See Appendix II: Repertoire/Resource List for suggestions of solo flute music.

There are a number of places in the ritual where acclamations could be sung or spoken. To encourage singing, you could provide the musical introduction and the cantor the invitation. Some examples include an acclamation for use after the Blessing of the Water (e.g., "Who Calls You by Name"), an acclamation for use after each baptism (e.g., "You Are God's Work of Art"), and a sung Amen (see Example 100). Listen to these examples demonstrated on the CD (Track 50) with flute, cantor, and assembly.

EXAMPLE 100: EXCERPT FROM "WHO CALLS YOU BY NAME"

D. Haas

Cantor: Bless-ed be God!   O   Bless-ed be God!   *All:* Bless-ed by God!   O

Bless-ed be God! *Cantor:* Who   calls you by name! *All:* Who calls you be name!_____

Cantor: Ho-ly and cho - sen   one!_____ *All:* Ho-ly and cho - sen   one!_____

EXCERPT FROM "YOU ARE GOD'S WORK OF ART"

Ephesians 1:4, 2:10
The Rite of Baptism
RCIA

D. Haas

You are God's work of art, cre - at - ed in Je - sus the Christ.

"GREAT AMEN" FROM *LAND OF REST ACCLAMATIONS*

LAND OF REST
Adapt. R. Proulx

A - men, —— a - men, a - men.

Track 50: Samples of Baptismal Acclamations
"Who Calls You by Name" – refrain; "You Are God's Work of Art" – refrain; "Great Amen" – for each example: flute introduction, followed by flute, cantor, and assembly

Reconciliation

The Sacrament of Reconciliation in a communal setting, including First Reconciliation, is yet another opportunity for ministry for a liturgical flutist as well as other musicians. There are several forms to the Sacrament of Reconciliation. The focus here is on Form II, the communal rite most commonly used.

OUTLINE OF THE RITE OF RECONCILIATION
FORM II

Introductory Rites	{ – Song – Greeting – Opening Prayer
Celebration of the Word of God	{ – Readings – Homily – Examination of Conscience
Rite of Reconciliation	{ – General Confession of Sins – Individual Confession and Absolution – Proclamation of Praise for God's Mercy – Concluding Prayer of Thanksgiving
Concluding Rite	

As in Baptism, quiet music could be played as the assembly is gathering. Once all have gathered, the rite calls for an Opening Song. "Take, O Take Me As I Am" is one example (see Example 101).

EXAMPLE 101: EXCERPT FROM "TAKE, O TAKE ME AS I AM"

J. Bell

Take, O take me as I am; sum - mon out what I shall be; set your seal up-on my heart and live in me.

You could choose to play the melody as an introduction, either with or without keyboard accompaniment, and then stay on the melody when the assembly sings the refrain for the first time. After that, you might consider playing one of the other lines (in an appropriate flute range) as a descant.

When a psalm is used during the Liturgy of the Word, it should be sung. For ideas, look to the psalms used during the season of Lent, such as an arrangement of Psalm 51.

The Gospel Acclamation precedes the Gospel. As with Baptism, one possible choice is the Gregorian Chant "Alleluia" (see Example 99). For Reconciliation services during the season of Lent, consider Richard Proulx's "Lenten Acclamation" (see Example 102). If no one is singing the vocal descant, you might choose to play this line after the verse.

EXAMPLE 102: EXCERPT FROM "LENTEN ACCLAMATION"

R. Proulx

Vocal Descant

Glo - ry to you, O Word of God, Lord___ Je - sus Christ!

Melody

Glo - ry to you, O Word of God, Lord— Je - sus Christ!

It is highly suggested to provide music (sung or instrumental) during the Individual Confession and Absolution. For sung music, refer to music from the Iona Community, or psalm arrangements such as "Psalm 136: Love Is Never Ending" by Marty Haugen, or a Taizé mantra, such as "Nothing Can Trouble" (or in Spanish, "Nada te turbe"). Solo instrumental music can be found in *Liturgical Meditations* by Jacques Berthier. See Examples 103 and 104 for excerpts from two of the *Liturgical Meditations*: the first scored for flute and keyboard, and the other for flute alone.

EXAMPLE 103: EXCERPT FROM "YOU ARE THE IMAGE AND THE HOPE"
FROM *LITURGICAL MEDITATIONS*

J. Berthier

EXAMPLE 104: EXCERPT FROM "PEACE AND SILENCE"
FROM *LITURGICAL MEDITATIONS*

Copyright © 1987 by GIA Publications, Inc.

After Individual Confession and Absolution, the Proclamation of Praise for God's Mercy can be sung in the form of a psalm, hymn, or litany. Some suggestions include "Canticle of Mary" by Michael Joncas, Taizé "Magnificat," or a psalm arrangement such as "Psalm 136" mentioned above.

Although it is not necessary, there could be a Closing Song. It might be the same selection as the Opening Song, or it could be another appropriate piece (such as "Jesus, Remember Me," another Taizé mantra).

While an ensemble of several instrumentalists with cantor is ideal, at least one instrumentalist and cantor are needed to support the musical prayer of the assembly. A flutist can certainly fill this role. The musical suggestions listed above reflect the flute either as enhancement to keyboard and cantor, or as sole accompaniment for the cantor, as well as solo instrument.

Anointing of the Sick

Vatican Council II clarified the instruction regarding those who might receive the sacrament of Anointing of the Sick. Although it was always intended for those afflicted with serious illness, it had become the practice prior to Vatican II to postpone the sacrament until death was imminent. In the Constitution on the Sacred Liturgy, the Fathers of the Second Vatican Council spoke in these terms:

> *"Extreme Unction," which may also and more properly be called "anointing of the sick," is not a sacrament for those only who are at the point of death. Hence, as soon as any one of the faithful begins to be in danger of death from sickness or old age, the fitting time for that person to receive this sacrament has certainly already arrived.*
>
> —Constitution on the Sacred Liturgy, #73

Many parishes provide a communal Anointing of the Sick once or twice a year. In this way, the sacrament emphasizes that what happens to one member affects all. The sacrament may be celebrated either within or outside the Eucharist. Although the sacrament may be celebrated in a hospital or other setting, our focus here is on the communal celebration in a church setting.

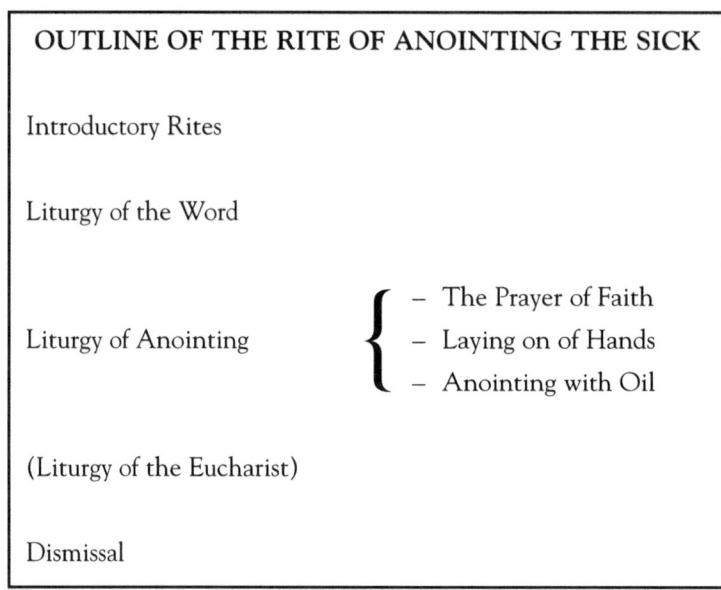

OUTLINE OF THE RITE OF ANOINTING THE SICK

Introductory Rites

Liturgy of the Word

Liturgy of Anointing
 { – The Prayer of Faith
   – Laying on of Hands
   – Anointing with Oil

(Liturgy of the Eucharist)

Dismissal

The Introductory Rites, Liturgy of the Word, and Dismissal follow the pattern of Mass (as does the Liturgy of the Eucharist when the sacrament is celebrated within Mass). Because of the communal nature of this celebration, most decisions concerning what and where to use music are usually made by the music director. As has been the focus for the other sacraments, we will center on the celebration of the sacrament itself.

During the Laying on of Hands and Anointing, there is opportunity to minister through music. Depending on the number of recipients of the sacrament, a variety of music could be used. There may be congregational singing, choir music, solo instrumental music (accompanied or unaccompanied)—or a combination of the above. Appropriate choices for flute solo literature during this sacrament would be similar to those appropriate for the Sacrament of Reconciliation. The choices for the other types of music would usually be made by the music director.

Marriage

The Sacrament of Marriage is celebrated either within Eucharist or outside the Eucharist.

As noted in Chapter 3, musical choices for prayer depend on three judgments: musical, liturgical, and pastoral. Regarding marriage, the liturgical judgment implies a familiarity with both the scriptures that have been chosen for the celebration and the liturgical season. The pastoral judgment takes into account the general makeup of the assembly: who they are, where they are from, their cultural background, etc. The musical judgment takes into consideration the quality of the music and its accessibility to the assembly celebrating a marriage. Since music is normative to every worship experience, select those pieces that would support the assembly in their prayer, sung and spoken. It is uncommon for a flutist to assist the couple in making their musical selections. However, such opportunities may arise, so it is necessary to understand the ritual to be able to provide *catechesis* for a couple at those times. It is imperative that you (and all music ministers) remember that this is a ministry, not a performance.

As with Sunday celebrations, weddings include a procession and a recession. You may or may not be involved in playing these selections. Weddings are also similar to the Sunday Eucharist in regard to the Liturgy of the Word, which includes spoken scriptures, sung psalmody, and Gospel acclamation. For weddings that are celebrated within the Eucharist, the Liturgy of the Eucharist follows the same pattern as on Sundays with the Preparation of the Gifts, Eucharistic Prayer, and Communion Rite. (See Appendix II: Repertoire/Resource List for repertoire suggestions.) It is the Rite of Marriage itself, which is celebrated after the homily, that differs from Sunday celebrations.

OUTLINE OF THE RITE OF MARRIAGE

Introduction
Questions
Consent
Blessing of Rings
Exchange of Rings

Our primary focus here is music within the Rite of Marriage itself. First, there could be a sung acclamation (i.e., an Alleluia, except during Lent) after the consent (vows) and/or after the exchange of rings. Another possibility would be to use a hymn tune after the exchange of rings. Examples include "Now Thank We All Our God" or "Hear Us Now, Our God and Father," the latter set to the tunes HYFRYDOL or NETTLETON. This gives a liturgical voice to the assembly at the moment when there is a community desire to get up and cheer for the newly married couple! It emphasizes that which is important in this rite: the sacramental moment itself—the bride and groom giving this sacrament to each other in the presence of God and the assembly.

The Nuptial Blessing is part of the marriage rite, although there is some variation in its placement within the service. For example, it often immediately follows the Lord's Prayer, but it may also occur at the time of the assembly's Final Blessing. Regardless of its placement, the blessing could be sung. Michael Joncas has an arrangement titled "A Nuptial Blessing." Because of its length, you may wish to weave only the sung refrain between the spoken text of the blessing. The keyboardist could begin the music and then accompany the flute, cantor, and assembly at the appropriate time, while continuing the music softly underneath the spoken text. With each successive repetition of the refrain, the flutist could vary the descant by playing one of the choral lines (see Example 105), or one of the instrumental parts from the C Instrument book (see Example 106), or an improvised descant of your own creation. Listen to this example on the CD (Track 51).

EXAMPLE 105: EXCERPT FROM "A NUPTIAL BLESSING"

V. Klima, adapt. M. Joncas and G. Szews

M. Joncas

EXAMPLE 106: EXCERPT FROM "A NUPTIAL BLESSING"
(FROM THE C INSTRUMENT BOOK)

M. Joncas

Track 51: Flute within the Nuptial Blessing
"A Nuptial Blessing" – refrain, flute and piano with spoken text, cantor and assembly

There are a variety of other opportunities for music within the celebration of marriage that can be offered as options to the bridal couple:

- Preservice music or Prelude music
- Gathering Hymn following the procession
- A song after the homily
- Sung response to the Intercessory Prayers
- Music during the Sign of Peace
- Postlude

In addition, sometimes there are cultural adaptations to which music can provide support.

- During the sign of unity expressed through the lighting of a single candle from two smaller candles or through the Hispanic *lazo ceremony*, both done after the consent (vows) and exchange of rings
- During devotions to the Blessed Mother
- When flowers are presented to the bride's and groom's mothers; etc.

Although these moments are not part of the rites, they are commonly experienced within the service and can be very meaningful to particular couples.

If any of the above options are chosen, the following repertoire is suggested:

- The preservice and/or postlude selections are usually taken from Classical repertoire.
- To gather and focus the assembly after the procession of the wedding party, or to give reflection time after the homily, a hymn might be appropriate. Some choices include "When Love Is Found" and "Love Is the Sunlight" by Jeanne Cotter and David Haas; "God in the Planning," text by John Bell; or "Covenant Hymn" by Rory Cooney and Gary Daigle.
- If the couple has chosen to spend time in prayer to the Blessed Mother, often a solo such as the Schubert "Ave Maria" is used. This piece could be sung by a vocalist or played as an instrumental solo with accompaniment.

Finally, there are times during the liturgy or during the marriage rite itself when an unaccompanied flute selection underscoring the ritual movement or the spoken text could provide quiet, simple musical support (provided it does not obliterate the spoken prayer).

The flute is an appropriate instrument for any of these moments within the celebration of marriage. However, remember that constant use is equivalent to too much frosting on the cake! As in all instances, use sensitivity when choosing where, when, and what to play.

Confirmation, First Eucharist, Ordination

Of the remaining three sacraments, First Eucharist and Ordination are celebrated within the context of the Eucharist. Confirmation is usually celebrated within the Eucharist, but not always. All three sacraments require preparation by the music director, who is ultimately responsible for the ongoing musical formation of the assembly. In other words, although the flutist is frequently invited to be part of the music ensemble for these special events, the main planning for the music rests with the music director.

If you are asked to bring solo repertoire, there are several considerations. For example, you must take into account the ritual moment during which the piece would be played: Prelude, during the sacramental action, Preparation of the Gifts, Communion Meditation, Postlude. In addition, you must consider the season of the church year. If the celebration takes place during Lent, the choices would likely be different than when the sacrament is celebrated during the Easter season. (See Appendix II: Repertoire/Resource List for repertoire suggestions.)

You may also need to take the initiative to make sure there is adequate rehearsal time with the accompanist prior to the service.

The Liturgical Use of the Flute
in Other Prayer Forms

The flute is an instrument whose versatility can call people to prayer in a variety of situations: in transition moments, in ordinary moments, in the pivotal moments of their lives. As such, flute music can be uplifting, soothing, celebrative, supportive, healing. Sometimes the plaintive tone of the flute is a powerfully sustaining instrument for peace, a sound that can invite courage and hope even within those who are deep in the throes of mourning and loss. In many ways, the presence of the flute (and by inference the instrumentalist parish minister) becomes like a comforting friend, appreciated for its constancy and its familiarity.

It is not possible in these pages to consider all of the variety of prayer situations encountered within a parish community. Imagine, for instance, the use of the flute at the prayer for the first viewing of the deceased, or at a communion service provided by a minister of care at a nursing home. It is our hope, however, that by discussing one or two prayer forms in some detail, your imagination will be stimulated to explore other possibilities in your particular worship community. We have chosen to look at the various stations surrounding the Funeral Rites and the Liturgy of the Hours.

Funerals

The Church provides prayers for each station in the family's journey from the point of their loved one's death to burial. Some of these moments are more public prayer; some are more private. Our focus is the ministry of the liturgical flutist in the public prayer settings:

> *The time immediately following death is often one of bewilderment and may involve shock or heartrending grief for the family and close friends. The ministry of the Church at this time is one of gently accompanying the mourners in their initial adjustment to the fact of death and to the sorrow this entails.*
>
> —**Order of Christian Funerals, #52**

- Gathering in the Presence of the Body
- The Vigil
- The Transfer of the Body
- The Funeral Liturgy (within the Eucharist or outside of the Mass)
- The Rite of Committal

According to *Music in Catholic Worship,*

> *Music becomes particularly important in the new burial rites. Without it the themes of hope and resurrection are very difficult to express.*
>
> —**Music in Catholic Worship, #83**

It becomes the responsibility of all the music ministers, including the liturgical flutist, to support the assembly in this expression.

Rather than taking the Funeral Rites in order, we have chosen to start with the public prayer setting in which a flutist most commonly participates—namely, the Funeral Liturgy. The other stations of the Funeral Rites will be considered in the order in which they are experienced: Gathering in the Presence of the Body, the Vigil, the Transfer of the Body, and the Rite of Committal. Each of these rituals (as well as the Funeral Liturgy Outside of Mass) allows for either ordained or lay presiding. These rites also provide numerous ministerial opportunities for a liturgical flutist, either with or without a cantor or accompanist.

Let's consider the following.

Funeral Liturgy:

The Funeral Liturgy is the high point of the Roman Catholic funeral rites. It can take place within the Eucharist or outside the Mass. It is the time when the community gathers in its place of worship to mourn the loss of the deceased and to support the family in their grief. Just as with Sunday celebrations, music is normative and gives voice to the assembly in their grief.

The greeting of the body is a poignant moment for the entire assembly. The potential for music to touch the soul and to tenderly embrace the mourners is ripe with possibility. Below is a common scenario.

> The priest/presider greets the body at the door of the church. It is here that the Introductory Rites take place, followed by the invitation to the assembly to gather in song as they process to their pews. As is normative during the Opening Song at the Sunday Eucharist, the assembly's song is supported by the organ/keyboard, cantor, and/or other instruments.
>
> This is the situation most often experienced by a liturgical flutist. On the other hand, if you are able to memorize and/or improvise, one of the following possibilities might be considered:
>
> - Stand with the priest/presider in greeting the body near the door of the church. After the Introductory Rites, lead the procession into the body of the church. Either the melody of the Opening Song or an improvisation in the key of the Opening Song can be played. After reaching the front, (while still playing) pause briefly in reverence before the altar and then proceed to the music area. Once most of the assembly is in the pews, the organ/keyboard dovetails with the flute music, the Opening Song is announced, and all sing with the support of the cantor and instruments.
>
> – or –
>
> - Stand with the priest/presider and play while the assembly gathers in the narthex. Continue playing quietly during the Introductory Rites, taking care not to obscure the spoken prayer. A particularly poignant moment occurs during the Placing of the Pall. Here is an opportunity to increase volume and intensity of your sound, flowing directly into the organ/keyboard introduction for the Opening Song. While walking in procession, continue to play, supporting the gathering of the assembly in song. Listen to the CD (Track 52) for an example of this approach using the selection "Jesus Christ, Yesterday, Today and Forever" by Suzanne Toolan (see Example 107).

EXAMPLE 107: EXCERPT FROM "JESUS CHRIST, YESTERDAY, TODAY AND FOREVER"

S. Toolan, SM

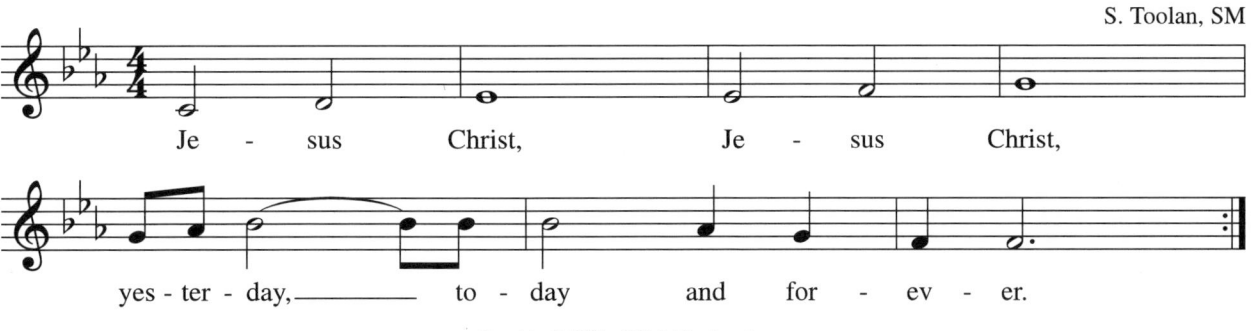

Je - sus Christ, Je - sus Christ, yes - ter - day,_____ to - day and for - ev - er.

Copyright © 1988 by GIA Publications, Inc.

Track 52: Flute within the Introductory Rites of the Funeral Liturgy
"Jesus Christ, Yesterday, Today and Forever" – flute and piano with spoken and sung voice

The funeral liturgy follows the same pattern as Sunday Eucharist: Introductory Rites, Liturgy of the Word, and Liturgy of the Eucharist (only for funerals that are celebrated within the Mass). Here, the Liturgy of the Eucharist follows the same pattern as Sunday liturgy with regards to the Preparation of the Gifts, Eucharistic Prayer, and Communion Rite. (See Appendix II: Repertoire/Resource List for repertoire suggestions.) What is unique to funerals is the Final Commendation. This ritual can occur at any one of several different times: after the Communion Rite at the Eucharist, after the Lord's Prayer if the funeral is celebrated outside of the Eucharist, or during the Rite of Committal at the cemetery.

OUTLINE OF FINAL COMMENDATION
Invitation to Prayer
Silence
Signs of Farewell   – Incensing and/or sprinkling with Holy Water
Song of Farewell
Prayer of Commendation

The Song of Farewell is always sung by the assembly. One appropriate selection is Steven R. Janco's "Song of Farewell/Saints of God." If the song is done at the cemetery, a flutist and cantor could support and lead the assembly without the need for keyboard accompaniment.

Following the Song is the Prayer of Commendation. If this ritual has taken place in the church, it is usually followed by the Procession to the Place of Committal. This is akin to the recessional of the Sunday Eucharist. Musical possibilities are numerous. Choose from your parish's repertoire of songs of hope in the resurrection. You may choose to walk in procession while playing.

Let's now consider a few of the other rituals that are part of the funeral rites.

Gathering in the Presence of the Body:

This ritual occurs when the family first views the body of their deceased loved one—often taking place when the family arrives at the funeral home. The presence of the parish's ministers can provide a sense of community support in this sensitive moment.

> *The family members, in assembling in the presence of the body, confront in the most immediate way the fact of their loss and the mystery of death.*
> —Order of Christian Funerals, #109

> ### OUTLINE OF THE RITE
>
> Sign of the Cross
> Scripture Verse
> Sprinkling with Holy Water
> Psalm
> The Lord's Prayer
> Concluding Prayer
> Blessing

The flutist could be present with the parish ministers (presider and cantor) at the funeral home before the arrival of the family, playing quiet, *a cappella* music that would greet the family and be a source of comfort. At the opportune time, you could then segue into a song that gathers the group in prayer. The psalm could also be accompanied as previously discussed. Or a closing song or mantra could be sung after the blessing.

Vigil for the Deceased:

> *The vigil for the deceased is the principal rite celebrated by the Christian community in the time following death and before the funeral liturgy—or if there is no funeral liturgy, before the rite of committal. It may take the form either of a liturgy of the word or of some part of the office for the dead.*
> —Order of Christian Funerals, #54

OUTLINE OF THE RITE

Introductory Rites
- Greeting
- Opening Song
- Invitation to Prayer
- Opening Prayer

Liturgy of the Word
- First Reading
- Responsorial Psalm
- Gospel
- Homily

Prayer of Intercession
- Litany
- The Lord's Prayer
- Concluding Prayer

Concluding Rite
- Blessing

According to the *Order of Christian Funerals,*

> *Music is integral to any vigil, especially the vigil for the deceased. In the difficult circumstances following death, well-chosen music can touch the mourners and others present at levels of human need that words alone often fail to reach. Such music can enliven the faith of the community gathered to support the family and to affirm hope in the resurrection.*
>
> —Order of Christian Funerals, #68

The Vigil is often experienced at the funeral home or in the church, but it could also be celebrated in any suitable place (e.g., the home of the deceased or a nursing home). Regardless of location, the vigil provides opportunity for the ministry of a liturgical flutist, either alone, with a cantor, or with other instrumentalists. For example, appropriate prelude music could set the tone for the vigil service. Because the rite is basically a Liturgy of the Word, other musical choices are much the same as at the Sunday Eucharist: Opening Song, Psalm, Gospel Acclamation, and perhaps a Closing Song. It is imperative to apply the wisdom of the three judgments (musical, liturgical, and pastoral) when choosing music to be used for this service.

Transfer of the Body to the Church or to the Place of Committal:

These prayers usually take place at the funeral home. The body is then transferred to the church for the funeral liturgy or occasionally directly to the cemetery, but always in procession.

> *Processions can express God's abiding presence among us as well as our journey toward the reign of God—our final destiny and the fulfillment of all our rituals. Since processions are accompanied by singing or instrumental music, they name in audible as well as visible form the goal of our life and the stages in the journey toward that goal.*
>
> —"Walking Our Prayer: With God on the Way to God," by Gordon E. Truitt, *Pastoral Music*, August–September 2002

The *Order of Christian Funerals* states the following on the subject of processions:

> *The procession to the church is a rite of initial separation of the mourners from the deceased; the procession to the place of committal is the journey to the place of final separation of the mourners from the deceased. Because the transfer of the body may be an occasion of great emotion for the mourners, the ministers and other members of the community should make every effort to be present to support them. Reverent celebration of the rite can help reassure the mourners and create an atmosphere of calm preparation before the procession.*
>
> —Order of Christian Funerals, #120

The outline of the rite provided in *Order of Christian Funerals* is shown below. The prayers leading up to the Procession to the Church or Place of Committal can vary greatly. Thus, your role as flutist would vary accordingly.

OUTLINE OF THE RITE

Invitation

Scripture Verse

Litany

The Lord's Prayer

Concluding Prayer

Invitation to the Procession

Procession to the Church or to the Place of Committal

After the prayers leading up to the procession, you could play quiet music as the mourners walk past and view the body one last time. If the funeral home is very near to the church, often the assembly will walk in procession to the church; you could continue to play while leading the procession of the assembly and the body of the deceased. If the church is some distance away, you could get to the church ahead of the mobile funeral procession and play the same music as at the funeral home. For added continuity, this music may also be what is chosen as the Opening Song of the Funeral Liturgy.

Note: You could minister in a similar way if the Committal Service takes places immediately following the Funeral Liturgy. In this instance, whatever music is played as the Closing Song of the funeral liturgy could be echoed at graveside or cemetery chapel.

It is clear that there are many ministerial opportunities for the liturgical flutist within the various funeral rites. To summarize but a few:

- The flutist could set the tone for any of the ritual moments by making appropriate choices of unaccompanied music.

- Solo flute music could be interwoven with spoken text or could segue into sung selections by choosing a piece in the same key as the assembly's song. (See Chapter 9 for more about weaving text and music.)
- There are many opportunities for psalmody; make application based on previously discussed approaches.
- The flutist could walk in procession, making the journey with the mourners from one station of the funeral rites to the next.

Liturgy of the Hours

Liturgy of the Hours (also known as the "Divine Office") is prayer centered around giving praise and honor to God all throughout the day. It is a way of marking time as holy and as gift. Its roots are in Judaism and in the prayer life of the monastic. Only since Vatican II has this prayer form become more accessible to the parish community, second only to the Eucharist as the community's way of worshipping God together.

> *If the faithful come together and unite their hearts and voices in the Liturgy of the Hours, they manifest the Church celebrating the mystery of Christ.*
>
> —Liturgy of the Hours, #22

While there are prayers for every part of the day within the Liturgy of the Hours, the Morning Prayer (lauds) and Evening Prayer (vespers) rituals are the ones most commonly done within a parish setting, with the occasional praying of Night Prayer (compline). Sometimes a parish will do Evening Prayer once a week during the seasons of Advent/Christmas and/or Lent/Easter. Often parishes do Morning Prayer during the Triduum days of Holy Thursday, Good Friday, and Holy Saturday. Night Prayer might be experienced at the end of the vigil on Holy Thursday. Sometimes circumstances occasion a fasting from the Eucharist during the week, and Morning Prayer is done as a way of gathering the community in prayer each day. The flexibility and adaptability of the Hours (there are options within the ritual for lengthening or shortening the prayer) make them ideal for many occasions when the worshipping community gathers to pray. In fact, most parishes have not as yet chosen to utilize fully this beautiful, restful, and comforting prayer.

Liturgy of the Hours provides an opportunity for a trained and qualified layperson to preside over the public prayer. It is also an opportunity for a flutist to give support to the assembly song, usually along with other musicians, but at least with organ/keyboard and cantor.

Each liturgy within the Liturgy of the Hours has its own prayer form, but all of the liturgies center around the singing of the psalms and the reading of Scripture. Below

> *Since the Office (Hours) is the prayer of the whole People of God, it has been drawn up and prepared in such a way that not only ecclesiastics but also religious and even laymen [sic] can take part in it. By introducing various forms of celebration, the attempt has been made to meet the specific requirements of persons of different order and degree. The prayer can be adapted to the different communities that celebrate the Liturgy of the Hours, according to their condition and vocation.*
>
> —Paul VI, November 1, 1970,
> **Apostolic Constitution on the Breviary *Laudis Canticum***

are the outlines of service for Morning, Evening, and Night Prayer. There are published musical settings for these prayers, and most hymnals have sections devoted to these rituals. As a pastoral minister, you should be familiar with this music and with this prayer form.

MORNING PRAYER

Introductory Rites
{
- Greeting
- Morning Hymn (emphasis on morning, light, praise)
- Water Ritual (optional)
- Morning Thanksgiving (optional)

Psalmody
{
- Psalm 63 (traditional morning psalm)
- Silence
- Collect Prayer
- Second Psalm (optional – usually a psalm of praise, thanksgiving, or creation, followed by Silence and Collect Prayer)

Scripture
{
- Brief Reading
- Silence
- Canticle of Praise (Canticle of Zachary or Glory to God)

Intercessory Prayer
{
- Intercessions (for needs of world, the community, and to dedicate the day's work to God)
- The Lord's Prayer

Concluding Rite
{
- Concluding Prayer
- Blessing
- Dismissal (exchange of peace)

EVENING PRAYER

Light Service

Optional
{
- Procession with Paschal Candle
- Proclamation
- Lighting of Assembly's Candles

OR

{
- Introductory Proclamation (in place of above)
- Evening Hymn
- Evening Thanksgiving

Psalmody
{
- Offering of Incense
- Psalm 141 (invariable)
- Silence
- Collect Prayer
- Second Psalm (optional – psalm of trust, peace, or thanksgiving, followed by Silence and Collect Prayer)
- Third Psalm or New Testament Canticle (optional)

Scripture
{
- Brief Reading
- Silence
- Responsorial Song or Short Response (optional)
- Canticle of Mary (Magnificat) (invariable)

Intercessory Prayer
{
- Intercessions
- The Lord's Prayer

Concluding Rite
{
- Concluding Prayer
- Blessing
- Dismissal (exchange of peace)

NIGHT PRAYER

Introduction
{
- Greeting
- Penitential Rite
- Hymn

Psalmody
{
- Psalm (traditional compline psalms: Psalm 4, Psalm 90 (91), and Psalm 133 (134)
- Silence
- Collect Prayer

Scripture
{
- Brief Reading
- Silence
- Responsory
- Canticle of Simeon

Intercessory Prayer

Concluding Rite
{
- Concluding Prayer
- Dismissal (anthem to Mary, such as "Salve Regina")

Some of the repertoire from your parish's Sunday Eucharistic celebrations could also be used in the celebration of the Liturgy of the Hours. For example, the Opening and Closing Songs could be taken from the parish repertoire, as could sung Intercessions and the Lord's Prayer. Other pieces, such as any unfamiliar psalm settings and canticles, could become a standard part of parish repertoire, and certainly part of the common repertoire for the music ministers, by celebrating the Hours on a regular (or at least seasonal) basis.

For more information about Liturgy of the Hours, consult *Morning and Evening: A Parish Celebration* by Joyce Ann Zimmerman, CPPS, published by Liturgy Training Publications.

Conclusion

When we think about all of the different prayer forms used in Catholic/Christian worship, there is not even one instance in which the use of the flute is inappropriate. A skilled liturgical flutist can be an integral part of the celebration of any sacrament. As noted, you could also play for the various funeral rites and the Liturgy of the Hours. You could also add **May Crownings** and other Marian devotions, as well as **Benediction**, **Quinceñero**, and Taizé Prayer to the list of the variety of prayer situations in the parish that invite a flutist's ministry and still not exhaust those possibilities. Just remember that although it is possible to play for any and all of these occasions, it is important to guard against overkill. Use discretion within any of these rituals, and first and foremost, embody the prayer.

In each of the settings outlined above, it is clear that part of the flute's versatility is its portability. The flute works equally well in large spaces such as churches and halls; in intimate settings like homes, small chapels, or funeral parlors; and in outdoor venues such as graveside committal services. The trained flutist is also equally comfortable in a stationary setting as in a procession.

A word of caution: When the ritual takes place outdoors, you need to be prepared for the weather. In cold temperatures, fingerless gloves could be very helpful. On windy days, be sure to use a sturdy music stand and wind clips or clothespins to prevent your music from blowing away. If the outdoor elements are less than ideal, you might consider using a cheaper, older flute if available, keeping your "good" flute exclusively for indoor use. If the weather is severe (e.g., rain, snow, or extremes of temperature), you may need to respectfully decline the opportunity to play. Weather of this nature could damage your instrument, to say nothing of the toll it may take on you! Fortunately, outdoor liturgies are usually scheduled at warmer times of year or in warmer climates, so some of the effects of nature are thereby avoided.

As you can see, the flute is a versatile and colorful instrument whose mystical qualities transcend the pedestrian. Take time at this point to become rooted in solid technique and liturgical vernacular. When this becomes second nature, you may choose to explore in-depth both the advanced techniques of improvisation and additional ways you might affect the assembly's prayer experience. This is the work of the next section—"The Advanced Liturgical Flutist: Going Deeper."

Section III

The Advanced Liturgical Flutist:
Going Deeper

Chapter 7
Improvisation Skills

Heightened Awareness of Creativity
Freedom for Interpretation
Seeing through Your Mind's Eye

Reflect on this poem about improvisation before reading Chapter 7.

It will take on
a musical life
of its own
because you have
the power
to hear the sounds
connecting
sparking
relating

With tingling fingers
and pronounced anticipation
you take what is known
and make it
your voice
fresh and alive
past concrete notes
and feared mishaps

You are free
free to create
what is all inside
giving way to
a process that
coincides with
your momentum
your confidence
your passion

Improvise and find
your own beginning
Improvise and find
your own end
Improvise and find
your own peace

—Rachel C. Ready

Improvisation allows you to be composer and arranger "in the moment." You are "off the page" and free to plummet to the depths of your spirit. Such freedom can be exhilarating and scary. It can bring us to the shores of our own peace or to the brink of feared mishaps. In time, we realize this is one gift of improvisation—that in doing it we can expect to make mistakes, and that then we are free to create something new. This tension between our fears over mishaps and the peace of being creatively free is a point of discovery—about ourselves, about our music-making, about our relationship with other musicians. We learn to listen better. We learn acceptance and humility. We learn trust. And, hopefully, we pray more deeply.

The liturgy requires of its handmaids that they should stimulate "prayer within beauty," not that they should "foster beauty within prayer."

—Joseph Gelineau

Webster's Dictionary says the following about improvisation:

> extemporaneous composition; to bring about, arrange, or make on the spur of the moment or without preparation; to construct or fabricate out of what is conveniently at hand.

It is clear that improvisation is not for the faint of heart. In the language of psychology, this is the world of the "right-brained." It involves a letting go, a tapping into a deep creativity, a trust in one's own musical instincts. All of this is borne of being rooted in certain knowledge and sensibilities. In other words, it is "in the moment" and "extemporaneous," yet in a very real way, there have been years of preparation and many steps in the process. Let us together remind ourselves of what these steps have been.

- Knowledge of scales (both major and minor), triads (major, minor, diminished, and augmented), seventh and ninth chords
- Ability to read and play both treble clef and bass clef parts (in the appropriate octave for flute)
- Sensitivity to the style and period in which the music was composed (see Appendix I: The History of the Use of the Flute and Other Instruments in Worship)
- Reflection on the song text as a catalyst for a deeper immersion into the nuances of the music
- Familiarity with the rites, their flow and rhythms
- Experience in memorizing and adapting flute parts to different situations
- Awareness of space and acoustics
- Attentiveness to who the assembly is and what occasion gathers them together
- Knowledge of repertoire
- A spirit of prayer

You can see that the groundwork for improvisation has already been established in the preceding chapters of this book, and you have probably already been through these steps in one way or another, even if you have not named them as such. So in many ways, this chapter will strengthen and expand on what you already know and are doing. But it will also demand a more serious approach to doing improvisation with greater complexity. Ask yourself if this is something that appeals to you. (For more about discerning your own readiness for improvisation, see Appendix V: Me, Improvise?!)

It is important to note that when improvising, each musician should possess a sense of individual authority in relationship with others. This does not imply musical arrogance or cockiness, but it does imply a sense of the importance of your instrument's voice in the mix of the whole. In some ways this is a paradox: it is both intimate (trying to find ways to express that which is personal) and detached (trying to step away from it enough to be present to others). This implies strong listening skills, a willingness to let go of too much focus on ego, and a desire to be co-creative and collaborative—all the while keeping the assembly primary. In other words, you must remember during improvisation that you are always a part of something bigger than yourself.

Only you will know when you are ready to begin seriously using improvisation. On one level you might think you will never be ready. Yet part of the process is being willing to let go of fear, doubt, and insecurities, and to risk making mistakes—just doing it and trusting your musicality.

Elements of Improvisation

As we approach the nuts and bolts of improvisation, it is important to keep in mind that there are as many different ways to improvise a descant as there are people who make music. The written descants that follow should be used as a guide and catalyst for creating your own parts. Each time you revisit this chapter, you will probably come up with another descant or another version of an old descant. This is not to say that the old is bad and the new is good, or that yours is good and someone else's is bad. There are numerous good ways of creating a pleasing descant. Begin by writing your descants on paper. With practice, you will reach a comfort level that will allow you to eliminate the written step.

Let's now focus on several elements that are integral to improvisation: harmony, melody, and rhythm.

Harmonic Considerations

When you decide to write or improvise a descant, there will almost always be a given harmonic structure within which you must remain. It is rare that you would need to create the harmonization by writing a keyboard or choral arrangement of a melody. Therefore, this discussion will focus on some ways of creating a descant when the harmonies are already supplied, thus continuing the work begun earlier in this book (see "Playing from a Guitar Score/Lead Sheet" in Chapter 4).

As you will recall, a basic understanding of chord analysis is necessary for the improviser. If you are reading from a guitar score, the analysis is already spelled out in the chord symbols. Keyboard music provides a bit more of a challenge because the chord symbols are often not present (This latter scenario will be addressed later in this chapter).

Let's first examine the refrain from "We Are Called" (see Example 108). Notice that the keyboard accompaniment also includes the guitar chords. In this case, you have the best of both worlds with the benefit of both keyboard and guitar accompaniment. Now look at one possible option for a flute descant, also shown in Example 108. Listen to the first 8 measures of this example on the CD (Track 53).

EXAMPLE 108: EXCERPT FROM "WE ARE CALLED" (INCLUDING FLUTE DESCANT #1)

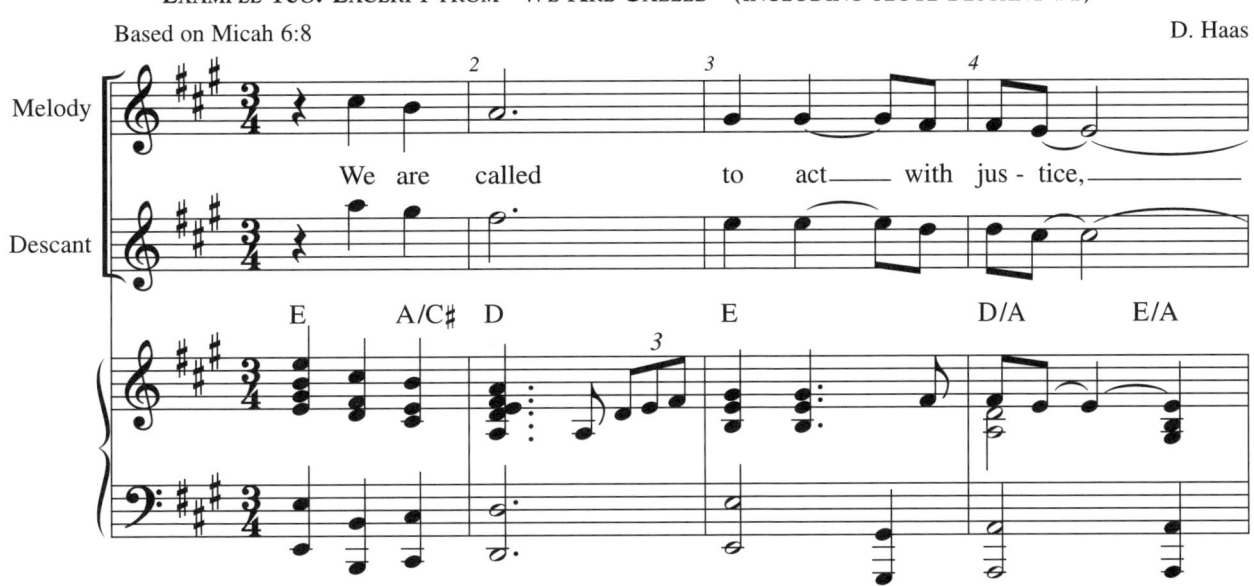

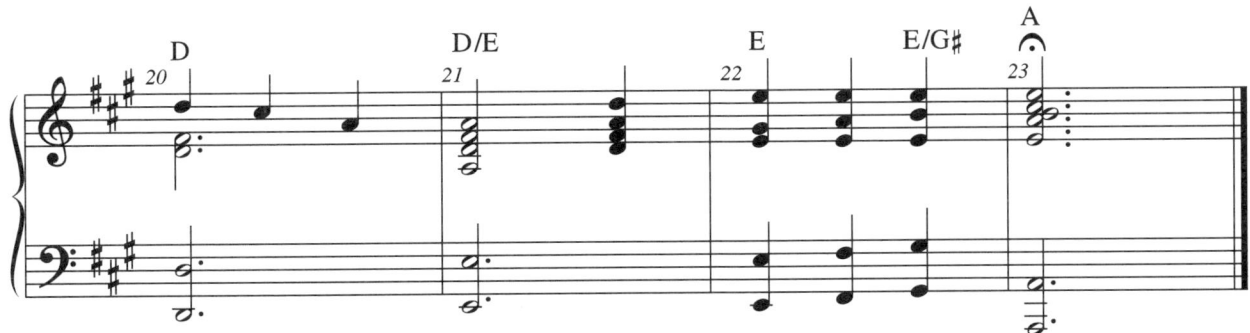

Track 53: Improvisation 1

"We Are Called" – piano introduction; mm. 1–8 of refrain, one flute on melody and one flute on descant #1 with piano

Notice that the above descant stays in rhythmic unison with the melody. In other words, all of the notes of the descant change at the same time as the notes of the melody. While this doesn't always have to be the case, it is certainly one option.

Notice, too, that the interval between the descant and the melody stays constant throughout. This device is known as *parallel motion*. In this instance, the descant is written a sixth higher than the melody line. You might not choose to use a constant interval in your descant, but it is one possible choice that works with this particular piece. It is interesting to note that if a fellow flutist is playing the melody *8va* while you are playing the descant, the interval between descant and melody changes to a third (see Example 109). Listen to the first 8 measures of this piece on the CD (Track 54). Notice how this change of interval affects the sound.

EXAMPLE 109: EXCERPT FROM "WE ARE CALLED" (WITH FLUTE DESCANT #1)

D. Haas

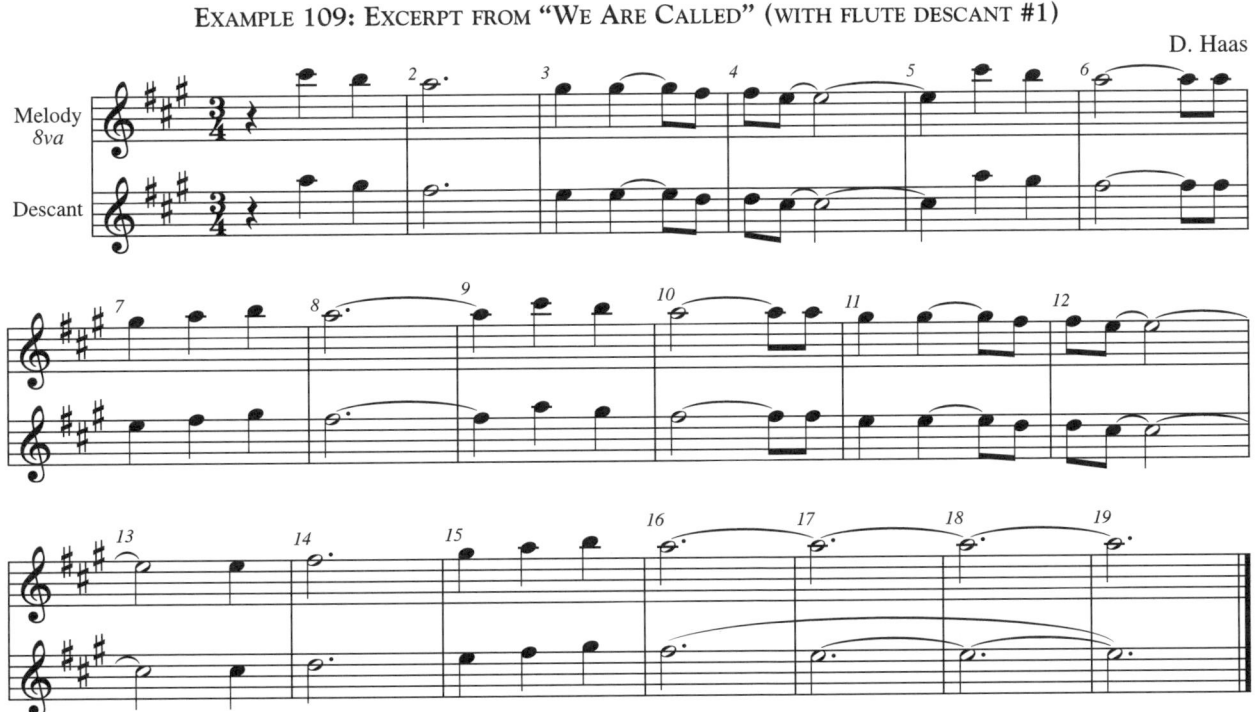

Track 54: Improvisation 2
"We Are Called" – mm. 1–8 of refrain, one flute on melody *8va* and one flute on descant #1

Thirds and sixths are common intervals used in descant writing. As you have just seen, they can be used with consistency for some pieces as long as the notes of the descant fit with the chord of the accompaniment. In measure 17 in Examples 108 and 109, the interval changes. If it had remained the same as the previous measure, the descant note, F♯, would no longer fit with the E/A chord in the accompaniment.

Now it's your turn to write a descant using primarily parallel thirds.

EXERCISE

Below you will find the melody and chord symbols for "Joyful, Joyful We Adore You" (see Example 110). On the empty staff line, write your descant in rhythmic unison with the melody, using the interval of a third lower than the melody line whenever this note is part of the accompanying chord. If this note is not part of the chord, move to a nearby chordal note. The first measure has been done for you.

If you feel the need, you may use the manuscript paper at the back of this book to write out the notes of the chords first. Then use this as a reference for the notes of your descant.

EXAMPLE 110: EXCERPT FROM "JOYFUL, JOYFUL, WE ADORE YOU"

HYMN TO JOY
L. van Beethoven

Perhaps your work looks something like this.

EXAMPLE 111: EXCERPT FROM "JOYFUL, JOYFUL, WE ADORE YOU" (WITH FLUTE DESCANT)

HYMN TO JOY
L. van Beethoven

As you can see, the first two measures of the descant work very well in parallel thirds. However, the beginning of measure 3 does not. The first two beats of this measure use a G major chord. With the melody note being a G, the descant note would be an E if you chose to simply play a third lower than the melody. Because the E is not a chordal note, it is not a good choice here. It would be better to have the descant double the G of the melody. It is good to double the root or the fifth of a chord, but not the third. By choosing the G for the descant, the descant line flows well from the F♯ at the end of measure 2 into the G at the beginning of measure 3 (see Example 112). F♯ is the leading tone, the seventh degree, in the key of G major. The leading tone is so named because of its strong tendency to lead to the tonic. Hence in this case, the F♯ at the end of measure 2 leads nicely to the G at the beginning of measure 3.

EXAMPLE 112: EXCERPT FROM "JOYFUL, JOYFUL, WE ADORE YOU" (PROGRESSION OF LEADING TONE TO TONIC)

HYMN TO JOY
L. van Beethoven

This descant may also be played *8va*. Now the prevailing interval becomes parallel sixths instead of parallel thirds. This is another viable choice.

Other parallel intervals can be used but with caution. Intervals of a fourth or fifth can create sounds that are rather hollow in nature as compared to the richness generated by the use of thirds or sixths. Parallel fifths should always be avoided. Return to "We Are Called" to see how *not* to write a descant (see Example 113)!

EXAMPLE 113: EXCERPT FROM "WE ARE CALLED" (WITH FLUTE DESCANT #2)
HOW NOT TO WRITE A DESCANT

Copyright © 1988 by GIA Publications, Inc.

There are a few reasons why this example doesn't work. First, every interval is a fifth, thus creating a series of parallel fifths—a harmonic movement that should be avoided. Second, there are several notes that don't fit with the accompanying chord. In measure 3, the underlying chord is E major. The C♯ notes in the descant don't belong to this chord. Thus, the previous examples that used parallel sixths and thirds (Examples 108 and 109, respectively) are better choices than this one.

Other intervals such as seconds and sevenths should be used only sparingly because of the dissonances they can create (see Example 114). Listen to the following example on the CD (Track 55).

EXAMPLE 114: EXCERPT FROM "WE ARE CALLED" (WITH FLUTE DESCANT #3)
HOW NOT TO WRITE A DESCANT

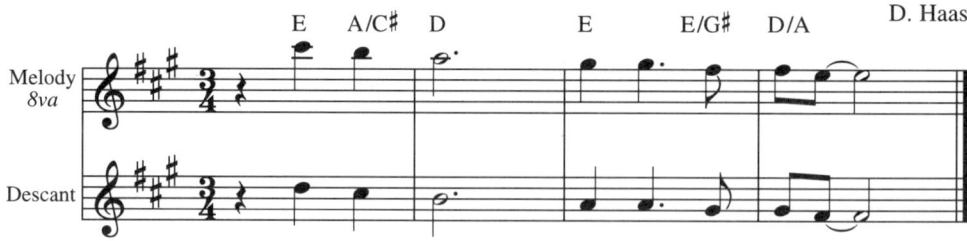

Copyright © 1988 by GIA Publications, Inc.

 **Track 55: Improvisation 3: How *Not* to Write a Descant**
"We Are Called" – mm. 1–4 of refrain, one flute on melody and one flute on descant #3

This series of parallel sevenths creates continual dissonances that can make an assembly feel very uncomfortable. Hence, this pattern should be avoided.

Now listen to the same example with the melody played an octave lower (see Example 115), as demonstrated on the CD (Track 56).

EXAMPLE 115: EXCERPT FROM "WE ARE CALLED" (WITH FLUTE DESCANT #4)
HOW NOT TO WRITE A DESCANT

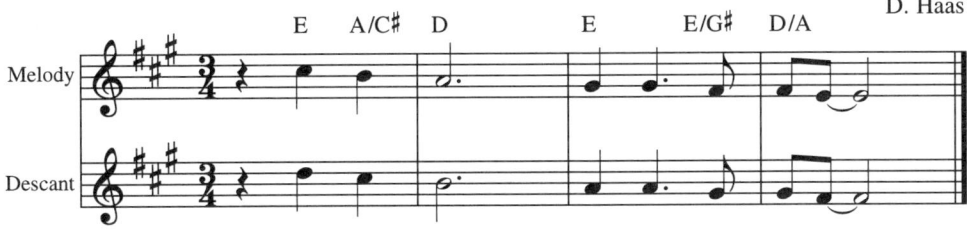

Track 56: Improvisation 4: How *Not* to Write a Descant
"We Are Called" – mm. 1–4 of refrain, one flute on melody and one flute on descant #4

In this case, each interval is a second. Once again, the assembly would not be comfortable with this descant because it uses so many dissonances. Hence, avoid the consistent use of parallel seconds. Of the above examples, only the ones that use parallel sixths and thirds are good choices (see Examples 108 and 109).

Let's now examine the tune NICAEA, (traditionally paired with the text "Holy, Holy, Holy! Lord God Almighty") written by John Bacchus Dykes (1823–76), shown in Example 116.

EXAMPLE 116: EXCERPT FROM "HOLY, HOLY, HOLY! LORD GOD ALMIGHTY"

NICAEA
J. B. Dykes

This time the keyboard accompaniment does not include chord symbols. Now it becomes helpful to analyze the chordal structure before creating a descant. The chordal analysis has been done for you in Example 117. You may wish to apply this procedure to other hymn tunes, using the techniques for chord analysis presented in Chapter 1 under "Chords."

EXAMPLE 117: EXCERPT FROM "HOLY, HOLY, HOLY! LORD GOD ALMIGHTY" (WITH CHORD ANALYSIS)

It is important to remember that the analysis of the chords of a keyboard accompaniment may not necessarily match the chords written on a guitar score, even if the parts are taken from the same hymnal. Example 118 shows the last four measures of "Holy, Holy, Holy" taken from the Guitar Accompaniment Book.

EXAMPLE 118: EXCERPT FROM "HOLY, HOLY, HOLY! LORD GOD ALMIGHTY" (WITH GUITAR CHORDS)

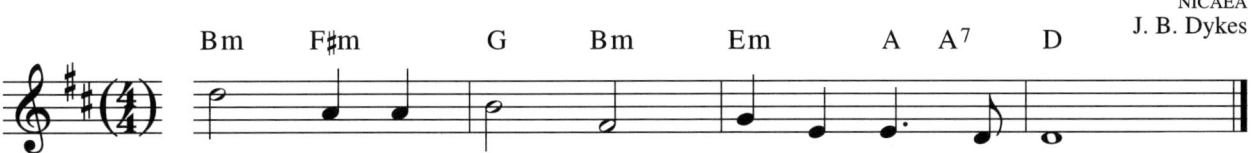

NICAEA
J. B. Dykes

As you can see, the chords are similar but not exactly the same. Therefore, if you are playing with keyboard accompaniment, it is best to use the analysis of the keyboard chords. If you are playing with a guitarist, then it is wise to read from the guitar score. For those occasions when you are reading from the opposite part, a rehearsal ahead of time will save some potentially embarrassing moments.

Let's get back to our analysis of "Holy, Holy, Holy" from the keyboard accompaniment (see Example 117). In this piece, the primary chordal changes occur every two beats (for the most part). There is more harmonic activity as you approach the **cadences**, the natural resting places where the music comes to a conclusion. The first cadence occurs in measure 8, with the speed of the harmonic changes increasing in measures 6–7. This cadence concludes with a dominant seventh chord at the end of measure 8. Since this piece is in the key of D, the dominant seventh is an A7 chord. Recall that dominant seventh chords usually lead back to the tonic, in this case, D major. An examination of measures 8–9 in Example 119 verifies this. (See Chapter 4 for more on dominant seventh chords.)

EXAMPLE 119: EXCERPT FROM "HOLY, HOLY, HOLY! LORD GOD ALMIGHTY" (WITH CHORD RESOLUTION)

NICAEA
J. B. Dykes

The second (and final) cadence occurs in measure 16. Notice the heightened number of chordal changes in measures 13–15.

You will also notice that measure 8 consists only of a whole note chord, with two half notes in the upper voice of the left hand. Since the rhythmic movement of this measure is rather slow, this place may provide opportunity for you to play a moving line. Armed with the above information, let's begin the process of improvisation.

EXAMPLE 120: EXCERPT FROM "HOLY, HOLY, HOLY! LORD GOD ALMIGHTY" (WITH FLUTE DESCANT #1)

NICAEA
J. B. Dykes

The descant shown in Example 120 is but one good way of creating a flute part for this piece. Let's analyze the elements that make this a good descant.

- Almost all of the notes in this descant are chordal; that is to say, they belong to the chord that is being played in the accompaniment.
- The notes of the melody have been deliberately avoided in the descant, although this doesn't always have to be the case. If the decision is made to double a melody note, remember to avoid doubling the third degree of the chord. For example, there is a G major chord in measure 3. Throughout the measure, the melody note is B, which is the third degree of the G major chord. Thus, you should avoid playing the B in the descant since it is already being sounded in the melody line.
- The descant often moves by step and only occasionally by skip. Wide intervals are used only sparingly.
- The descant often changes pitches when the melody stays on the same pitch (e.g., measure 2). This type of harmonic movement is called **oblique motion**, with one voice staying on the same pitch while the other voice moves.

All of the above techniques combine to make this a pleasing descant. It's your turn now.

EXERCISE

Try your hand at writing a descant for "Holy, Holy, Holy." For the moment, keep the rhythms simple, primarily half notes and quarter notes. When the melody uses notes of longer values (i.e., half notes and whole notes), then use rhythms of quicker values in the descant. In this way, you will create a rhythmic line that is different from the rhythms used in the melody. Stick to chordal notes, but avoid moving by parallel fifths. Also avoid doubling the melody note if the melody is the third degree of the chord. Work on a phrase-by-phrase basis if it seems overwhelming to work on the piece in its entirety. The first few notes have been done for you (see Example 121).

EXAMPLE 121: EXCERPT FROM "HOLY, HOLY, HOLY! LORD GOD ALMIGHTY"

NICAEA
J. B. Dykes

Track 57: Improvisation 5
    "Holy, Holy, Holy! Lord God Almighty" – piano introduction and one verse, piano alone

When you have completed your descant, then play it with the keyboard accompaniment on the CD (Track 57).

Before moving on, take a moment to congratulate yourself on a job well done! You have already accomplished a great deal!

Now let's examine a more detailed descant (see Example 122).

EXAMPLE 122: EXCERPT FROM "HOLY, HOLY, HOLY! LORD GOD ALMIGHTY" (WITH FLUTE DESCANT #2)

Even a quick glance will reveal that this descant is more complex than descant #1. A deeper look reveals that this descant is merely an ornamented form of the previous version (see Example 120). It includes non-chordal tones—notes that do not belong to the chord. Take measure 2, for example, which begins with an A major chord. The first note of the descant, E, belongs to this chord; however, the second note of the descant, D, does not. The subsequent note, C♯, once again belongs to the A major chord. In this case, the second note, D, is a passing tone—a specific type of non-chordal note that passes between one chordal note and another.

Now look at measure 15. There is an A7 chord on beat 3. The descant for this beat begins with an A but moves up to B and then back to A. The two As are both chordal tones, but the intervening B is not; this is another form of non-chordal note known as a **neighboring tone**. Neighboring tones move up or down by step from a chordal note, and then return to the same chordal note. Notice that in each example, the chordal notes occur on the stronger portions of the beat, while the non-chordal notes come on the weaker portions. Although this doesn't always have to be the case, it is one way of emphasizing the chordal notes while using the non-chordal notes to create interest and variety.

Here is another chance for you to write your own descant.

EXERCISE

This time, try writing a descant using some non-chordal notes. You might choose to elaborate on the descant you just wrote, or write another from scratch. Once again, the first few notes have been provided for you (see Example 123).

EXAMPLE 123: EXCERPT FROM "HOLY, HOLY, HOLY! LORD GOD ALMIGHTY"

NICAEA
J. B. Dykes

When you have finished, try playing your descant with the keyboard accompaniment on the CD (Track 57).

Now that you have a few different descants for "Holy, Holy, Holy," you might consider the following design:

Verse 1	Play the melody *8va.*
Verse 2	Play descant #1 or *your* first descant.
Verse 3	Tacet.
Verse 4	Play descant #2 or *your* second descant.

The possibilities really are numerous! Enjoy the spontaneity and the variety it can provide!

Sometimes the smallest alteration in the harmonic structure can change the whole mood of a piece. Take the example of a **Picardy third**. This harmonic change occurs at the end of a piece that has been entirely set in a minor key. The final chord is changed to a major chord, altering the quality of the sound from the minor to the major mode. Listen to the conclusion of "I Heard the Voice of Jesus Say" on the CD as an example. Track 58 ends the piece as written in the key of E minor (see Example 124). On Track 59, the final chord is changed to E major (see Example 125). The choice of concluding chords is a judgment call to be made by the music director.

Note: In Examples 124 and 125, the keyboard accompaniment is printed without chord symbols. If you so desire, do a chordal analysis of these excerpts.

EXAMPLE 124: EXCERPT FROM "I HEARD THE VOICE OF JESUS SAY" (FINAL 4 MEASURES WITHOUT PICARDY THIRD)

KINGSFOLD
Harm. R. Vaughan Williams

Track 58: Ending a Piece without a Picardy Third
"I Heard the Voice of Jesus Say" – final 4 measures, flute and piano

EXAMPLE 125: EXCERPT FROM "I HEARD THE VOICE OF JESUS SAY" (FINAL 4 MEASURES WITH PICARDY THIRD)

KINGSFOLD
Harm. R. Vaughan Williams

Track 59: Ending a Piece with a Picardy Third
"I Heard the Voice of Jesus Say" – final 4 measures, flute and piano

You will need to know in advance whether or not the music director intends to use the option of a Picardy third. It is best not to be caught off guard, playing one ending while another musician is playing the other. A simple consultation in advance with the music director will avoid any unnecessary dissonance. However, if you are not able to consult with the music director in advance, then avoid playing the third and simply end on the tonic or fifth degree. This is a safe solution.

Melodic Considerations

When writing or improvising a descant, it is important to remember that a good descant is also a good melody in its own right. After writing a descant of your own, try playing the descant by itself to see if it can stand alone as a good melody. The following melodic considerations will help.

Let's examine a descant written for "The God of All Eternity" (see Example 126).

EXAMPLE 126: EXCERPT FROM "THE GOD OF ALL ETERNITY" (WITH WELL-WRITTEN FLUTE DESCANT)

Tune: © 1989, WGRG, Iona Community, Scotland, GIA Publications, Inc., exclusive N. American agent

There are several melodic qualities that make this a good descant. First, it has a melodic range of a ninth—from middle octave D to high E. Avoid writing descants that hover around the same two or three notes. See Example 127 for an example of a poorly written descant.

167

EXAMPLE 127: EXCERPT FROM "THE GOD OF ALL ETERNITY" (WITH POORLY WRITTEN FLUTE DESCANT)

O WALY WALY

The descant in Example 127 lacks a sense of direction. By using the same three notes over and over, it can become boring very quickly.

A second quality that makes the descant in Example 126 a good one is its use of non-chordal notes. In measure 1, the F♯ on the "and" of beat 2 is a neighboring tone. The Gs that flank it are both chordal tones. In measure 3, the F♯ on beat 2 is a passing tone, moving from the E (which is the third degree of the C chord) to the G (which is the seventh of the A^{m7} chord).

Certain notes have strong tendencies to lead to other notes. As was discussed previously, the leading tone (seventh scale degree) has a strong tendency to move to the tonic (first scale degree). Let's go back to the F♯ on the "and" of beat 2 in the first measure. As the leading tone, it has a strong tendency to lead to the tonic, G. And so it does (see Example 128).

EXAMPLE 128: EXCERPT FROM "THE GOD OF ALL ETERNITY" (PROGRESSION OF LEADING TONE TO TONIC)

O WALY WALY

Measure 7 of Example 126 highlights another example of notes with strong tendencies. The C on beat 3 leans heavily toward the B on beat 1 of measure 8 (see Example 129). The C is the fourth scale degree in the key of G major. This scale degree has a strong tendency to go to the third scale degree, in this case, the B in the final measure.

EXAMPLE 129: EXCERPT FROM "THE GOD OF ALL ETERNITY"
(PROGRESSION OF FOURTH SCALE DEGREE LEADING TO THIRD SCALE DEGREE)

O WALY WALY

To demonstrate the tendency of the fourth degree to lead towards the third, think of the *plagal cadence*, sometimes referred to as the "Amen" cadence (see Example 130). This cadence consists of two chords: the subdominant chord (a major chord built on the fourth scale degree) and the tonic chord. Listen to this example demonstrated on the CD (Track 60).

EXAMPLE 130: PLAGAL CADENCE (OR "AMEN" CADENCE)

Track 60: Plagal Cadence
"Amen" cadence (IV–I), piano alone

Try your hand at using these tendency tones in a descant.

EXERCISE

Example 131 gives you a keyboard harmonization of a G major scale. The first few notes of a descant are also given to you. Now that you are aware of the melodic pull of the fourth scale degree towards the third, incorporate this into your descant.

EXAMPLE 131: DEMONSTRATION OF TENDENCY TONES

Now play your descant with the keyboard accompaniment on the CD (Track 61).

Track 61: Create Your Own Descant Using Tendency Tones
Harmonization of G major scale, piano alone

Your descant may or may not look like the one shown in Example 132. Remember that there are as many possibilities for writing good descants as there are musicians. If yours doesn't look exactly like this, you may still have a very fine descant.

EXAMPLE 132: DEMONSTRATION OF TENDENCY TONES

Study the descant shown in Example 132. Identify the places in the descant at which the melodic line moves from the fourth scale degree, C, to the third scale degree, B. There are two places. The first occurs at the end of measure 1 leading into the beginning of measure 2. The second occurs on the last two notes of the descant.

Another melodic device that is related to this one is the suspension (see "Reading from a Guitar Score" in Chapter 4). Look back to the first descant for "The God of All Eternity" (see Example 126). The G in the descant on the downbeat of measure 4 provides harmonic suspension, as noted in the chord symbol, Dsus4, of the accompaniment. Remember that "sus" is an abbreviation for the word "suspension." Moving upwards from D, the fourth degree is G. The G resolves to the F♯ of the D chord on beat 2 of measure 4 (see Example 133). The strong tendency of the suspended fourth is to go to the third of the next chord.

EXAMPLE 133: SUSPENSION

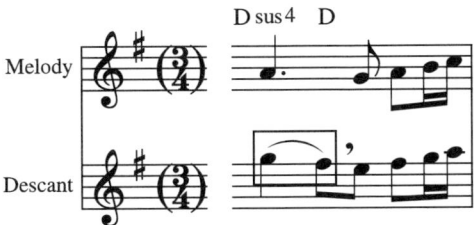

Let's return to Example 126 and our analysis of "The God of All Eternity," comparing the original descant to the melody. The melody contains melodic interest and direction that climaxes with the downbeat of measure 5. The descant also includes melodic interest but climaxes one measure later, on the downbeat of measure 6. Variety is created when the descant climaxes at a different place than the melody.

The descant is also rhythmically independent from the melody. Notice that the descant starts two beats later than the melody. When the melody sustains a note, the descant is moving. These elements provide variety, interest, and a feeling of continuity from one phrase to the next.

Finally, when parallel motion is used, the intervals are not fifths. In measure 4, for example, there are several ascending parallel sixths on beats 2 and 3. There are also descending parallel thirds on beats 2 and 3 of measure 6, even though the interval is actually an octave plus a third. Another effective harmonic tool, **contrary motion**, occurs in measure 5. In this technique, the lines move in opposite directions.

Listen to the overall effect as this piece (as shown in Example 126) is played on the CD (Track 62).

Track 62: Melodic Considerations for a Well-Written Descant
"The God of All Eternity" – one verse, flute on descant from Example 126 with piano

---

EXERCISE

When you are ready, try writing your own descant for this piece (see Example 134). Use some of the melodic and harmonic devices just described. If you need help getting started, use the same first measure as the example here. Play your descant with the keyboard accompaniment on the CD (Track 63). Have fun with it!

EXAMPLE 134: EXCERPT FROM "THE GOD OF ALL ETERNITY"

O WALY WALY

Track 63: Create and Play a Descant
"The God of All Eternity" – piano introduction; one verse, piano alone

Melodic variety can also be achieved through the use of embellishments. The light nature of the sound of the flute lends itself well to the use of musical ornamentations such as **grace notes**, **glissandos**, **trills**, **mordents**, and **turns**.

Grace notes, sometimes called **appoggiaturas**, come in a variety of notations (see Example 135). Single short grace notes are written as small eighth notes with a slash mark through the stem; two or more short grace notes are written as small sixteenth notes, without a slash through the stem.

EXAMPLE 135: SHORT GRACE NOTES

Short grace notes receive no rhythmic value of their own. They are played as rapidly as possible before the beat, with the purpose of decorating the principal note that follows it. In other words, the time it takes to play these grace notes is taken from the previous note. The rhythmic value of the following principal note is not affected. Listen to the short grace notes (shown in Example 136) played on the CD (Track 64).

EXAMPLE 136: EXCERPT FROM SERENADE
(WITH SHORT GRACE NOTES)

F. J. Haydn

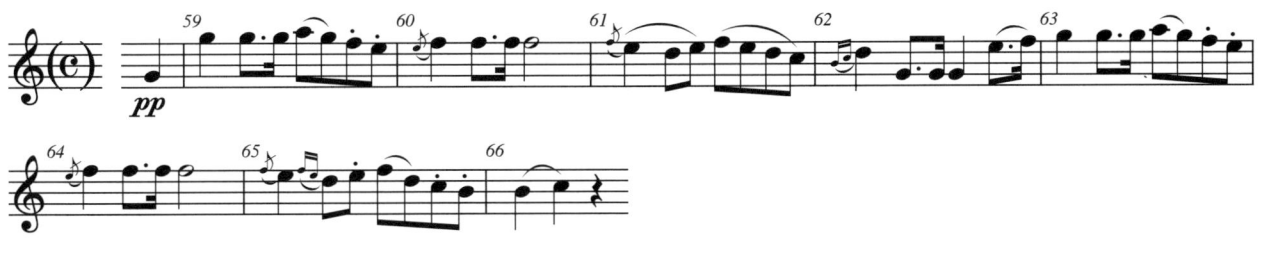

Track 64: Short Grace Notes
Haydn's *Serenade* – mm. 59–66, flute alone

Long grace notes can take many forms (see Example 137). They can be written as any kind of note—whole, half, quarter, eighth, sixteenth, etc.—and do not have a slash through the stem.

EXAMPLE 137: LONG GRACE NOTES

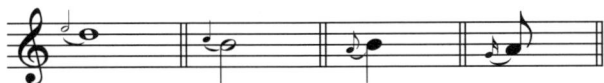

When you come across a long grace note, it is necessary to play the grace note for its specified value, subtracting that value from the principal note that follows. In Example 138, both notes are played as quarter notes.

EXAMPLE 138: RELATION OF LONG GRACE NOTES TO ACTUAL NOTE VALUES

This system of notation was used primarily in the Baroque and early Classical eras of music history. Composers who lived during that time used this notation to indicate that the grace note was a non-chordal note, while the principal note was the one that fit with the chord.

Example 139 demonstrates both long and short grace notes. Listen to this example on the CD (Track 65).

EXAMPLE 139: EXCERPT FROM *ALLEGRO ALLA TURKA*
(WITH LONG AND SHORT GRACE NOTES)

W. A. Mozart

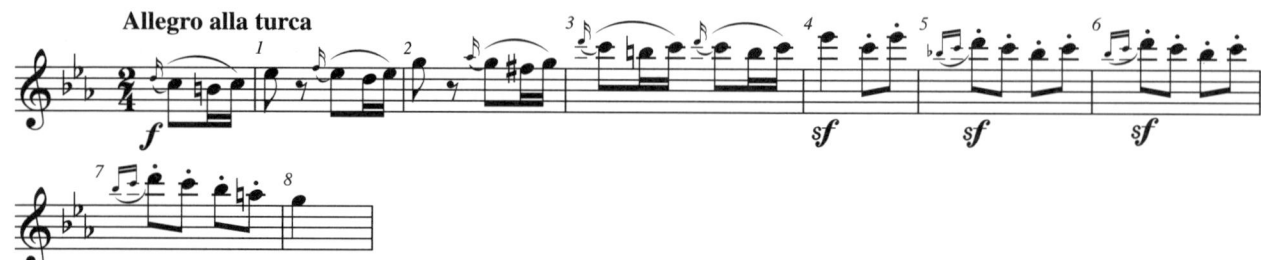

Track 65: Long and Short Grace Notes
Mozart's Allegro alla Turca – flute alone

The pick-up measure, as well as measures 1, 2, and 3, contain examples of long grace notes. They are written as single, small sixteenth notes and are played as sixteenth notes, with their value being subtracted from the eighth note to which they are attached. Thus, this passage is played as straight sixteenth notes. Measures 5–7 demonstrate short grace notes. They, too, are written as small sixteenth notes; however, they are played before the beat, taking care not to disturb the rhythm of their principal notes that follow.

This example from the Classical era presumes the performer understands how to determine whether a grace note is short or long. In general, grace notes written during the Baroque and early Classical eras are meant to be played as long grace notes. Grace notes written since that time are almost always meant to be played as short grace notes. Therefore, the grace notes that occur in most *liturgical* flute music are short and should be played before the beat. (See Appendix I: The History of the Use of the Flute and Other Instruments in Worship.)

Example 140 shows a flute descant written against the melody of "The King of Love My Shepherd Is." It demonstrates short grace notes. Listen to this excerpt played on the CD (Track 66).

EXAMPLE 140: EXCERPT FROM "THE KING OF LOVE MY SHEPHERD IS"
(DESCANT WITH SHORT GRACE NOTES)

ST. COLUMBA
Irish Melody

Track 66: Varieties of Short Grace Notes
"The King of Love My Shepherd Is" – one verse, one flute on melody and one flute on descant in Example 140

You should have noticed short double grace notes in measures 1, 2, and several others. There are also short single grace notes on beat 3 of measures 5, 12, and 14. Notice the slash mark through the stem of these notes in the printed music. Contrast the playing style of these grace notes with those you heard in the previous example by Mozart (Example 139, CD Track 65).

Now listen to the CD (Track 67) as this tune receives further embellishments, namely glissandos, trills, mordents, and turns (see Example 141). Of course, it would be very uncommon for all of these ornamentations to occur in the same descant. They have been included together here for demonstration purposes only.

EXAMPLE 141: EXCERPT FROM "THE KING OF LOVE MY SHEPHERD IS"
(DESCANT WITH ADDITIONAL EMBELLISHMENTS)

ST. COLUMBA
Irish Melody

Track 67: Varieties of Embellishments
"The King of Love My Shepherd Is" – one verse, one flute on melody and one flute on descant in Example 141

Measures 3, 9, and 12–13 demonstrate the use of glissandos. This is a form of embellishment that moves quickly from one principal note to another, playing as many notes in between the two as possible. The two notes are connected by a diagonal wavy line (see Example 142).

EXAMPLE 142: GLISSANDO

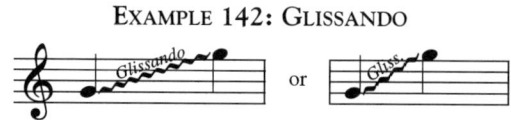

Care must be taken to keep the rhythmic integrity intact and to stay within the key signature when executing the glissando.

Measures 4 and 8 provide an example of the use of trills, one of the most common types of ornamentation. In general, trills begin on the printed note, and move back and forth as quickly as possible between this note and the note immediately higher in the key signature. (Exceptions are found mostly in Baroque and early Classical eras, where trills can begin on the note above the principal note.) Trills are symbolized by the letters "tr," sometimes followed by a wavy line (see Example 143).

EXAMPLE 143: TRILL

In many instances, fundamental fingerings are used for trills. However, if the use of fundamental fingerings would make the trill cumbersome, there is usually an alternative fingering designed specifically for trills. Reference the trill chart at the back of this book for the options. When more than one fingering is given, experiment with what fingering works best in each instance for the continuity and flow of the melodic line.

Trills that are very short, only encompassing the principal note, its neighboring note, and the principal note again, are called "mordents." You hear them in measures 7 and 16 of the descant in Example 141 (CD Track 67). They are symbolized by short wavy lines (see Example 144).

EXAMPLE 144: MORDENT GOING TO UPPER NEIGHBORING NOTE

When a vertical line occurs in the middle of the mordent (as in measure 16), the middle note of the mordent moves to the lower neighboring tone instead of the upper neighboring note (see Example 145).

EXAMPLE 145: MORDENT GOING TO LOWER NEIGHBORING NOTE

Sometimes several embellishments can be combined. For example, a mordent could be paired with double grace notes, as seen on beat 3 in measure 3 of the descant in Example 141. Notice the symbol that resembles a sideways "S." This symbol, which represents the particular combination of a mordent and double grace notes, receives a new name—a **grupetto**—more commonly known as a "turn." The turn involves a total of five different notes. The first, third, and fifth notes are the same principal note, in this case, G. The second note is the upper neighboring note, an A in this example. The fourth note is the lower neighboring note. In this instance, the lower note becomes F♯ because of the key signature. Thus, this turn is actually a mordent (G–A–G) followed by double grace notes (F♯–G) (see Example 146).

EXAMPLE 146: THREE WAYS TO WRITE THE SAME SOUND

The use of ornaments can provide another vehicle for improvisation of a melodic line. Now it's your turn to add embellishments to an existing melody, shown in Example 147. Use embellishments as a way of emphasizing certain melody notes.

EXERCISE

Add embellishments to the melody, which appears on the second staff in Example 147. Then use the blank staff line above it to compose a descant for the melody, perhaps even adding embellishments to the descant as well.

EXAMPLE 147: EXCERPT FROM "ONWARD TO THE KINGDOM"

MARIE'S WEDDING
Irish traditional
Arr. David Haas

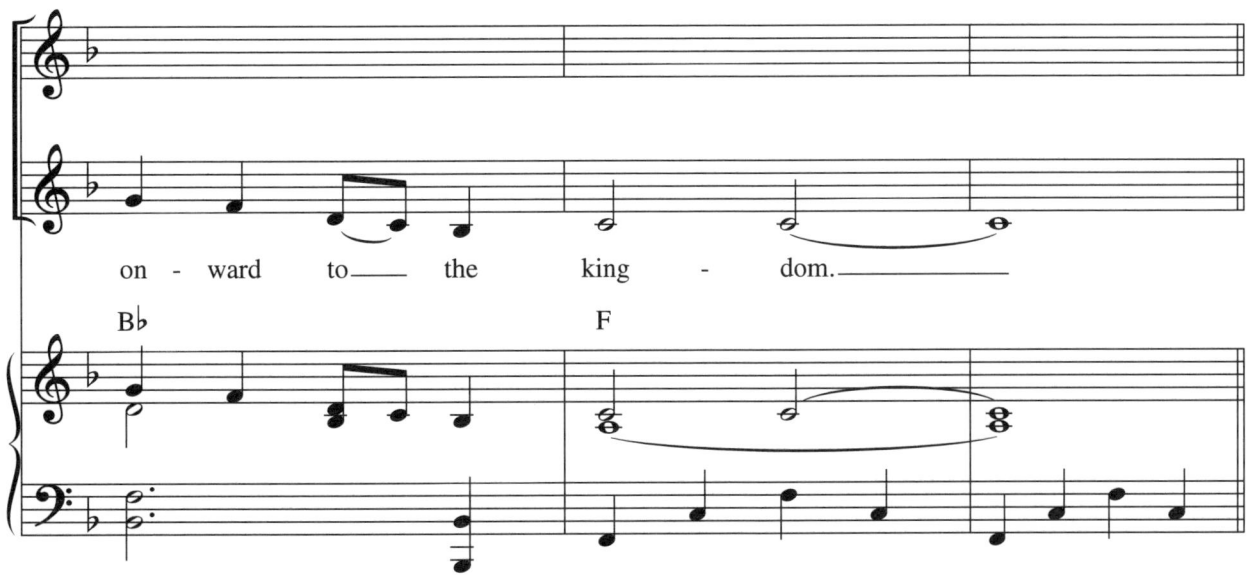

on - ward to —— the king - dom. ——

B♭   F

Track 68: Add Your Own Embellishments
  "Onward to the Kingdom" – piano introduction and one refrain, piano alone

Now consider recording yourself playing your ornamented melody, an octave higher than written, of course. Have some fun by playing your descant against your own recording. Also play either your ornamented melody or your descant with the accompaniment on the CD (Track 68).

Rhythmic Considerations

The above examples have given illustrations of both rhythmic unison and rhythmic variety. There are appropriate times for each of these techniques. As we saw earlier in this chapter with the first descant for "We Are Called" (see Example 108), rhythmic unison (the movement of the melody and descant in the same rhythms) can provide a very effective approach for writing a descant.

On the other hand, rhythmic variety can be achieved in a number of ways. One way is to begin the descant after the melody, as demonstrated in both of the descants provided for "Holy, Holy, Holy" (Examples 120 and 122), as well as the descant for "The God of All Eternity" (Example 126). Variety is also accomplished by creating a moving line in the descant while the melody sustains a note. Again, both "Holy, Holy, Holy" and "The God of All Eternity" illustrate this concept.

You can also achieve rhythmic variety by using a descant of less complex rhythms on an early verse, and then playing a more complex descant on a later verse. The two different descants for "Holy, Holy, Holy" (Examples 120 and 122) demonstrate this point.

Recurring rhythmic patterns can also be an effective tool when used in appropriate circumstances (see Example 148). Listen to the following descant on the CD (Track 69).

EXAMPLE 148: EXCERPT FROM "HOLY, HOLY, HOLY! LORD GOD ALMIGHTY" (FLUTE DESCANT IN TRIPLETS)

NICAEA
J. B. Dykes

Track 69: Rhythmic Patterns
"Holy, Holy, Holy! Lord God Almighty" – one verse, one flute on melody and one flute on descant in triplets

Be careful to avoid too much use of this technique; it can be very successful when used in moderation. However, it can become monotonous if used too frequently. The verse in Example 148 could be played successfully for Prelude as a flute duet, especially if "Holy, Holy, Holy" is also going to be sung as the Gathering Song. This verse could also be used during the Gathering Song as an introductory verse or an interlude, either with or without keyboard accompaniment.

Now try your hand at writing this type of descant.

> ### EXERCISE
>
> A simplistic descant is given to you in Example 149. Let these notes be your anchor as you add a recurring rhythmic pattern to this line. You can write your notes directly into Example 149 or use the blank manuscript paper at the back of this book. At some points you may find yourself outlining the chord. In these instances, you would be moving by skip: D–F♯–A, for example. At other places you may decide to add non-chordal notes, such as passing tones and/or neighboring notes, usually moving by step: D–E–F♯ or D–C♯–D, for example.

EXAMPLE 149: EXCERPT FROM "HOLY, HOLY, HOLY! LORD GOD ALMIGHTY" (SIMPLISTIC FLUTE DESCANT)

 **Track 70: Compose Your Own Descant: Focus on Rhythmic Patterns**
"Holy, Holy, Holy! Lord God Almighty" – one verse, flute alone on melody

Listen to the CD (Track 70). You will hear just the melody line played by the flute. Add your rhythmic descant to this part, creating another duet version for this piece.

Example 150 shows one realization of this exercise. Triplets are again used for the rhythmic pattern, with the first note of every triplet coinciding with the pitch of the quarter notes in the descant in Example 149. Again, your descant undoubtedly won't look just like this one. It will be a different, yet worthy, descant for this piece.

EXAMPLE 150: EXCERPT FROM "HOLY, HOLY, HOLY! LORD GOD ALMIGHTY" (FLUTE DESCANT)

NICAEA
J. B. Dykes

Another technique to aid in improvisation is rhythmic imitation. Take a look at "Laudate Dominum," shown in Example 151. The descant begins one measure after the melody, using the same rhythmic pattern for the descant in measures 2 through 5 as the melody in measures 1 through 4, with the slight exception of the last descant note of measure 5. This use of rhythmic imitation is especially effective with music that has a percussive character in the melody, such as this one does.

EXAMPLE 151: EXCERPT FROM "LAUDATE DOMINUM"

J. Berthier

Take a look at measures 5–7 of the descant. These measures repeat the same rhythmic pattern, but each measure begins one step lower than the previous measure. This compositional device is known as a **sequence**. Sequences can be written in either ascending or descending patterns, and can proceed along intervals of any size. In this case, there is a descending sequence in which each measure begins one step lower than the previous measure. It is usually wise not to use more than three repetitions of a sequenced pattern. In this instance, the third repetition (in measure 7) changes slightly, leading into the return of the beginning of the melody.

Example 152 uses the familiar refrain from "Angels We Have Heard on High." An analysis of the melody (found in the upper voice of the keyboard accompaniment) reveals a recurring rhythmic pattern consisting of one half note followed by four eighth notes. Notice that this pattern is written in sequential form, with each measure beginning one step lower than the previous measure. The sequence is only repeated three times before new melodic material is introduced. Because of all of these features, this piece lends itself beautifully to a variety of descants.

EXAMPLE 152: EXCERPT FROM "ANGELS WE HAVE HEARD ON HIGH"

GLORIA
French carol, 18th c.

Now it's your turn.

EXERCISE

Write a descant for the refrain of "Angels We Have Heard on High" on the empty staff in Example 152. Use an imitative rhythmic pattern in sequential style. Try to also incorporate non-chordal notes.

Track 71: Compose Your Own Descant: Focus on Sequences
  "Angels We Have Heard on High" – piano introduction; refrain, piano alone

Once you are finished, play your descant with the keyboard accompaniment on the CD (Track 71).
   Here is one possible descant for this refrain.

EXAMPLE 153: EXCERPT FROM "ANGELS WE HAVE HEARD ON HIGH" (WITH FLUTE DESCANT)

Look at measures 1–3 of Example 153. Notice that the descant imitates the rhythm of the melody, using recurring patterns consisting of four eighth notes and one half note. Notice, too, that the descant uses an ascending sequence, with each measure starting one step higher than the previous measure. This pattern contrasts the descending sequence used in these same measures in the melody. In measure 3 of the descant, the sequence has been altered ever so slightly, so that the second note is F. Without this adjustment, the second note would have been E, which would not fit with the F major chord in the accompaniment. In the melody, the tune starts over again beginning with measure 7. At this point, you might choose to repeat your descant using the same notes as at the beginning of the refrain, or you could choose to go in a different direction entirely. The descant printed here uses the same material over again.

Your descant probably looks very different from this one. Just remember that both are good options for this piece.

Conclusion

This chapter provided opportunity to develop skills in improvisation through more serious exploration of harmonic, melodic, and rhythmic elements. By nature, liturgical music needs to be repetitious. Music repeated over and over moves into the heart and out of the head, opening us to our deeper selves. However, instrumentalists can add variety to the constancy of the sung melodic line. Before moving to the next chapter, test your knowledge and your confidence once more. As a way of collecting all that has been previously discussed, look at the music and selected text for "Bread to Share" by Marty Haugen in Example 154. Take time with the score, considering the harmonic, melodic, and rhythmic elements. Embrace the spirit of the words through some reflection on them.

EXAMPLE 154: EXCERPT FROM "BREAD TO SHARE"

share; Plen - ty of bread at the feast of life, there is

plen - ty of bread to share. share.

To Verses *Last time*

B♭7   E♭   A♭6   E♭ B♭/D Cm A♭m/C♭

E♭/B♭   Fm7/B♭   *To Verses* E♭   *Last time* E♭

bread of grace and mer - cy:_____
bread of strength and jus - tice:_____
bread for free - dom's jour - ney:_____
bread of love and wel - come:_____

(Hum)

You have plen - ty to share, you have

plen - ty of bread to share.

Notice any other markings, like the **D.C.** at the end of the verses. D.C. stands for the Italian words "da capo"—in English, "the head"—and indicates a return to the beginning of the piece.

Note: This is not to be confused with **D.S.** (*"dal segno"*), which translates as "from the sign" and indicates a return to the % marking.

What would you do to add variety to this long piece that would probably be used at the Communion of the Mass? How would you embellish and enhance it? Would you play all the time or just on certain verses? Make your decisions based on everything you have learned in these pages, and then have fun playing along with the CD (Track 72).

Track 72: Create Your Own Part
"Bread to Share" – piano introduction; refrain and 4 verses, piano and vocals

After the first time you play with the CD, think about how you might play your part differently the next time, learning from one experience to the next. You will notice that there is no empty staff line this time. Try your hand at playing without the benefit of writing your work down first. However, if you feel the need to commit your part to writing, you may choose to use the empty staff paper at the back of this book.

You have had a variety of hands-on experiences in this chapter. The next chapter includes a number of opportunities to experiment with tone color to create even more interesting and inspirational sounds during worship.

Chapter 8
Exploring the Flute's Language

Interior Awareness of Shades of Sound
Subtle Gradations of Dynamics and Color
Heightened Listening Skills

The power of language is profound. Storytellers, for instance, can use language to put us on the edge of our seats, to cause us to hold our breath in anticipation or in sudden surprise, to paint a picture every bit as colorful as a work of art by one of the great master painters. What a flutist does with the color of the tone can be just as provocative, just as inviting. Yet it is part of the paradox of making music that to establish the most colorful and rich tone to the outside ear, the flutist must go deep inside and listen with a different ear. This is so much more than the usual listening we all do every minute of our day. It is rather like having an inner ear attached to our soul—an ear tuned to Divine Beauty. Listening in this capacity requires a quieting inside, a slowing down, an acute attentiveness and mindfulness to how well the quality of our sound matches the depth of the written music or the depth of the text. If, as Aldous Huxley states, "After silence, that which comes nearest to expressing the inexpressible is music," then we bridge silence and music when we go deep inside and find within us the heartbeat of the universe, responding to it in the shape of our sound. In this way, we are willing to connect with all of creation—expressing the inexpressible—receiving and giving a glimpse of Divine Beauty.

A human soul may reveal its mysteries through direct expression, simple speech, simple gesture, simple painting, just as the soul of the brook is expressed in full simplicity and economy.
—Johann Sebastian Bach, 18th c.

The flute's voice is its sound, of course, and its language the notes it plays. Each flutist has an individual sound. However, even within this unique sound, there is such a multitude of emotion that can be expressed by experimenting with the tone—in

Music is the shorthand of emotion.
—Leo Tolstoy, from *Music Sourcebook* (LTP)

other words, a language that is often not explored for all its possibilities. The development of this "language"—that is, the way the notes are played—can add so much delight to our playing.

This chapter takes a more nuanced look at tone color, using repertoire from different musical periods as one way of reinforcing this concept. The chapter also helps to develop the skill of listening for the shape of the tone by focusing on training the ear through a variety of techniques and exercises.

The Nuances of Tone Color

As has been stated already, the voice of the flute speaks its own language, and each flutist's sound is uniquely his/hers. James Galway is instantly recognizable to the listener's ear as being different than Jethro Tull. Your sound also has its own special quality that makes it different than the sound of any other flutist. In addition, portions of the range of the flute are similar to the range of the human voice, making its timbre uniquely capable of touching the soul at a deeper level than the spoken word alone. There is no limit to how your "flute voice" can be developed and expressed. This section will allow you to imagine all kinds of possibilities.

Let's expand on our exploration of tone color begun in Chapter 1. Tone color, like the artist's palette, comes complete with its many hues. When describing a flutist's tone color, words such as bright, delicate, lilting, dark, somber, or haunting might be used. As noted in Chapter 1, tone color can be varied in many ways: by adjusting the placement of the flute on the lips, the size of the aperture, the direction of the airstream, the speed and breadth of the vibrato, just to name a few.

The photo below depicts the normal placement of the flute on the lips.

NORMAL FLUTE PLACEMENT ON THE LIP

To achieve a lighter, more delicate sound, experiment with placing the lip plate slightly higher on your lip.

HIGHER FLUTE PLACEMENT ON THE LIP

In addition to adjusting the placement of the flute, try also using a shallow vibrato, one that almost disappears into the lightness of the texture. For *pp* at the end of a phrase, think of lifting your facial muscles, even raising your eyebrows, to achieve an ethereal quality in your sound while simultaneously slowing and eventually eliminating the vibrato. Focus the sound, imagining a target (such as a bull's-eye) at the top of your music stand. In this way, you can allow the volume to fade into nothingness without sacrificing intonation. Listen to the CD (Track 73), which illustrates this effect using the concluding phrase of *Serenade* by Franz Joseph Haydn (1732–1809).

EXAMPLE 155: EXCERPT FROM *SERENADE*

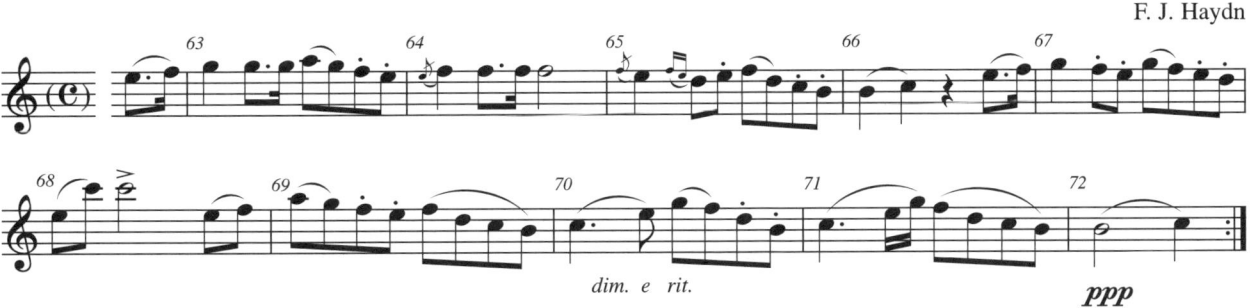

Track 73: Applying Tone Color Techniques to the Music
Haydn's *Serenade* – last phrase, flute alone

It is of critical importance to be sensitive to the style of the music and the historical era from which it comes. Example 155 comes from the Classical era, which generally requires a sound that is delicate and intimate. Let us look at one more example (see Example 156) from this era.

EXAMPLE 156: EXCERPT FROM "GOD, WHOSE ALMIGHTY WORD"

ITALIAN HYMN
F. de Giardini

"God, Whose Almighty Word," shown here with full keyboard score, was written by Felice de Giardini who lived from 1716–96. Being from the Classical period, it has a very light, delicate character. One of the ways this is achieved on the flute is by the lightness of a well-placed, forward tongue. Strive for a delicate attack, articulating just behind your top teeth, and emphasizing the "t" aspect of the attack. Use vibrato only sparingly, primarily on the dotted-half notes at the cadences. As noted in Chapter 1, your articulation will differ from the printed page, in keeping with the needs of the instrumental musician. Be attentive to how you would sing the tune, and imitate this style in your interpretation.

Try playing the melody of this piece several different ways—possibly adding slurs, **staccatos**, and accents—to achieve the most desirable effect. For the quarter notes that you choose to tongue, play them lightly and in a lilting style, with a slight separation between them. (By now it goes without saying that the flutist will be playing the melody an octave higher than written.)

Listen to the interpretation on the CD (Track 74). Let your ear tell you which notes have been slurred, accented, etc.

 **Track 74: Classical Style of Playing**
"God, Whose Almighty Word" – piano introduction; one verse, flute on melody *8va* and piano

Let's now jump forward in music history to the nineteenth century, to the Romantic era. In general, music written during this period calls for a larger, more emotion-filled sound, especially when compared to the chamber style of music written during the Classical era. To achieve this type of sound, use a larger aperture, a more intense vibrato, and a faster airstream.

EXAMPLE 157: EXCERPT FROM CONCERTATO ON "O GOD, BEYOND ALL PRAISING"

THAXTED
Setting by R. Proulx

Setting copyright © 1988 by GIA Publications, Inc.

The tune THAXTED, shown with keyboard score in Example 157, was written by Gustav Holst (1874–1934). He used this tune very effectively in the orchestral suite, *The Planets*, in the movement titled, "Jupiter." This lush melody calls for a full, dark sound, resplendent with a strong vibrato and legato articulation. For the flutist, these effects can be achieved by placing the lip plate slightly lower on your chin, and aiming the airstream down into the flute.

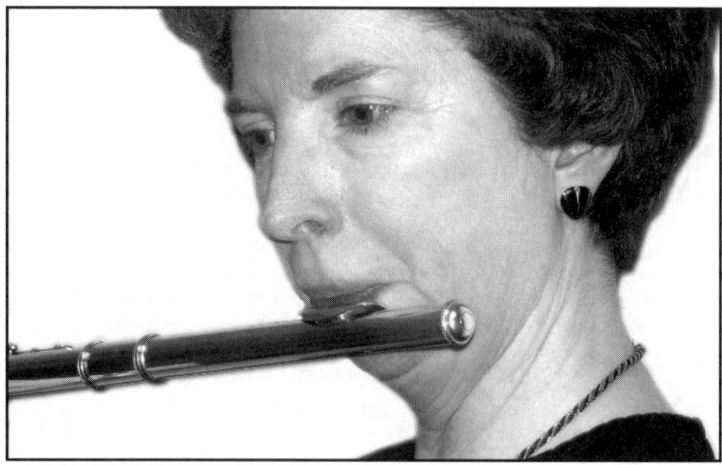

LOWER FLUTE PLACEMENT ON THE LIP

An open throat and strong diaphragmatic support both become very important for sustaining the necessary intensity. To achieve proper articulation, place the tongue further back in the mouth, using more of a "d" sound than a "t" sound. Listen to hear these techniques demonstrated on the last phrase of this piece on the CD (Track 75). (Once again, notice that the flutist is playing the melody an octave higher than written.) Try to decipher which notes have been slurred. Listen, too, to the style of vibrato and the intensity of the sound.

 **Track 75: Romantic Style of Playing**
Concertato on "O God, beyond All Praising" – mm. 17–25, flute on melody *8va* and piano

As you can see, there is much more to music-making than playing the notes on the printed page. Years of study and experience in tonal development and its many

> *In performing the work with the correct style and tone, your individuality and personality will always come through.*
> —Donald Peck, "The Color of Music," *Flute Talk*, January 2003

nuances are necessary for developing that broad array of colors from which to choose for any given piece.

EXERCISE

Take a look at other pieces of music of your choosing. Note the composer and the era of music history from which the piece comes.

- Experiment with variations in your tone color based on your knowledge of the style of the piece.
- Try adjusting the placement of the lip plate on your lip and the direction of your airstream.
- Change the size of your aperture by firming or relaxing the muscles around your lips.
- Experiment with different speeds of vibrato and different styles of articulation.

Listen to recordings of master flutists such as James Galway, Jean-Pierre Rampal, Julius Baker, Carol Wincenc, and Eugenia Zukerman. Listen, too, to great singers such as Marilyn Horne, Beverly Sills, Placido Domingo, and Luciano Pavarotti. Listen to solo violinists, cellists, trumpeters, and clarinetists—not only in the Classical genre but also in jazz, gospel, and other styles as well. In the comfort and security of your own home, you might try playing your flute with some of these recordings. This technique is great for developing your aural skills. It might take a little experimenting to find first the right key and then the correct pitches, but you would really hone your listening skills with this exercise. Also listen to recordings of well-known liturgical musicians. Pianist Jeanne Cotter is a wonderful example. Her albums, *After the Rain* and *Coming Home* are good illustrations of her work. Although printed music is available for these recordings, no flute parts are included. Just have fun listening to her and playing along with her beautiful music!

No matter the genre, there is much to be learned by listening to master musicians. Strive to imitate those aspects of their music-making that you find appealing. By doing this, you will eventually develop your own palette of tone colors from which you can pick and choose as you wish.

Training the Ear for Improvisation

Here is another method for developing your aural proficiencies. Try writing a familiar melody without looking at it; in other words, this is the written equivalent to playing by ear.

EXERCISE

Write the refrain of "The First Nowell" by ear using the following steps:

1. Listen to the tune on the CD (Track 76) several times. Then hum or sing the melody with the CD several more times.

2. Look at Example 158, where the pick-up notes and first full measure are written for you. (The key signature and time signature are also given.) Determine the first note of the second measure and all subsequent pitches by asking yourself the following questions:

   - Is the next note long or short? In other words, keeping in mind that the time signature is 3/4, is this note a half note, quarter note, eighth note, or something else?
   - Does the note move up or down from the previous note? Or is it the same pitch as the previous note?
   - If it is a different pitch, did it get there by step or by skip? If by skip, how wide?
   - Is it the same pitch as any of the previous notes that are already identified?

In spite of asking yourself this litany of questions, you may still be guessing at notes using the trial-and-error method. That is perfectly okay. Here are some helpful hints to assist you in this process.

- If trying to write the entire refrain seems overwhelming, break it down into its component parts, proceeding phrase by phrase (or even measure by measure, if necessary).
- Try playing the piece on the keyboard or on your flute if this helps you find the notes.

EXAMPLE 158: EXCERPT FROM "THE FIRST NOWELL"

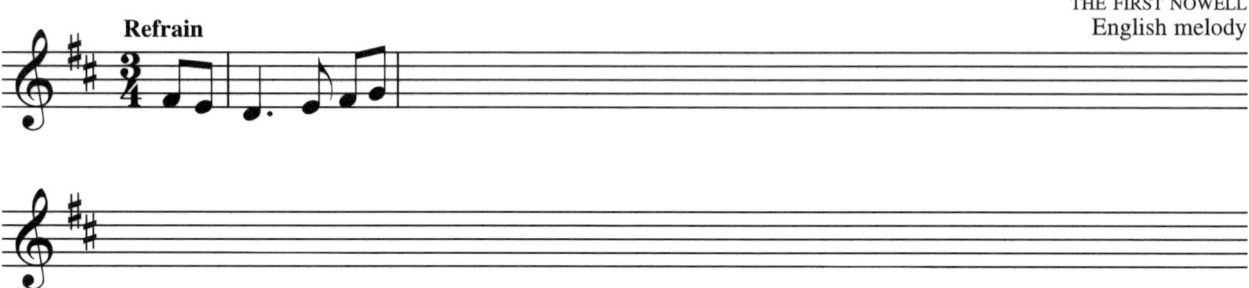

Track 76: Ear Training I

"The First Nowell" – refrain, flute alone

You can check your work by turning to the end of this chapter, where the refrain is printed in Example 162.

Let's examine "The First Nowell" in greater detail. This tune does not begin on the tonic. Rather, it begins on the third scale degree: F♯ in the key of D. Now look at the last note of the melody. "The First Nowell" is an example of the exception to the rule that the last note of the melody determines the key of the piece. In this tune, the last note of the melody is F♯—not the tonic, D. So in this case, the melody not only begins on the third scale degree but also ends on that same pitch.

Now try the same type of dictation exercise using a different approach.

EXERCISE

Write the melody of "Joyful, Joyful We Adore You" by ear. Start the melody on third line B on the treble staff. This time, there is no CD track to assist you. See if you can find your pitches by singing the tune to yourself or playing it on your flute. Listen to determine if the melody stays on the same pitch or goes up or down. Listen, too, for the proximity of the intervals. In other words, decide if the melody moves by step or by skip. Use the empty staff in Example 159 for your work. The first note and the time signature of ⁴⁄₄ are given to you.

EXAMPLE 159: EXCERPT FROM "JOYFUL, JOYFUL, WE ADORE YOU"

HYMN TO JOY
L. van Beethoven

You can check your work by turning to the end of this chapter, where the melody of "Joyful, Joyful, We Adore You" can be found in Example 163. Notice that the key signature for G major has been added at the beginning of the line. Since there are no Fs or F♯s in the melody of this piece, it can be rather difficult to determine the key using the dictation process alone. However, now that you know that the melody ends on G and you are in a major key, you can conclude that the key is G. Therefore, the key signature will have one sharp, F♯. Just as in "The First Nowell," the melody does not begin on the tonic but rather on the third degree of the scale, which is B.

Now that you have completed the dictation of two familiar tunes, try some others. You will benefit greatly from this process.

Here is another exercise for developing your listening skills. Let's return to THAXTED, Concertato on "O God, beyond All Praising," this time to study the vocal score (see Example 160).

EXAMPLE 160: EXCERPT FROM CONCERTATO ON "O GOD, BEYOND ALL PRAISING"

THAXTED
Setting by R. Proulx

On the CD (Track 77), you will hear the keyboard accompaniment with flute improvising a counter-melody based on the harmonies of the vocal parts. For the purposes of this exercise, the flute part will never stray from the printed page. It will simply jump from line to line of the choral score.

Note: Take a close look at the tenor voice (the third staff) in Example 160. Notice that it is written in the treble clef with the number "8" appearing under the clef sign. The "8" indicates that the pitches should be sung one octave lower than written. This is a common way to write tenor parts.

EXERCISE

Listen to the CD (Track 77). Your task is to mark the path of the flute part as it moves from one vocal line to another (of course, in appropriate octaves for flute!).

Track 77: Ear Training II
Concertato on "O God, beyond All Praising" – mm. 43–66, flute playing various vocal lines and piano

Check your work by looking at Example 164 at the end of this chapter. The path of the flute part is high-lighted there. You will notice that the flute part on the CD sometimes observes the rhythms of the printed page, but often does not. Many times vocal parts repeat several notes in a row on the same pitch, where the flutist may instead choose to play these as one or two sustained notes. This is another viable option you may wish to explore.

Here is yet another opportunity to develop aural proficiencies. Listen to the CD (Track 78), on which the refrain of James Moore's "Taste and See" is played with keyboard accompaniment and flute descant.

EXERCISE

Listen to James Moore's "Taste and See" on the CD (Track 78). The melody is provided in Example 161. Your task is to write the flute descant on the empty staff line above the melody. The first few measures of the descant have been given to help you get started.

EXAMPLE 161: EXCERPT FROM "TASTE AND SEE"

J. E. Moore, Jr.

James E. Moore, Jr. Copyright © 1983 by GIA Publications, Inc.

Track 78: Ear Training III
James Moore's "Taste and See" – refrain, flute on descant and piano

Check your work by referring to Example 165 at the end of this chapter. The complete descant is printed there.

James Moore's setting of "Taste and See" is meant to be played in a gospel style. Admittedly, the previous descant does not portray this style. It was used as an example for ear training purposes only.

Listen now to the CD (Track 79), which much more closely portrays the intended style for this piece. As you can see, knowing the intended style of a piece can make all the difference in the world. Although both of the previous examples are indeed descants for "Taste and See," the second one more closely matches the gospel flavor of this piece.

Track 79: Gospel Style of Playing
James Moore's "Taste and See" – refrain in gospel style, flute playing improvised descant and piano

Note: As just demonstrated, it is important to honor the intended style of the piece. It is equally important to understand that gospel *liturgical* music is different from gospel style used in a concert, just as jazz music we hear on the radio is different than a jazz-style piece of *liturgical* music. Regardless, it is extremely helpful to listen to these styles of playing in other contexts to immerse yourself in the genre before using these styles in liturgical playing.

As an additional means for developing your ear training skills, try a free improvisation. Track 80 on the CD provides only an improvised keyboard part.

EXERCISE

Listen to the CD (Track 80) several times.

- Determine the time signature of the piece. Play with the CD to determine the key signature (using the trial-and-error method). (The correct time and key signatures are printed below.)
- Listen for style and design. Is the piece played in a lyrical manner, an accented manner, or somewhere in between? Are there repetitive phrases? Does the music restate the opening chord progression at some later point in the piece?

This exercise is just for you, in the comfort of your own home. Play your improvisation with the CD (Track 80), without writing anything first. Be open to your own creativity. In other words, be open to the Spirit within you. Play with the CD several times, each time discovering a new improvisation.

Now listen to Track 81 on the CD, with an improvised flute part added to the keyboard part. Try to play your improvisation against the improvisation on Track 81, thus creating a second improvised flute part. Did the parts work together, or did you need to make adjustments in your descant?

As you see, there are many different ways of improvising. Each time you improvise with either of these tracks, your part will be different.

Time signature: ⁴⁄₄   Key signature: D major

Track 80: Free Improvisation I
Improvised piano accompaniment alone

Track 81: Free Improvisation II
Improvised flute and piano

Conclusion

This chapter has given you various techniques for broadening the scope of your tonal palette. It has also encouraged you to play and write melodies without benefit of the printed page. It has attuned your ear to a number of different styles of music and musicians. You have additionally been encouraged to explore free improvisation which, as you have discovered, creates a different playing experience each and every time. That is part of its delight, its playfulness, its mystery.

In Chapter 9, you will find still other opportunities to "fly" on your own even more and experience a greater depth of prayer, a greater level of creativity, and a greater sense of intimacy with yourself and with your flute.

Musical Examples Referenced in Chapter 8

EXAMPLE 162: EXCERPT FROM THE REFRAIN OF "THE FIRST NOWELL"

EXAMPLE 163: EXCERPT FROM "JOYFUL, JOYFUL, WE ADORE YOU"

EXAMPLE 164: EXCERPT FROM CONCERTATO ON "O GOD, BEYOND ALL PRAISING"

Example 165: Excerpt from "Taste and See"

J. E. Moore, Jr.

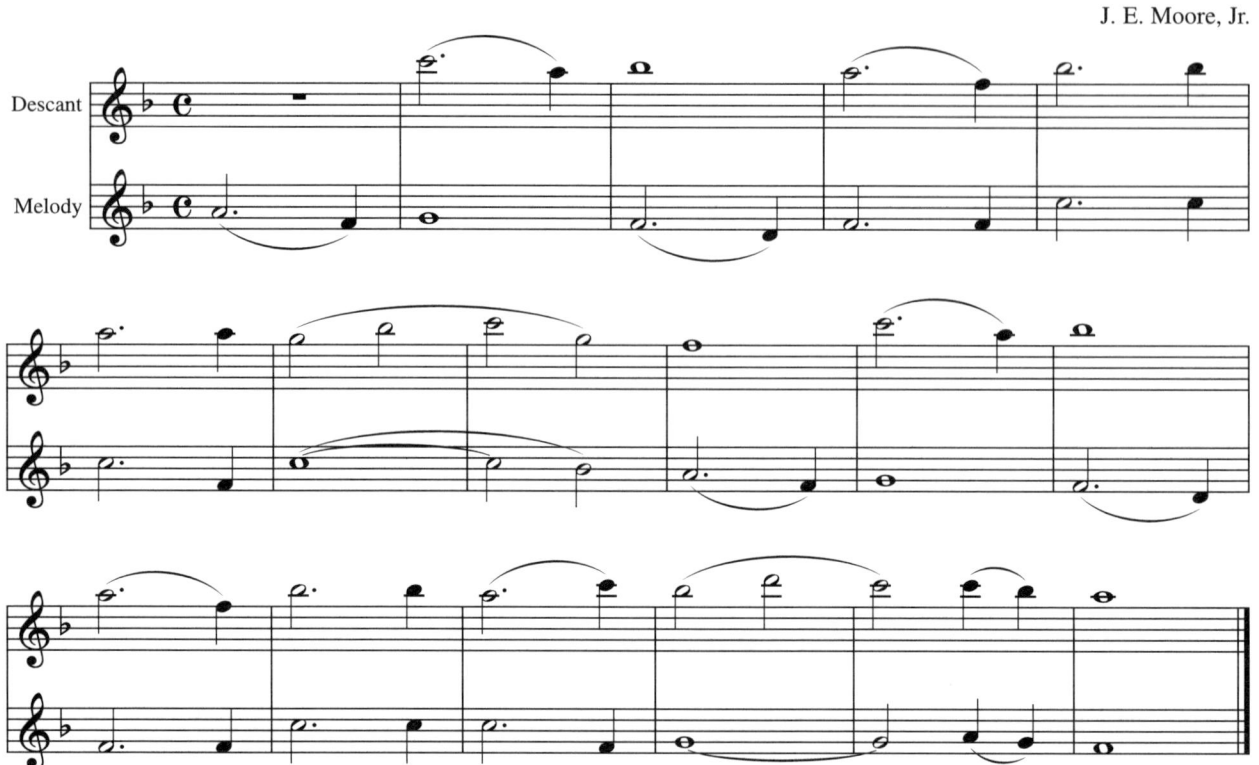

Chapter 9
Expanding the Role of the Parish Flutist

Weaver
Interpreter
Ritual Connector

Consider the following story. It has been rendered in several ways, so this is one telling:

There is a ritual practiced by a tribe in Africa. Upon coming of age and upon realizing a desire within herself to bring forth life, a woman of the tribe goes off by herself and listens until she hears the song that is the spirit of the child who wants to be born. Then the woman chooses the man who will join her in the creation of the child and she teaches him the song. Singing the song together is their marriage rite, and so the whole village learns the song that is to be the new life their union creates. Once this new life is conceived and born into the world, the father and the mother and the whole village sing the song—the beautiful, melodious and rhythmical sound that is the child—over and over throughout all the growing years until the child knows the song, too. Sung throughout life, finally this song is sung at the moment the child/adult leaves the physical body to be birthed into a new life in the spirit.

This story implies there is always the presence of the song. The song is past, present, future. Every part of creation is an "embodied song" with its own patterns, rhythms, and melodies, and all are part of the Universal Song. The song is eternal. When playing the flute, with its unique sound, the song within you is given expression. The invitation to you is to listen more carefully to the song within you and allow its many facets to find voice in the way you play your instrument. Knowing yourself better allows you to be a greater gift to the world. Let us give thanks, then, that music is one road given us to self-knowledge.

Nothing is better than music. When it takes us out of time, it has done more for us than we have the right to hope for. It has broadened the limits of our sorrowful lives; it has lit up the sweetness of our hours of happiness by effacing the pettiness that diminishes us, bringing us back pure and new to what was, what will be, and what music has created for us.

—Nadia Boulanger

Creativity knows no bounds. Now that you have jumped with both feet into improvisation, this chapter provides some interesting ideas for interpretive improvisation. There are also a variety of opportunities for getting beyond written descants and doing more "free" improvisation. The ideas presented in this chapter will continue to go deeper as we expand the role of the parish flutist. We will also explore various ways the flute can be used to create a rich tapestry of sound, the possibilities of using the flute as the common thread between rituals, and its use as a means of opening the spoken text in ways unexpected.

All it takes is some imagination and the conviction that music is powerful beyond measure—a gift from God. As Eric Werner says in *The Sacred Bridge*, "…music is not so much a thing of beauty as an ethical force." Then it becomes our responsibility to bring to bear all the resources we have considered in these pages—musical, spiritual, pastoral, liturgical—to awaken the soul (our own and others') by creating an ever more inviting ritual prayer.

Weaving Various Musical Selections

There may be occasions when you are called upon to play solo flute music for an extended period of time—such as during a Communal Reconciliation Service or Communal Anointing of the Sick. In these instances, sometimes seemingly disparate pieces of music can be woven together in a very effective manner. Consider Examples 166 and 167, one piece coming from the liturgical repertoire and the other from the standard flute solo literature.

EXAMPLE 166: EXCERPT FROM "AMAZING GRACE"

NEW BRITAIN
Virginia Harmony, 1831

EXAMPLE 167: EXCERPT FROM *MORCEAU DE CONCOURS*

G. Fauré

Let's first examine the similarities between these two pieces. They are both in the key of F major. Both are in 3/4 meter. The tempos of both pieces are similar. In spite of the fact that both pieces are usually played with keyboard accompaniment, they both work well as unaccompanied solos. In other words, these pieces complement each other very well. Try intermingling these tunes in the following way.

Begin with one verse of "Amazing Grace" as written. Next play the first excerpt of *Morceau de Concours*, followed by another verse of "Amazing Grace." Play measures 1–4 of this verse in the printed octave, switching to *8va* in measure 5. Add embellishments as desired. Conclude with the second excerpt of the *Morceau de Concours*.

Listen to this example as played on the CD (Track 82). The end result is a beautiful new composition for flute alone, in which *Morceau de Concours* almost becomes a variation on "Amazing Grace." This new work can also be a very appropriate prelude if "Amazing Grace" happens to be the Gathering Song.

 **Track 82: Weaving Two Musical Selections I**
"Amazing Grace," 1 verse; Fauré's *Morceau de Concours*, mm. 2–9; "Amazing Grace," 1 verse; Fauré's *Morceau de Concours*, mm. 30–33 – flute alone

A similar result occurs with the juxtaposition of two liturgical pieces: "We Three Kings" and "What Child Is This" (see Examples 168 and 169).

EXAMPLE 168: EXCERPT FROM "WE THREE KINGS"

KINGS OF ORIENT
J. H. Hopkins, Jr.

EXAMPLE 169: EXCERPT FROM "WHAT CHILD IS THIS"

GREENSLEEVES
English melody, 16th c.

Again, these pieces have several similarities. They are both in the key of E minor. They have complementary tempos and styles. The time signatures, while not identical, are related. Because of these factors, these two pieces work well together.

Begin with the music for "We Three Kings." Continue with an embellished verse of "What Child Is This," followed by its refrain melody. Conclude with an ornamented rendition of "We Three Kings." (See Example 170.)

This piece is very appropriate for Epiphany celebrations. Let it spark your further imagination and exploration of other possibilities. Then see what other pieces of music you can find that lend themselves to being "woven" together.

EXAMPLE 170: EXCERPT FROM "EPIPHANY MEDITATION"

A. O'Shea

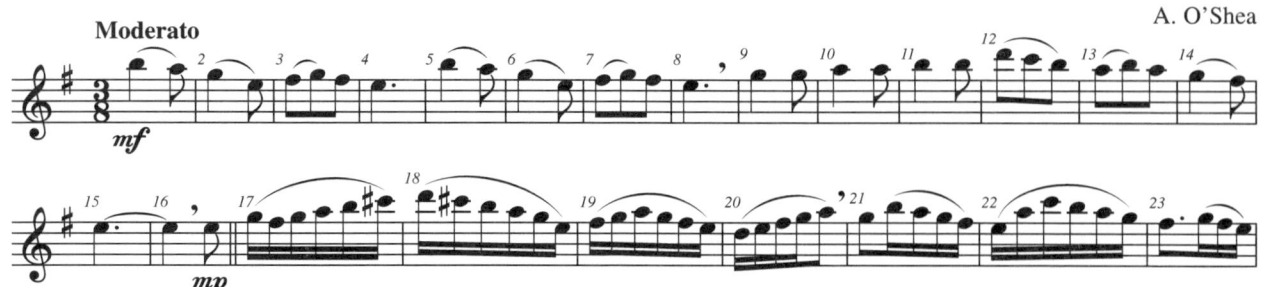

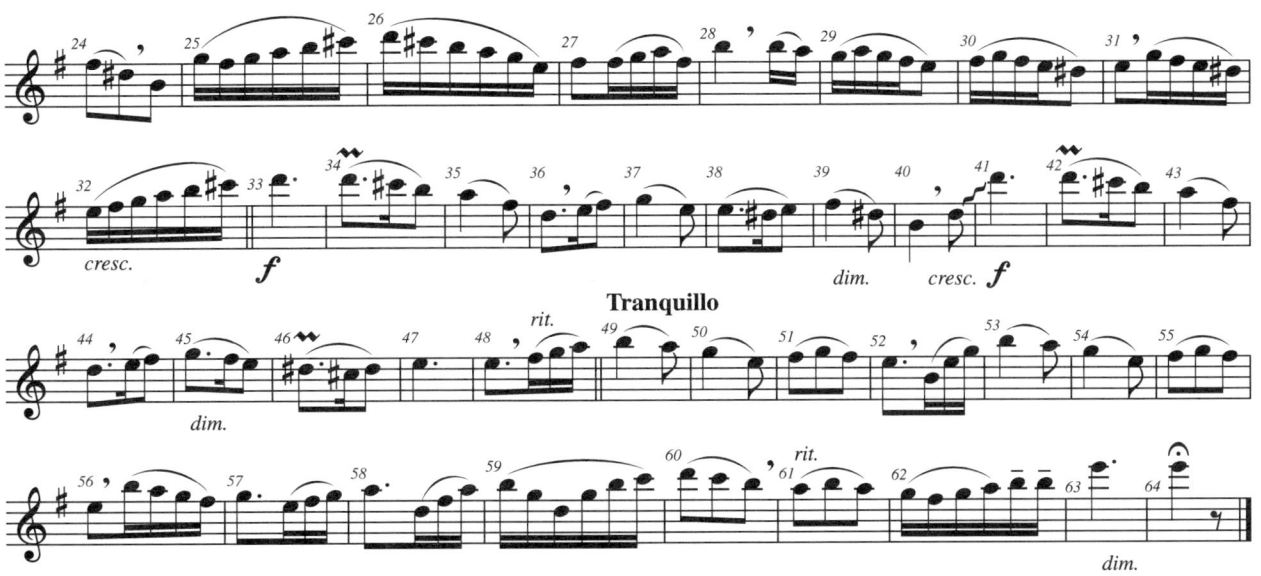

Another way to approach this weaving of two musical selections is to use two flutes placed in separate areas of the worship space. One might be in front and one in back or at the midway point; or one in the front and another in the choir loft; or both in front, but one on the left side of the sanctuary and another on the right.

Let's look again at the "Epiphany Meditation" in Example 170. One flutist could play the opening section (mm. 1–16), the other flutist the next section (to the downbeat of m. 31), and so on, weaving back and forth seamlessly, one picking up where the other left off. Both musicians should be of similar tone quality and ability. And because of the distance, rehearsal together in the space is a must. This technique has the stunning effect of "wrapping" the assembly in sound, and so is worth the effort needed for blending and proper timing. Listen to this effect on the CD (Track 83).

Track 83: Weaving Two Musical Selections II
　　"Epiphany Meditation" – 2 flutes in antiphonal style

Weaving Music and Text

Solo flute music can also be interwoven with spoken text (see Examples 171 and 172). The reading can be taken from Scripture or another source. Imagine how the following example could be used during a Day of Reflection for Ministers of Music.

EXAMPLE 171: "O SPIRIT ALL-EMBRACING"

O Spirit all-embracing and counselor all-wise,
unbounded splendor gracing a shoreless sea of skies:
unfailing is your treasure, unfading your reward;
surpassing worldly pleasure, the riches you afford.
Come, stream of endless flowing, and rescue us from death;
Come, wind of springtime blowing, and warm us by your breath.

O Beauty ever blazing in flower, field, and face,
you show yourself amazing in unexpected place.
We see you and remember what once our dreams had been;
you fan the glowing ember and kindle hope within.
Come, fire of glory gracious, bless all who trust in you;
undying flame tenacious, burn in your world anew.

Come, passion's power holy, your insight here impart,
and give your servants lowly an understanding heart
to know your care more clearly when faith and love are tried,
to seek you more sincerely when false ideals have died:
for vision we implore you, for wisdom's pure delight;
in prayer we come before you to wait upon your light.

Text: Delores Dufner, OSB; © 1995, 2003, GIA Publications, Inc.

EXAMPLE 172: "PRAYER IN ALLELUIA, FORM II"

Copyright © 1987 by GIA Publications, Inc.

There are several methods for weaving spoken text and music. Simple alternation between sections of text and music is one method, using the music as a commentary on the text. Listen to this technique applied to these two works on the CD (Track 84).

Track 84: Weaving Music and Spoken Text I
"O Spirit All-Embracing," stanza 1; "Prayer in Alleluia," Form II, mm. 1–8; "O Spirit All-Embracing," stanza 2; "Prayer in Alleluia," Form II, mm. 9–14; "O Spirit All-Embracing," stanza 3; "Prayer in Alleluia," Form II, mm. 15–22 – spoken voice in alternation with flute

Underscoring the text—playing music softly in the background under the spoken text—is also very effective, provided the music doesn't detract from the text. Listen to this effect on the CD (Track 85) with "Canticle of Daniel," from *I Will Sing Forever* (see Example 173) interspersed with free improvisation.

EXAMPLE 173: EXCERPT FROM "CANTICLE OF DANIEL" I

Bless our God,
beyond all stars and things in space.
Praise, glory, honor!
Bless our God,
all the heavens, all the earth.
Praise, glory, honor!

Bless our God,
all the angels.
Praise, glory, honor!
Bless our God,
in the heavens.
Praise, glory, honor!

Bless our God,
through the teeming waters.
Praise, glory, honor!
Bless our God,
spirits and heavenly beings.
Praise, glory, honor!

Bless our God,
darkness and shining light.
Praise, glory, honor!
Bless our God,
thunder and lightning.
Praise, glory, honor!

Bless our God,
all of the earth and sea.
Praise, glory, honor!
Bless our God,
towering mountains and hills.
Praise, glory, honor!

Bless our God,
all things that grow.
Praise, glory, honor!
Bless our God,
bubbling fountain and spring.
Praise, glory, honor!

Bless our God,
rapid river and ocean.
Praise, glory, honor!
Bless our God,
all things that swim.
Praise, glory, honor!

Bless our God,
all who serve.
Praise, glory, honor!
Bless our God,
all who minister.
Praise, glory, honor!

Bless our God,
all the faithful and just.
Praise, glory, honor!
Bless our God,
holy and lowly ones.
Praise, glory, honor!

Bless our God,
all the galaxies.
Praise, glory, honor!
Bless our God,
all creation in the cosmos.
Praise, glory, honor!

—David Haas/Daniel 3:56–88
from *I Will Sing Forever* (GIA Publications, Inc., 2001)

Track 85: Weaving Music and Spoken Text II
"Canticle of Daniel" – recited verses underscored with free improvisation, flute and spoken voice

In this example, instead of solo flute music taken from the standard repertoire, the flutist responds with a free improvisation. Here it was played by one flutist, but it could also be done with one or more other instruments. In this example, the flutist looked at a copy of the spoken text and improvised against the images presented or at times simply out of the spirit of the entire reading.

On the CD (Track 86), you will hear four additional spoken verses of "Canticle of Daniel" (see Example 174), specifically verses 4, 5, 13, and 14. Use your creativity to do your own musical interpretation with a free improvisation against the text.

EXAMPLE 174: EXCERPT FROM "CANTICLE OF DANIEL" II

Bless our God,
the sun and the moon.
Praise, glory, honor!
Bless our God,
all heavenly stars.
Praise, glory, honor!

Bless our God,
the rains and the dew.
Praise, glory, honor!
Bless our God,
the winds, rapid and slow.
Praise, glory, honor!

Bless our God,
all flying creatures.
Praise, glory, honor!
Bless our God,
all earthly beasts.
Praise, glory, honor!

Bless our God,
all children of God.
Praise, glory, honor!
Bless our God,
people of Israel.
Praise, glory, honor!

—David Haas/Daniel 3:56–88
from *I Will Sing Forever* (GIA Publications, Inc., 2001)

Track 86: Try Your Own Interpretive Playing
"Canticle of Daniel" – 4 verses, spoken voice alone

Look to other poetry or scripture. Tape your voice speaking your favorite passages, and then improvise interpretively on your flute against the text. In general, long, slow notes (perhaps in a minor key) work well for a more somber text. Faster, more embellished and articulated playing (perhaps in a major key) works better for a more uplifting text.

Weaving Music, Text, and Ritual

As previously stated, the flute can be played effectively against a scripture reading, but this should be done only sparingly during a worship service lest it become overdone. Remember that the text always takes precedence: the music supports it. Any improvisation must hold the tension between spontaneity and intentionality, and must never be approached for its own sake. Even improvisation is servant to the prayer.

This being said, there are occasions when the flute could be very effectively used to interpret the text and weave text and music. Consider using the flute underneath portions of the Passion on Palm Sunday or during the reading of the Creation Story at the Easter Vigil. The flute could also be used as interpreter of the text during the proclamation of the Psalm on any given Sunday. There could be a lovely interchange between the cantor singing a chanted Psalm and the flutist using free improvisation. The flute could underscore the images presented, as shown in Psalm 116: "I Will Walk in the Presence of the Lord" by Richard Proulx (see Example 175), with the Proulx psalm tones on the verses. Notice on the CD (Track 87) the way the flute varies the improvisation between harmonic embellishment and countermelody.

EXAMPLE 175: EXCERPT FROM "PSALM 116" (ANTIPHON II)

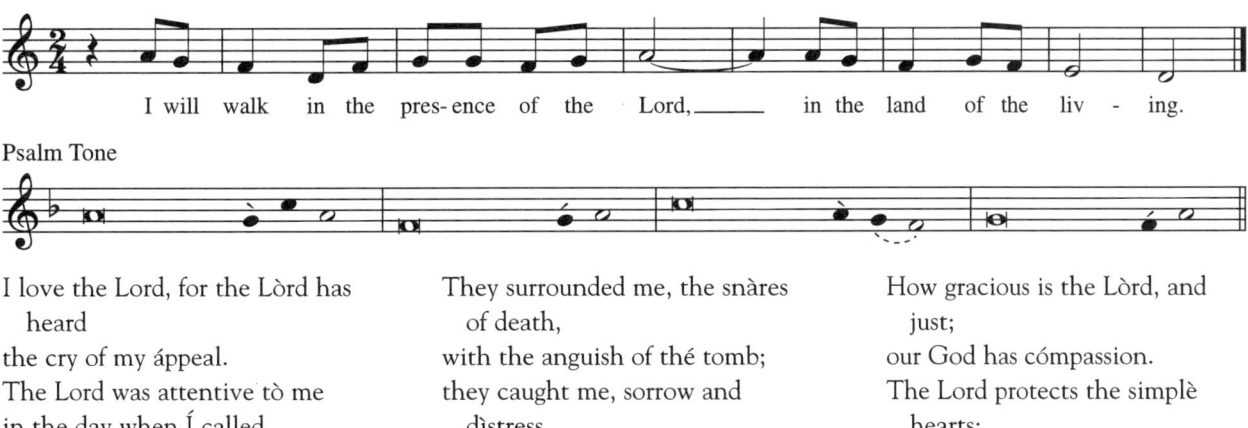

I will walk in the pres-ence of the Lord,____ in the land of the liv - ing.

Psalm Tone

I love the Lord, for the Lòrd has heard
the cry of my áppeal.
The Lord was attentive tò me
in the day when Í called.

They surrounded me, the snàres of death,
with the anguish of thé tomb;
they caught me, sorrow and dìstress.
I called on the Lord's name.
O Lord, my God, déliver me!

How gracious is the Lòrd, and just;
our God has cómpassion.
The Lord protects the simplè hearts;
I was helpless so Gód saved me.

Text: Psalm 116:9; Copyright © 1963, The Grail, GIA Publications, Inc., agent
Music: Richard Proulx, © 1975 by GIA Publications, Inc.
Psalm Tone: Richard Proulx, © 1986 by GIA Publications, Inc.

Track 87: Interpreting the Psalms
Proulx's "Psalm 116," Antiphon and Psalm tone – refrain and 3 verses, flute, cantor, and guitar

The flute could also be the "common denominator" or the weaving element between several rituals that are connected yet spread out in relation to time. For instance, the Taizé mantra "Jesus, Remember Me" could be used at each of the funeral liturgy stations. (See Chapter 6 for discussion on funeral liturgies.) The flute could introduce the piece at the vigil service, play it in procession when entering the church for the funeral liturgy, play it again as everyone leaves the church, and play it one more time at the cemetery.

Consider also the days of the Triduum. A way to highlight the Triduum as one major liturgy (within which the Paschal Mystery is expressed in several ways over the three days) would be to use the flute as a thread within the liturgies.

- On Holy Thursday, the flutist might lead the procession to transfer the Holy Eucharist, supporting the assembly's singing of "Pange Lingua."

- On Good Friday, the flutist might lead a procession that brings the cross to be used for veneration into the body of the church. The ritual calls for the procession to stop three times, with the presider leading an acclamation (with an assembly response) at each station. One possibility would be to use the song "Behold the Wood of the Cross" by Dan Schutte. In this example, the flutist improvises in the key of the music (D minor), ending on the first note of the refrain—indicating the pitch for the presider. Another option for this ritual would be for the presider to sing the acclamation as a chant tone pitched higher at each successive station. The flutist could improvise in a manner similar to the first example, this time ending each improvisation on a different pitch to coordinate with the first note of the presider's acclamation.

- Finally, at the Easter Vigil, the flutist might lead the procession to the door of the church from the spot outside where the blessing of the fire and the lighting of the Easter candle have taken place. "Jesus Christ, Yesterday, Today and Forever" by Suzanne Toolan, SM, works well for this procession.

All of the ideas presented above regarding free improvisation have been done in parish settings but only after several years of flutist and music director working and ministering together, growing in trust. As has already been said, the use of free improvisation allows for a more spontaneous response to the spirit within us during any given moment. Be open to this gift and nurture it. Be adventurous and imaginative. Little by little, explore improvisation's many possibilities. However, try not to rush the process of growing into this skill; it does take time.

Conclusion

Keep in mind that at whatever level you play and in whatever way you use the flute in prayer, ultimately it is God who is present within your music-making. What you continually are about is doing whatever you can in your life and in your music-making to cooperate with God's spirit in bringing beauty into the world and deepening the prayer of the assembly at worship.

> *There is no doubt that Christian liturgy benefits from the presence of skilled musicians even as it calls forth from them a new and necessary discipline. This discipline, seldom taught in our universities or conservatories, puts musicianship in an auxiliary role, handmaid to the liturgy. As noted in Liturgical Music Today, church musicians are called to be disciples first and then ministers.*
>
> —from *The Milwaukee Report*, #72

Postscript

Completion of these materials is surely a milestone. It implies that you have considered not only many technical aspects of playing the flute, but that you have also focused on using the flute within the context of prayer and within the context of liturgy. You have named yourself as pastoral musician on your own spiritual journey, yet as part of a community of believers.

In many ways, the completion of this book is but a beginning, much like a graduation ceremony signals an end as well as the start of something new. Consider that we are just 40+ years post-Vatican II. All that this Council opened up to us is in its infancy. We are still so new in our interpretation of the Council documents and their application to our liturgies. In other words, we are living in a unique time when what we do as pastoral musicians can add to the insight surrounding this historical evolving of interpretation and application. If we recognize this, then we will know our part is important to the whole. We will better understand that we are never finished with our formation. We will recognize the need (and even responsibility) to take advantage of continuing education and regularly avail ourselves of workshops and conferences. We will see the wisdom in asking questions and seeking answers.

We hope this book has been a helpful tool in your development; yet the book is not exhaustive. We are confident you will take the ideas presented here and expand on them. We urge you to find a way to talk about this with other musicians and, particularly, to share your learnings with other flutists. Be a good leader, balancing musical professionalism and liturgical competency with authentic ministry and deepening spirituality—"helping the assembly to rejoice, to weep, to be of one mind, to be converted, to pray." (from *Liturgical Music Today*, #58)

Yours is a vocation shared with composers, text writers, music directors, cantors, and choir members, as well as other instrumentalists, to shepherd the sung prayer of the people of God at worship. This is a process over a lifetime. Be patient in this vocation even as you continually challenge yourself. Take time along the way to notice and mark your growth in all the areas we have considered. One way to do this is through ritual, such as the one outlined below:

- Light a sweet-smelling candle.
- Play your favorite piece on the flute or perhaps improvise a melody out of your own sense of joy in accomplishment.
- Listen carefully to the wonderful musical sound you make.
- When you finish, take a few moments of silence to get in touch with gratitude for such a marvelous gift.
- Pray the following blessing prayer aloud:

O glorious and gracious God,
You have made me your hands and feet, your eyes and ears and voice in this world.
I am your work of art, a jewel of your abundant creation.
May my mind, heart, and spirit always be open to your grace.
May I live my life witnessing gratitude for your faithful love.

It is such mystery that you should anoint me as music-maker.
I can hardly find words to thank you for such an abundance of music to delight my heart—
*   yet I offer my desire to reflect a deeply abiding love for you whenever I play my instrument.*
I ask for your blessing, ever-present God, on all that I do and say, on all that I am.
Amen.

—Denise La Giglia

A new inspiration springs forth with every time, with every age, with every place. In the song of the church there is always one more measure, one more note, one more verse, more lyrics, and above all, more deeds to perform, deeds that build the temple of the kingdom of God.

—Ricardo Ramirez (from "Fiesta, Worship and Family,"
found in *Liturgy Sourcebook* (LTP))

Appendix I
The History of the Flute and Other Instruments in Worship

The flute is one of the most ancient of instruments. Its history dates back thousands of years before the birth of Christ. The earliest flutes were probably bamboo shoots of varying sizes, which produced different pitches depending on the length of the tubing. Numerous notes could also be produced on a single piece of bamboo by poking several holes in it, and then covering some or all of the holes with the fingers.

There is evidence of instruments being played in the worship services of the ancient Hebrews. Psalm 150 tells us, "Praise God with flutes and strings." During the worship services of that era, instrumental music was usually played in unison with vocal music, with the instruments supporting the assembly's song.

During Jesus' lifetime, professionally trained singers and instrumentalists served in the temple. In Herod's temple, for example, the trumpet and shofar (a ram's horn) were often used to signal the entrance of the priests, while string and wind instruments doubled the vocal lines or accompanied the choir.

First century Christians continued the lyrical style of their Jewish ancestors in their psalms, their blessing prayers, etc. They carried the traditions of Judaism into the Gentile world. But as Christians began to include the memory and example of Jesus, variations began to surface. Paul emphasized that all gifts should serve the common good, thus suggesting a preference for responsorial rather than solo singing, a dialogue rather than a monologue. Therefore, while professional musicians undoubtedly did participate in early worship, they did not dominate the prayer. The emphasis of the music at worship was on the primacy of the assembly's voice.

The early centuries of the Church saw a shift in the location of the community's prayer from domestic settings to churches. Bit by bit the assembly was removed from the action of the priest. During the Romanesque era/Early Middle Ages (500–1000 AD), *monophony* (also known as plainsong or chant) dominated the music of the Church. It was usually sung by choirs in which only men were allowed to participate, and there was very little opportunity for assembly participation. There is almost no evidence of sacred instrumental music at this time, with the exception of the use of the organ (as early as 800 AD), and the drone bass, which sometimes accompanied sacred monophony. In general, instruments were prohibited in the Church during the Romanesque Era. Instruments were much more commonly used in the secular music of this time—especially dance music—where wind, percussion, and string instruments abounded.

During the Gothic era/Late Middle Ages (1100–1430 AD), monophony gradually gave way to *polyphony*, which often used a *cantus firmus* in the tenor line, with upper voices moving more quickly and in a more ornamented style. Often three different texts were sung simultaneously, sometimes in three different languages, thereby obscuring the importance of the text. Because the text could not be understood, it became commonplace for the cantus firmus to be played by an instrument instead of being sung. At times, instruments were also used to double the other vocal lines.

During the Renaissance era (1400–1600), many significant developments occurred in the evolution of music. In 1517, Martin Luther led the Protestant Reformation. He called for, among many other things, the inclusion of congregational singing in the vernacular in liturgy. This led to the emergence of Germany and Austria as dominant forces in the music world from 1650 to 1900. As a counterattack on the Reformation, the Fathers of the Catholic Church convened the Council of Trent (1545–1563). The Council called for the abolition of the use of all secular texts for liturgical use and also kept Latin as the official language of Roman Catholic liturgy.

At the beginning of the Renaissance era, what little sacred instrumental music there was usually duplicated or was substituted for an existing vocal line. In the fifteenth and sixteenth centuries, independent parts began to appear for keyboard instruments, specifically organ, harpsichord, and clavichord. Preludes, which functioned as an introduction to a liturgical service, became the first truly instrumental music. String and wind ensembles also became popular, due in part to the architecture of St. Mark's Cathedral in Venice. This church, built in the shape of a cross, fostered the style of antiphonal music known as the *canzona*, placing one group of musicians in each of the "arms" of the cross. Venetian composer Giovanni Gabrieli (c.1557–1612) became a master of the canzona. He ranks among the first composers to write works for voices and instruments in which the instrumental parts do not duplicate the vocal lines.

During the Baroque era (1600–1750), composers still wrote sacred music specifically for liturgical purposes. However, more and more instrumental religious music was being written for non-liturgical use (e.g., preludes, postludes, musical backgrounds for marriage ceremonies, etc.). It was also written in the florid, embellished style that was characteristic of Baroque music. Major and minor tonalities also developed during this time and are still in use today.

Scientific developments during the Baroque era led to improvements in the manufacture of instruments, especially string instruments, leading composers to write idiomatically, with the characteristics and limitations of a specific instrument in mind. However, it was still common practice to interchange instruments of like range (e.g., bassoon for cello, recorder for violin). This era also saw the development of equal-tempered tuning, a system in which an equal distance occurs between each half step. This discovery allowed musicians to play music in any key without stopping to retune the instrument, which led to a freer use of both chromaticism and dissonance.

Composers continued to write music for Mass settings during the Baroque era, but in a dramatic fashion, with the addition of orchestral accompaniment. The *oratorio*, the sacred counterpart to opera, used extensive combinations of voices and instruments.

In contrast to the Baroque era, composers in the Classical era (1725–1800) intentionally wrote music that lacked an expression of emotion. The function of music shifted to the world of entertainment. Musicians became employed in palaces and courts in addition to churches. The introduction of the concert hall and opera house also created new venues for musicians, with all classes of people now being able to enjoy live performance. For the first time in history, the church ceased to be the main patron of the arts; however, the church still needed sacred music in spite of the prevalence of secularism. Composers continued to write Mass settings, but more and more often these settings were meant for the concert hall rather than for liturgical use. Masses, therefore, took on a symphonic nature, using orchestras, choirs, and soloists.

By the nineteenth century, the church was no longer a patron of music. Composers of the Romantic era (1800–1900), in contrast to their forerunners in the Classical era, wrote music filled with emotion, reflecting the composer's own personal convictions instead of the desires of his patron (be that the emperor or the church). Music of this era became technically very demanding. The art of improvisation all but disappeared during this time, since all stylistic marks were clearly indicated in the music by the composer. Sacred music was most often written for the combination of orchestra and choir, and usually with a symphonic rather than a choral bent. The role of the orchestra became increasingly important, with the text more or less "fitting in" to a symphonic work. Composers wrote sacred works of grand scale, almost always with the concert hall—not the church—in mind.

In contrast, music that was really intended for liturgical use in the Roman Catholic Church had changed very little for hundreds of years prior to the Second Vatican Council (1962–1965). The Fathers of Vatican II made conscious efforts to return the Church to its roots, restoring not only the rites as originally intended but also music as originally intended. The primacy of the assembly's voice is now the focus, which differs from the mindset of previous centuries when congregations listened to the beauty of music performed by others. With the reforms of Vatican II also came the renewal of the use of many instruments other than the organ for Roman Catholic worship. "Folk music" (music of the people) is now commonplace, as is the use of popular instruments such as piano, guitar, winds, brass, strings, and percussion.

To the twenty-first century liturgical musician, the appearance of instruments other than organ may appear to be "new"; however, it now becomes apparent that the current music of the Roman Catholic Church has merely returned us to our roots. As the psalmist wrote three thousand years ago,

> Give praise with blasts upon the horn,
>   praise him with harp and lyre.
> Give praise with tambourines and dance,
>   praise him with flutes and strings.
> Give praise with crashing cymbals,
>   praise him with sounding cymbals.
> Let everything that has breath
>   give praise to the LORD!
> Hallelujah!
>   —Psalm 150:3–6, New American Bible

Appendix II
Repertoire/Resource List

Collections for Flute Alone

Hymn Variations for Solo Flute, Victoria Jicha (Music Makers, Inc.; copyright transferred Charlotte, NC: Alry Publications, 2002)

More Hymns for Solo Flute, Victoria Jicha (Music Makers, Inc.; copyright transferred Charlotte, NC: Alry Publications, 2002)

Solos for Flute Alone

Four Moments of Prayer, Joseph Gelineau (Chicago: GIA Publications, Inc.)

Les Folies d'Espagne, Marin Marais (New York: Bärenreiter Kassel)

Partita in A Minor, J. S. Bach (New York: Bärenreiter Kassel)

Reflections, Katherine Hoover (New York: Papagena Press)

Solfeggietto, C. P. E. Bach, arranged by Arthur Frackenpohl (Delevan, NY: Kendor Music, Inc.)

Sonata in A Minor, C. P. E. Bach (New York: Bärenreiter Kassel)

Twelve Fantasies, G. P. Telemann (San Antonio, TX: Southern Music Company)

Unaccompanied Meditations, Richard Proulx (Chicago: GIA Publications, Inc.)

Collections for Flute and Accompanying Instrument

Baroque Music for Solo Instrument & Keyboard, Sets I and II, edited and arranged by S. Drummond Wolff (St. Louis, MO: Morning Star Publishers)

Church Instrumentalist Series, Books I and II, arranged and edited by Arthur Ephross and Janann Stark (San Antonio, TX: Southern Music Company)

Classic Solos for Flute & Keyboard: A Collection for Weddings & Recitals, compiled and arranged by Jane Holstein (Carol Stream, IL: Hope Publishing Company)

Eight Pieces for Flute & Organ, Richard Slater (Chicago: GIA Publications, Inc.)

Five Carols, David Moore (Chicago: GIA Publications, Inc.)

Great Classics for Flute Solo, arranged by John Hollins (Pacific, MO: Mel Bay Publications)

Liturgical Meditations, Jacques Berthier (Chicago: GIA Publications, Inc.)

Play Before God (for C instrument, guitar, keyboard), Bobby Fisher (Chicago: GIA Publications, Inc.)

Sacred Solos for C Flute with Piano Accompaniment, compiled, arranged, and edited by Clair W. Johnson (Miami, FL: Rubank, Inc.)

Sacred Solos for the Flute, Volumes I and II, compiled and arranged by Dona Gilliam and Mizzy McCaskill (Pacific, MO: Cathedral Music Press)

Season of Peace (for C instrument, guitar, keyboard), Bobby Fisher (Chicago: GIA Publications, Inc.)

Solos & Duets for C Instruments & Accompaniments, Volumes I, II, and III, arranged by John Wilson (Carol Stream, IL: Hope Publishing Company)

Solos for Flute, compiled by Donald Peck (New York: Carl Fischer)

Songs of Faith, Volumes I and II, Bill Holcombe (West Trenton, NJ: Musicians Publications)

Thirty-Six Flute Repertoire Pieces with Piano Accompaniment, compiled and edited by Donald Peck (New York: Carl Fischer)

Three Marian Hymns, Brian Henkelmann (Chicago: GIA Publications, Inc.)

Twenty-four Short Concert Pieces, Robert Cavally (San Antonio, TX: Southern Music Company)

Wedding Music for Flute & Guitar, arranged by Mychal Gendron (St. Louis, MO: Cathedral Music Press)

Wedding Music, Volumes I–IV, edited by David Johnson (Minneapolis, MN: Augsburg Publishing House)

Solos for Flute and Keyboard

A Christmas Prelude for Flute & Organ, Charles Callahan (St. Louis, MO: Morning Star Publishers)

A Lenten Prelude for Flute & Organ, Charles Callahan (St. Louis, MO: Morning Star Publishers)

A Pentecost Prelude for Flute & Organ, Charles Callahan (St. Louis, MO: Morning Star Publishers)

American Hymn Medley, Victoria Jicha (Music Makers, Inc.; copyright transferred Charlotte, NC: Alry Publications, 2002)

An Advent Prelude for Flute & Organ, Charles Callahan (St. Louis, MO: Morning Star Publishers)

An Easter Prelude for Flute & Organ, Charles Callahan (St. Louis, MO: Morning Star Publishers)

An Epiphany Prelude for Flute & Organ, Charles Callahan (St. Louis, MO: Morning Star Publishers)

Christmas Medley, Mary Jean Simpson (Charlotte, NC: Pan Publications)

Easter Medley, Mary Jean Simpson (Charlotte, NC: Pan Publications)

Easter Sonata for Flute & Organ, Robert J. Powell (St. Louis, MO: Concordia Publishing House)

Five Liturgical Meditations (for flute, oboe, or violin and keyboard), Bob Moore (Chicago: GIA Publications, Inc.)

Flötenmusik, J. S. Bach (New York: Bärenreiter Kassel)

Flötenmusik, Telemann (New York: Bärenreiter Kassel)

Liturgical Suite (for flute and piano), Bob Moore (Chicago: GIA Publications, Inc.)

Pastorale for Flute & Organ, Charles Callahan (St. Louis, MO: Concordia Publishing House)

Rhapsody on American Folk Hymns, Charles Callahan (St. Louis, MO: Morning Star Publishers)

Sechs Sonanten, Quantz (New York: Bärenreiter Kassel)

Sonatas, Marcello (New York: Bärenreiter Kassel)

Sonatas, Volumes I and II, Handel (New York: Bärenreiter Kassel)

Suite Modale, Ernest Bloch (New York: Broude Brothers Limited)

Theresa's Canticle of Love (for C instrument and classical guitar or piano), Marie Therese Sokol (Chicago: GIA Publications, Inc.)

Flute Duets

Forty Short Duets for Beginner Flutists (for two flutes and piano), original compositions and transcriptions arranged in progressive order by Louis Moyse (New York/London: G. Schirmer)

Salve Regina (for flute, oboe, keyboard), Jacques Berthier (Chicago: GIA Publications, Inc.)

Suaimhneas (Peace): Irish Music for Flute, Violin, Guitar & Keyboard, C. McKinney/C. Whyte (Chicago: GIA Publications, Inc.)

The Faithful Flute Duo: Arrangements for Two Flutes and Piano, by Brent Olstad (Anderson, IN: Intrada Music Group)

Flute Trios

Be Thou My Vision, arranged by Gordon Schuster (Anderson, IN: Intrada Music Group)

Canon (for three flutes and keyboard, or three C flutes, alto, and bass flute), J. Pachelbel, arranged by Robert Webb (San Antonio, TX: Southern Music Company)

Favorite Wedding Classics for 1–3 Flutes (piano accompaniment book sold separately), edited by Carol Cuellar (Miami, FL: CPP/Belwin, Inc.)

Flute Quartets

American Hymn Medley, arranged by Victoria Jicha (Music Makers, Inc.; copyright transferred Charlotte, NC: Alry Publications, 2002)

Ave Maria (for two C flutes, alto, and bass flute), Franz Schubert, arranged by Victoria Jicha (Music Makers, Inc.; copyright transferred Charlotte, NC: Alry Publications, 2002)

Jesu, Joy of Man's Desiring, J. S. Bach, transcribed by Bill Holcombe (West Trenton, NJ: Musicians Publications)

Music for Weddings, Volumes I and II (for four C flutes and optional alto and bass flutes), arranged by Bill Holcombe and Paul Battles (West Trenton, NJ: Musicians Publications)

Ensemble Music

Gathered in the Love of Christ, Johann Pachelbel and Marty Haugen (Chicago: GIA Publications, Inc.) This piece combines an arrangement of Pachelbel's *Canon in D* (scored for flute, oboe, cello, and keyboard) with Marty Haugen's *Gathered in the Love of Christ* (which adds sung text for the assembly to the previous combination of instruments).

Music for the Contemporary Ensemble, Volumes I and II (for C instruments, guitar, keyboard, bass), Bob Moore (Chicago: GIA Publications, Inc.)

Music for Three, Volumes I and II, arrangements for trio with interchangeable parts by Daniel Kelley (Studio City, CA: Last Resort Music Publications, Inc.)

Flute Descants (To Be Used with Assembly Singing)

Catholic Community Hymnal: Instrumental Edition for C Instruments, 1 volume (Chicago: GIA Publications, Inc.)

Choral Descants, Volumes I–VI (optional flute and C trumpet descants included), arranged by Randall DeBruyn (Portland, OR: OCP Publications)

Choral Praise, Volumes I and II (with solo instrument descants) (Portland, OR: OCP Publications)

Gather Comprehensive: Instrumental Edition for C Instruments, Volumes I and II (Chicago: GIA Publications, Inc.)

Gather Comprehensive: Instrumental Edition for C Instruments, Volumes I and II, 2nd edition (Chicago: GIA Publications, Inc.)

I Am the Resurrection and the Life: Solo Instrument Edition (funeral music) (Portland, OR: OCP Publications)

People's Mass Book: Instrumental Edition for C Instruments (Franklin Park, IL: World Library Publications)

RitualSong: Instrumental Edition for C Instruments, Volumes I and II (Chicago: GIA Publications, Inc.)

Solo Instrument Book (companion to *Breaking Bread*) (Portland, OR: OCP Publications)

The Church Flutist: Obbligatos for 50 Hymn Tunes, Bp. Michael and Jane Bent (Appleton, WI: Expanded Musical Concepts)

Traditional Choral Praise (hymn arrangements for SATB choir, SAB choir, vocal and instrumental descants with keyboard accompaniment), arranged and edited by Dr. Randall DeBruyn (Portland, OR: OCP Publications)

When Love Is Found (wedding music), by Jeanne Cotter and David Haas (Chicago: GIA Publications, Inc.)

Worship: Instrumental Editions, 3d edition (Chicago: GIA Publications, Inc.)

Mass Settings with Flute Descants

Mass of the Angels & Saints (parts available for 2 C instruments), Steven R. Janco (Chicago: GIA Publications, Inc.)

Mass of Creation (parts available for 2 C instruments), Marty Haugen (Chicago: GIA Publications, Inc.)

Mass of Glory, Ken Canedo and Bob Hurd, solo instrument arrangement by Ken Canedo (Portland, OR: OCP Publications)

Mass of Light (parts available for 2 C instruments), David Haas (Chicago: GIA Publications, Inc.)

Mass of Redemption, Steve Janco (Franklin Park, IL: World Library Publications)

Sing Praise and Thanksgiving, Michael Joncas, flute part by Alan J. Hommerding (Franklin Park, IL: World Library Publications)

Liturgy and Liturgical Music Reference Books

A Sourcebook about Music, compiled by Alan Hommerding and Diana Kodner (Chicago: Liturgy Training Publications)

Handbook for Creative Church Musicians, Harold Owens (Chicago: GIA Publications, Inc.)

Handbook of Church Music for Weddings, Mary Ann Simcoe (Chicago: Liturgy Training Publications)

Handbook of Church Music for Weddings, 3d edition, Mary Beth Kunde-Anderson and David Anderson (Chicago: Liturgy Training Publications)

Instrumentation and the Liturgical Ensemble, Marty Haugen (Chicago: GIA Publications, Inc.)

Morning and Evening: A Parish Celebration, Joyce Ann Zimmerman, CPPS (Chicago: Liturgy Training Publications)

Pastoral Music in Practice, edited by Virgil C. Funk and Gabe Huck (a joint publication of The Pastoral Press, Washington, DC, and Liturgy Training Publications, Chicago)

The Liturgy Documents: A Parish Resource, 3d edition (Chicago: Liturgy Training Publications)

Pedagogical Reference Books

Advanced Method for Flute, Volumes 1 and 2, H. Voxman and William Gower (Miami, FL: Rubank, Inc.)

Do It! Play Flute, Books I and II, James O. Froseth (Chicago: GIA Publications, Inc.)

Flute, James Galway (New York: Schirmer Books)

Harmonic Materials in Tonal Music, Volumes I and II, 9th edition, Greg A. Steinke (Upper Saddle River, NJ: Prentice Hall)

On Playing the Flute, Johann Joachim Quantz (New York: Schirmer Books)

Performance-Based Ear Training (for all instruments), James O. Froseth (Chicago: GIA Publications, Inc.)

Performance-Based Ear Training (for flute), James O. Froseth (Chicago: GIA Publications, Inc.)

Practice Pages for Tonal & Technical Development on the Flute, Victoria Jicha (Music Makers, Inc.; copyright transferred Charlotte, NC: Alry Publications, 2002)

Scales and Arpeggios: 480 Exercises for Flute, Marcel Moyse (Paris: Alphonse Leduc Publications)

Seven Daily Exercises, Op. 5, M. A. Reichert (New York: Carl Fischer)

Seventeen Big Daily Finger Exercises for the Flute, Paul Taffanel and Philippe Gaubert (Paris: Alphonse Leduc Publications)

The Flutist's Handbook: A Pedagogy Anthology, compiled by the NFA Pedagogy Anthology Committee (Santa Clarita, CA: The National Flute Association, Inc.)

The Inner Game of Music: Workbooks for Individuals, Barry Green (Chicago: GIA Publications, Inc.)

Tone Development through Extended Techniques, Robert Dick (St. Louis, MO: Multiple Breath Music Company)

Tone Development through Interpretation for the Flute (and other wind instruments), Marcel Moyse (McGinnis & Marx Music Publishers)

Sources

Most pieces from the standard flute repertoire can be purchased from either of the following companies:

Flute World Co.
P.O. Box 250248
Franklin, MI 48025
phone: (248) 855-0410
24-hour fax: (248) 855-2525
online: http://www.fluteworld.com

Alry Publications, Etc., Inc.
P.O. Box 36542
Charlotte, NC 28236
phone: (704) 334-3413
fax: (704) 334-1143
online: http://members.aol.com/alrypbi

Publishers for Catholic resources and liturgical texts:

GIA Publications, Inc.
7404 S. Mason Avenue
Chicago, IL 60638
phone: (800) 442-1358 or (708) 496-3800
fax: (708) 496-3828
online: http://www.giamusic.com

World Library Publications
3708 River Road, Suite 400
Franklin Park, IL 60131
phone: (800) 566-6150
fax: (888) 957-3291
online: http://www.wlp.jspaluch.com

OCP Publications
5536 NE Hassalo
Portland, OR 97213-3638
phone: (800) 548-8749 or (503) 281-1191
fax: (800) 462-7329
online: http://www.ocp.org

Liturgy Training Publications
1800 N. Hermitage Avenue
Chicago, IL 60622-1101
phone: (800) 933-1800 or (773) 486-8970
fax: (800) 933-7904 or (773) 486-5630
online: http://www.ltp.org

Affiliated Organizations

Membership in each of the following organizations is highly recommended for all liturgical flutists. Both of these organizations have annual conventions, and both publish magazines with articles of interest to those in this field.

National Association of Pastoral
  Musicians (NPM)
962 Wayne Avenue
Suite 210
Silver Spring, MD 20910-4461
phone: (240) 247-3000
fax: (240) 247-3001
online: http://NPMSING@npm.org

National Flute Association (NFA)
26951 Ruether Avenue
Suite H
Santa Clarita, CA 91351
phone: (661) 299-6680
fax: (805) 299-6681
online: http://www.nfaonline.org

Appendix III
Sound Amplification for the Flutist

Microphones should be used sparingly to amplify the sound of the flute—only when the situation necessitates. If circumstances are such that you are playing with other acoustical instruments, you will likely not need a microphone to amplify your sound. There are other techniques you could use for sound amplification, such as playing an octave higher or playing with a fuller tone. However, be wary of overblowing or forcing the sound because that will cause intonation problems. If this were the case, then it would be better to use a microphone; however, it should be used cautiously and with preparation. Remember that the flute should never be overbearing or in any way take away from the prayer.

There are situations when a microphone will almost always be needed. For example:

- Playing with amplified instruments, such as electric guitar or keyboard;
- Playing in a space with little reverberation; or
- Playing in an open outdoor setting or even in a large indoor space.

Here are a few rules of thumb for using a microphone:

- The flute's sound is emitted from both the embouchure hole as well as the open keyholes. Therefore, place the microphone near the left-hand C key, the approximate midpoint of the length of the flute.
- Test the microphone ahead of time. A third party can assist you by listening from various locations in the space. Adjust the volume and/or your proximity to the microphone as needed.

If the microphone has an On/Off switch, be sure you are aware of how to use it. It is probably best to turn it off when not in use so any extraneous noises (such as page turns) are not heard.

Appendix IV
Compensation Issues

Stipend Guidelines

The pastoral flutist is almost never a full-time musician in a parish or any other institution. In fact, the vast majority of flutists are not professional musicians at all, but rather would consider themselves as amateurs or "apprentices." Music-making is a way of contributing to the parish, of offering time and talent as gift. Indeed, the most common situation is that the liturgical flutist is a member of the parish in which he/she ministers through music. This person might be a student musician of grammar school or high school age, or a young adult. Sometimes older adults who played musical instruments as children might begin to play again and contribute to the parish liturgical music program.

Usually it is the parish music director who makes the decisions regarding compensation for instrumentalists and singers. This is based on many factors, not least of which is the music budget and what it allows in terms of hiring musicians. It is important that professionalism in a musician is recognized, honored, and given value through just payment for service. There are professional pastoral musicians (including flutists) who depend on such compensation for their livelihood. This issue is so significant that there are some who believe that even if a professional musician wants to contribute time and talent to the parish, in fairness to all other professionals a stipend should be given, which could then be returned to the parish as gift or donation. Whatever the decision, raising consciousness in the parish about the matter of just compensation for professional musicians is to be commended.

Any musician who has a professional level of playing and is being hired to play at worship services will want to have a working knowledge of the stipend guidelines in his/her area so as to know what is equitable in any particular situation. Often help is provided through "paid-per-service guidelines" set up by a diocesan music commission or worship office, or even through talking with other professional musicians. This is especially important because often those doing the hiring will ask the musician about compensation first rather than initially offering an amount for consideration. So the professional flutist (or any other professional musician) should have a range in mind—in other words, an amount that seems just and appropriate and a lesser amount that is acceptable just in case financial resources are such that the initially suggested amount could not be met.

Following are some points for professional musicians to ponder when considering compensation:

- How much time will be involved?
- Is this event in my own area or am I traveling outside my locale? If so, how much travel will be involved?
- Are there extra rehearsals besides the practice immediately prior to the service?
- How much personal practice time was involved in getting ready for this event?

- Do I need to purchase new music specifically for this service?
- Was there consultation time involved as a help with preparing the prayer/liturgy/service?
- What are my own expenses to maintaining myself as a qualified and competent musician?
- What is the compensation paid to other musicians in the area?

It is important to remember that professionalism that is recognized with compensation and ministry that is offered as service and gift are not mutually exclusive. At core, all liturgical or pastoral musicians are part of the assembly and embody the prayer of that assembly. Whatever the situation, the musical offering must be the best any of us can give at any particular time in our life's journey.

Copyrights

"Music in Catholic Worship" (#78) states:

> *Likewise, to ensure that composers and publishers receive just compensation for their work, those engaged in parish music programs and those responsible for budgets must often be reminded that it is illegal and immoral to reproduce copyrighted texts and music by any means without written permission of the copyright owner. The fact that these duplicated materials are not for sale but for private use does not alter the legal or moral situation of copying without permission.*
>
> **—BCLN, April 1969**

The issue of copyright infringement should not be taken lightly. It is a matter of justice and honor. Many parishes have copyright licenses, having paid a yearly fee to a particular publisher for duplication permission. Check with the music director or business manager of your parish for this information. If your parish does not have such a license, a simple call to the publisher will facilitate the acquisition of copyright permission, either for a one-time use or more. Permission can be obtained either by an individual for his/her own use or by a parish or other organization.

Appendix V
Me, Improvise?!

If you find yourself reading this section, it is apparent that the possibilities inherent to improvisation fascinate you. If this fascination is enough to move you past any anxieties about improvisation, then you probably do not need to spend any time with the materials included in this appendix. If you see yourself requiring some added impetus, however, then spending some time here may provide what you need to take the leap into this style of playing.

First, consider the following idea as (in all likelihood) a new way of looking at this skill: Improvisation can be seen as a helpmate for our own spiritual journey. In other words, improvisation might be for you a spiritual practice. Just as the spiritual seeker must continually work at letting go of anything that blocks the path to going deeper within or that blocks the path from expanding beyond the known, so must the improviser be willing to let go of anything that binds up a free and creative "*muse*." Often these blocks or bindings come in the form of doubts, insecurities, and fears—like fear of failing or fear of making mistakes. As already mentioned within these pages, any movement away from such blocks and toward a greater level of trusting usually comes about only gradually and is in continual process. Naturally, along the way we all get stuck sometimes in a spiral of negative thoughts: "I can't do it." "I will never get it." "It's not in me; I'll never be ready for it." The truth is, there is so much more to us than what we allow most of the time—whether as musicians or in the rest of our lives. Thus, any openness to the gift of improvisation is in itself an opportunity to discover more of what is within us. It is a way of being present to new possibilities. And whether or not improvisation becomes our own playing style is not as important as how much growth will occur through the process of simply trying it—even just for our own enjoyment and within the safe confines of our own home.

One help we have found, both to foster a desire to be freed up enough to begin such a process as well as to move beyond any negativity, is to write our own story. Taking a little time to reflect on your journey as a pastoral musician can awaken you to see how much you have grown, expanded, and deepened already. In our cases, neither of us ever imagined improvisation as a goal or a given when we began our journeys as pastoral musicians, and certainly our individual paths have taken us on very different turns through the years. Yet we find that we both ended up at a similar point of recognizing how our spirituality has been nurtured and nourished through our music, as well as how much improvisation has freed us up—not only in our music-making but in other parts of our lives as well.

We believe our stories are a witness to how the Divine works in our lives—always inviting us to "more." We share these stories humbly in the hope that they will provoke your own reflection on your journey as a pastoral musician and how your development as a musician has been a part of your own spiritual path. We offer an invitation to you to enjoy your own story and to be open to what you can learn from it. Hopefully it will help you with the very intimate decision about whether or not you are ready either to begin or to more boldly continue with improvisation.

On the other hand, it just may be that along the way you recognize improvisation is not your gift. This open-eyed decision is far different than dismissing improvisation without even considering it.

After all is said, however, the most important thing to remember is simply to trust whatever choice you make at any point in time. Enjoy who you are and where you are while always staying present to your own inner movement. Such a posture is reflected in the song text from the Iona Community, "Take, O Take Me As I Am." You might want to ponder and meditate on it before reading our stories, or listen to it on the CD (Track 88) while writing your own story.

EXAMPLE 176: EXCERPT FROM "TAKE, O TAKE ME AS I AM"

J. Bell

Track 88: Embodying the Prayer
"Take, O Take Me As I Am" – flute, voice, and piano

My Pastoral Musician Story
Denise La Giglia

I knew I wanted to make music since I was nine years old. I played flute in grammar school and high school. The Catholic grammar school I attended had a sensational band program, which included private lessons. At the time of my graduation from grammar school, there were over 150 players in senior band alone! At one point in time, I played in three bands: the junior band as a saxophonist, and the senior band (grammar school) and community band (high school and adult level) as both flute and piccolo player. In the high school band, I played saxophone mostly because attending an all-girl Catholic high school meant there was already an abundance of flute players! Also, it was fun to try something new. Alongside these years of band were also eleven years of piano study and four years of theory classes during high school.

During college, I studied voice as part of my degree requirement in music. All these involvements provided a wealth of music-making too numerous to note. Even before I was an adult, I was gifted with the kind of abundant and diverse musical experience that develops a strong musicality.

I began ministry in music in my early twenties. It was not as a flutist, but rather as a cantor and an ensemble director. I played flute only sporadically for about twenty years, until around age forty a need for a flutist at a conference liturgy occasioned me to pick it up again and get more serious about it. I have been developing this ministry ever since. In those early years of being a pastoral flutist, there were either no flute parts written or the parts provided were at a very basic level. Sometimes I wrote my own parts, but mostly I started reading from the piano or guitar score. Since I had all those years of piano and theory study, I was able to adapt these scores for the flute. I found I had a good sensitivity to arranging, even "in the moment." I appreciated this gift for myself, especially since I was raising five children and didn't have any time to do much notating of music. (And music directors appreciated that they didn't have to write out parts for me either.)

It wasn't until a National NPM convention in Long Beach, California, in 1989 that I really began to appreciate and nurture my improvisational skills. Although I had been doing music ministry since 1970, it wasn't until the mid-1980s that I was freed up enough to pursue further study in liturgy and ritual. Going to this conference was just part of my quest for development in these areas.

At the convention, I attended a workshop given by Genevieve Noufflard, the flutist in Joseph Gelineau's parish in France. She gave me a glimpse of the flutist in a much broader context than I had at the time—a level of leadership and spirituality that fascinated and invited me. One most poignant moment was when she talked about the gift of having the ability to improvise. She did not see herself as having such a gift. Instead, she told us she painstakingly read over music during practice time so she would have a vast repertoire at her disposal to respond in the moment to the homily at Mass or some other part of the ritual where reflective music might be needed. She saw it as a richer and deeper experience to be able to respond spontaneously out of your own prayer, your own spirit, by simply beginning to play improvisationally.

I heard this as a call to share this gift that I was aware of in myself but had only thought about from a more practical perspective. I heard her words as an invitation to work at developing this skill for the sake of the assembly's prayer as well as my own, to stretch myself even more to ponder its possibilities and its freedoms. This commitment opened me to taking flute lessons again, to being more present to my ministry and to other ministers, to taking more risks with my playing, and to developing my spirituality through further study and through regular monthly sessions with a spiritual director. Now I recognize improvisation to be a gift to me that I could never have imagined for myself. It is very much connected to my spirituality and my prayer.

My Pastoral Musician Story
Anna Belle O'Shea

I have been a liturgical flutist since the early days of the post-Vatican II era. I was twelve years old when I entered music ministry at the urging of my mother and with the permission of my pastor. My mother was the parish organist for one Mass each Sunday, so I simply joined her in the choir loft. I read over her shoulder, playing the melody line on each hymn, instinctively playing everything an octave higher. At some point, I must have decided to try the alto line an octave higher and found it to be a lovely way of creating a flute descant. Although I was quite unaware at the time, these were the beginning steps of freeing myself from the printed page.

I had begun studying both piano and flute at age eight and, therefore, had a knowledge of bass clef as well as treble. As the years (and decades) progressed, I began to play tenor and/or bass parts, realizing that they gave me more possibilities for descant lines. But being a classically trained musician, I never deviated from the printed notes. I did, however, realize that keyboard parts and vocal lines use different articulation marks than do flute parts. So I began to articulate the way I felt the music should be played by a wind player rather than playing what I was reading on the printed page. This was another small step on the journey toward improvisation.

During my college and young adult years, I was not only a church musician, but for twelve years I was also a professional flutist, playing principal flute in a symphony orchestra. These years gave me wonderful opportunities to play with other instrumentalists, in both full orchestra and chamber settings. This is the time when I came to realize the importance of the church musician as a skilled player. This is also where I honed the critical listening skills of intonation, balance, and blend.

At that time, I was also a band director and general music teacher in several Catholic grammar schools. In these roles, I was responsible for working with children on the music for their school liturgies. I began to encourage the band students to play for school liturgies by writing out parts for them at a level they could handle and with the appropriate transpositions. Everything had to be written by hand since there were no published books for instrumental liturgical musicians at that time, nor were there any computer programs that would have made the process simpler.

In 1988, I suffered multiple nerve injuries to my jaw, neck, and upper torso as a result of a serious car accident. After a one-year leave of absence from the symphony, it became obvious to me that I was no longer going to have the endurance required for my job. Although this was a very difficult time for me, I can now look back on it in a positive light. A door may have closed, but God opened a window. In the years since that accident, I have felt called to move more deeply into music ministry, and hence, my journey has continued.

Somewhere along the way, I began to purchase books of vocal descants to prevent boredom from creeping into my work as a liturgical flutist. These descants provided me with enough variety to be able to play a different descant on each verse of a hymn. But I was still only playing the notes on the printed page with the necessary octave and articulation adjustments. Out of necessity, I also began to transpose on sight, for those times when the singer needed a piece played a step higher or lower and when I had found a vocal descant that was in a different key than the organist was playing. This was yet another step into freeing myself from the printed page.

Of course, there was a large body of music for which no vocal descants had been written. For those pieces, I began to write flute descants—simpler ones for the early verses and more involved ones for the final verse—till I had an entire folder filled with descants. It was inevitable that someday I would get to a job and the music director would decide to play a piece for which I hadn't written a part. I don't know exactly when that happened, but it was then that I began to improvise flute descants without first writing them out. It was a very freeing moment when I realized I could create a part on the spot without reading something on the printed page. It is now commonplace for me to improvise descants at each and every liturgy I play. By the time publishers such as GIA and OCP printed books for C instruments, I was very comfortable with creating my own parts. This has given me the space to use a published descant as a springboard from which to explore other possibilities.

As my journey has continued, I have had many and varied experiences that have pushed my envelope. There have been times when I have been asked to improvise on flute alone, either on a hymntune or simply in a given key. There have been other times when I have been asked to improvise with other instrumentalists or occasionally vocalists. It is the culmination of all my prior experiences that has brought me to this point.

Although many other aspects of my life have changed greatly since my childhood, one element that has always remained constant has been liturgical music. To this end, I have recently attained a Master of Arts Degree in Church Music and Liturgy, with an emphasis in flute. I pray for continued discernment to know the direction of my journey from here.

My Pastoral Musician Story

by _____

_____

_____

_____

_____

_____

_____

_____

_____

_____

Whatever else you find in your story, your journey has been enhanced by the time and effort you have given to the materials in this book.

Congratulations on being so attentive to your gift of music.

Flute Fingering Chart

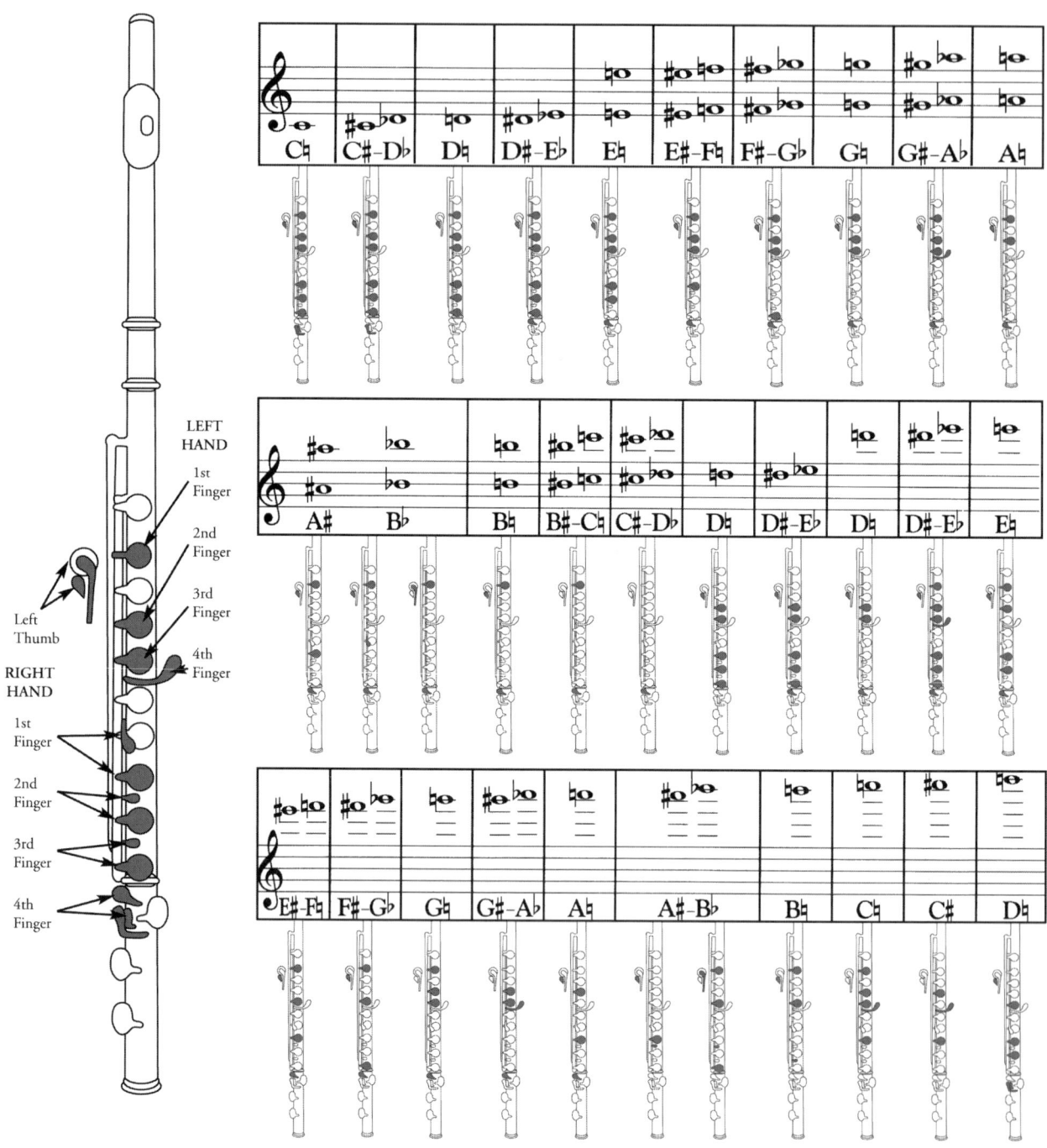

Flute Trill Fingering Chart

A trill should always go to the next note higher in the key signature, unless indicated by an accidental after the trill sign (ex. *tr♯* .)

Cover those keys shown in black. Trill those keys shown in grey, indicated with an arrow.

Used with permission. Gemeinhart Company, LLC, Executive Vice President of Sales, John Morgan.

Glossary

The terms included in this Glossary appear in *italics and boldface type*
throughout the text of this book.

Accent – A style of articulation, indicating a stronger attack on the affected note(s).

NOTES WITH ACCENT MARKS

Acclamation – A short, exclamatory response to Scripture or other prayer; generally sung by the entire
assembly.

Adjusting cork – The device inside the tip of the flute headjoint, regulating the pitch of the instrument.

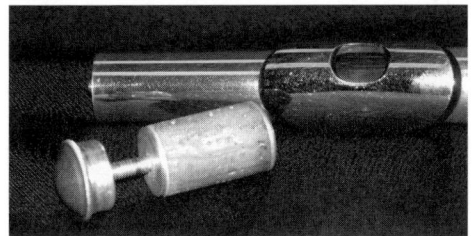

ADJUSTING CORK

Antiphon – A musical device in which alternation takes place between at least two musical entities (e.g.,
alternation between cantor and choir, between cantor and assembly, between instruments and voices,
between two sets of instruments, etc.). In liturgical settings, a short sentence that can be chanted or
recited and associated with a particular part of the service (e.g., Entrance Antiphon, Communion
Antiphon, etc.). *See also* **Refrain**.

Aperture – The opening between the lips formed by the embouchure. Air blown through this opening
enables the playing of a wind instrument.

Appoggiatura – *See* **Grace notes**.

Arpeggio – A broken chord, one in which the notes of the chord are played in succession rather than
sounded simultaneously.

Articulation – The clear definition given to the beginning of a note; achieved on wind instruments by
attacking the note with the tongue, hence, sometimes referred to as **tonguing** the note.

Augmented chord – A triad consisting of the first, third, and raised fifth degrees of the major scale.

C AUGMENTED CHORD

Bass clef – The symbol at the beginning of every line of music for low-pitched instruments—such as tuba, trombone, cello, string bass, bassoon, and low notes on keyboard instruments that are usually played by the left hand.

BASS CLEF

Benediction – Adoration of the Blessed Sacrament within a structured prayer service.

Cadence – A natural resting place at which the music comes to a conclusion, equivalent to a comma or period in a sentence.

Call-and-response – A form of liturgical music in which there is an interplay between the cantor and the assembly, with the cantor singing an acclamation or phrase and the assembly repeating it as an answer.

Cantus firmus – A melody identified by its long, held notes and its sacred text; popular during the Middle Ages; usually the tenor line to which two or more independent melodies of complex nature were added above it.

Canzona – A form of music originating in sixteenth century Italy, significant because of its use of instruments exclusively (without the addition of voices) and because of its common use of antiphonal groupings of instrumentalists.

Catechesis – Instruction on the teachings of a faith tradition.

Chant – A non-metrical, free form style of song using liturgical texts and strong, rhythmic emphases; dating back as far as the tenth century.

Chord – A series of three or four notes played in a set pattern, either simultaneously or successively, based on the first, third, and fifth scale degrees (sometimes also including other scale degrees, such as the sixth, seventh, or ninth).

Chromatic scale – A series of notes written at half-step intervals, either ascending or descending.

CHROMATIC SCALE

Circle of Fifths – A theoretical device that provides a visual reference for naming the major keys and their key signatures. The tonic of each scale is five scale degrees away from the tonic of the scales before and after it.

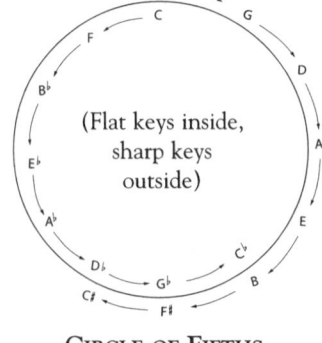

(Flat keys inside, sharp keys outside)

CIRCLE OF FIFTHS

Contrary motion – A technique used in harmonization in which the two voices move in opposite directions.

Da capo – A notation (abbreviated D.C.) that indicates a return to the beginning of the piece.

Dal segno – A notation (abbreviated D.S.) that indicates a return to the 𝄋 sign.

Descant – A countermelody, usually written higher in pitch than the existing melodic line.

Diminished chord – A triad consisting of the first, third, and lowered fifth degrees of the minor scale.

C DIMINISHED CHORD

Dominant – The fifth scale degree.

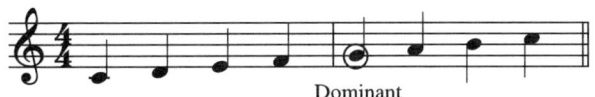

C MAJOR SCALE INDICATING G AS THE DOMINANT

Dominant seventh chord – A four-note chord whose root is the fifth step (dominant degree) of a major or minor scale, with the subsequent notes being a third, fifth, and seventh higher than the root. The dominant seventh chord usually resolves to the tonic chord.

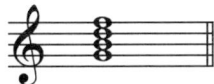

G7 CHORD (DOMINANT SEVENTH CHORD IN KEY OF C MAJOR OR C MINOR)

Embouchure – Formation of the lips and mouth to play an instrument.

Enharmonic – An alternate spelling of names of notes (e.g., F♯ = G♭).

First inversion chord – The term used to indicate a chord in which the third scale degree is the lowest sounding note.

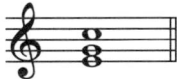

C MAJOR CHORD IN FIRST INVERSION

Glissando – A form of ornamentation, symbolized by *Glissando*, in which as many notes as possible are played between two principal notes.

Grace notes –A form of ornamentation, written as a small note(s), sometimes taking its rhythmic value from the preceding note, sometimes from the following note.

Gruppetto – *See* **Turn**.

Half step – The smallest interval used in Western music; consists of any two adjoining notes on the piano keyboard.

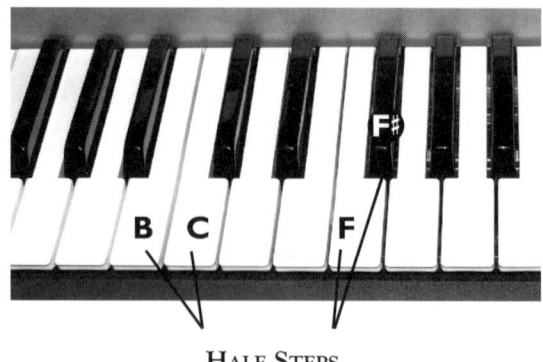

HALF STEPS

Harmonic minor scale – One of the three forms of the minor scale. The seventh degree of the harmonic minor scale is raised one half step, both ascending and descending.

A MINOR SCALE (HARMONIC FORM)

Headjoint – The mouthpiece portion of the flute.

Hymnody – A musical style that uses a lyrical, sacred text, set to a simple, metrical tune with a defined pulse.

Improvisation – A style of performing that allows the artist to ad lib or compose "in the moment" within some predetermined framework (e.g., harmonic structure, key signature, ritual context, etc.).

Interval – The distance between two notes.

Intonation – The flatness, sharpness, or accuracy of pitch.

Lazo ceremony – Ritual often included in a Hispanic wedding service after the sharing of vows and exchange of rings, wherein a lasso is loosely placed over the shoulders of the bride and groom, visually uniting the two.

Leading tone – The seventh scale degree, so named because of its strong tendency to lead to the tonic.

Leading Tone

C MAJOR SCALE INDICATING B AS THE LEADING TONE

Legato – A smooth, connected style of articulation.

Litany – A style of prayer, often sung, that consists of two parts done antiphonally.

Liturgical judgment – One of three judgments cited in *Music in Catholic Worship* as a criteria for making musical choices for liturgy. Liturgical judgment refers to knowledge of text, ritual, and movement, as well as other elements relating to the worship.

Major chord – A triad consisting of the first, third, and fifth degrees of the major scale.

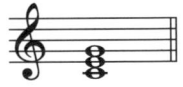

C MAJOR CHORD

Major scale – *See* **Scale.**

Mantra – A short song repeated over and over for the sake of deepening the prayer.

Marcato – A style of articulation that places a marked emphasis on each note, much like a strong accent.

May crowning – A Marian devotion in which a statue of Mary is ceremoniously crowned, usually within the month of May.

Mediant – The third scale degree.

Mediant

C MAJOR SCALE INDICATING E AS THE MEDIANT

Melodic minor scale – One of the three forms of the minor scale. The sixth and seventh degrees of the melodic minor scale are raised one half step in the ascending portion, with the accidentals being cancelled in the descending portion.

A MINOR SCALE (MELODIC FORM)

Metronome – A tool used for keeping a steady beat, as indicated in the tempo markings on the music (example: M.M. = 60 indicates a tempo of 60 beats per minute).

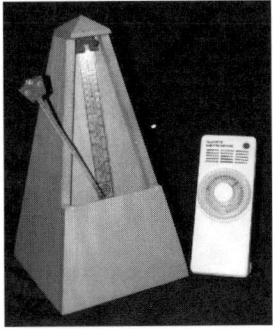

METRONOME

Minor chord – A triad consisting of the first, third, and fifth degrees of the minor scale.

C MINOR CHORD

Minor scale – *See* **Scale.**

Modality/mode – In Western music, a particular sound that can be identified by terms such as "major" or "minor," determined by its scalar pattern of intervals.

Monophony – A musical form in which only one melodic line is used (e.g., chant).

Mordent – A form of ornamentation, symbolized by ∿, that involves playing the printed note and its upper neighboring note, followed by the principal note again.

Muse – Source of artistic inspiration. In Greek mythology, there were nine goddesses or muses who guided poetry, the arts, science, etc.

Musical judgment – One of three judgments cited in *Music in Catholic Worship* as a criteria for making musical choices for liturgy. Musical judgment refers to an evaluation of music based on its inherent quality and on how it will stand the test of time, as well as its accessibility to the assembly.

Narthex – The gathering space of the church, as separate from the body (nave) of the church.

Natural minor scale – One of the three forms of the minor scale. The natural minor scale uses the same notes as its relative major scale, but starts on the sixth degree of the major scale.

A MINOR SCALE (NATURAL FORM)

Neighboring tone – A non-chordal note that is one scale degree higher or lower than the chordal note. Both its preceding and succeeding notes are the same chordal note.

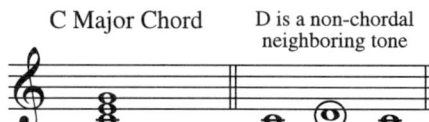

C MAJOR CHORD WITH D AS THE NEIGHBORING TONE

Non-chordal note – A note that does not belong to the chord being played in the accompaniment.

Oblique motion – A technique used in harmonization in which one part stays on the same pitch while the other part moves either up or down.

Octave – An interval of eight steps.

VARIOUS OCTAVES

Octavo – A printed form of music, generally associated with a specific size and/or with music written for choirs or choral groups. The word originates from the Latin *octavus*, meaning "eighth." It refers to the size of the piece of paper, which allows eight pieces to be cut from one sheet.

Oratorio – The sacred counterpart of opera; an elaborate composition for chorus and orchestra, performed without costumes or staging.

Parallel motion – A technique used in harmonization in which the two different parts move in the same direction and at the same interval.

Passing tone – A non-chordal tone that passes between two different chordal tones.

D and F are non-chordal passing tones

C MAJOR CHORD WITH PASSING TONES OF D AND F

Pastoral judgment – One of three judgments cited in *Music in Catholic Worship* for making musical choices for liturgy. Pastoral judgment refers to a sensitivity to the needs of the particular assembly, such as parish history, cultural make-up, familiarity with the rites, etc.

Phrase – A musical thought or idea, often four or eight measures in length.

PHRASES (INDICATED BY SLURS)

Picardy third – A harmonic change to major mode occurring at the final chord of a piece that has been set entirely in the minor mode. This is accomplished by raising the third degree of the last chord, thus changing this chord from a minor chord to a major chord.

Plagal cadence – A harmonic device in which the subdominant chord is followed by the tonic chord to form the conclusion of a section or of a piece. It is sometimes referred to as the "Amen" cadence.

IV - I

PLAGAL CADENCE

Polyphony – A musical form in which two or more independent, harmonious melodies occur at once.

Quinceñero – A religious ceremony within the Hispanic community, celebrated for a female as she matures from childhood to young womanhood, usually occurring at the time of her fifteenth birthday.

Refrain – A term used to identify a section of music (or music and text) that is recurring throughout a piece. In liturgical music, the refrain is often sung first by the cantor, then by the assembly, and then repeated after each verse.

Register – A portion of the range of an instrument (or voice) differing in quality from the other portions (i.e., high, middle, low register).

Root – The first degree of a chord.

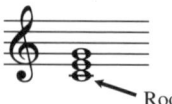

C MAJOR CHORD WITH ROOT OF C

Root position chord – The term used to indicate a chord in which the tonic is the lowest sounding note.

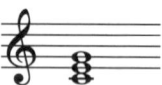

C MAJOR CHORD IN ROOT POSITION

Scale – A succession of notes moving in a specific ascending and/or descending order at stepwise intervals.

C MAJOR SCALE

A MINOR SCALE (MELODIC FORM)

Second inversion chord – The term used to indicate a chord in which the fifth scale degree is the lowest sounding note.

C MAJOR CHORD IN SECOND INVERSION

Sequence – The repetition of a musical pattern, usually two or three times, with each repetition ascending or descending at the same interval.

Seventh chord – A four-note chord comprised of the first, third, fifth, and lowered seventh scale degrees.

C⁷ CHORD

Slur – A curved line above or below two or more notes of different pitches to indicate that only the first of these notes is articulated (tongued), with the others following in a non-articulated, smooth style, played in one breath.

SLURRED NOTES

Staccato – A style of articulation, indicating notes of a light, delicate attack, and short, disconnected length.

STACCATO NOTES

Staff – The five lines and four spaces on which music is written.

Stanza – A verse of a hymn.

Staves – Plural of **staff**, the lines and spaces on which music is written.

Subdominant – The fourth scale degree.

C MAJOR SCALE INDICATING F AS THE SUBDOMINANT

Submediant – The sixth scale degree.

C MAJOR SCALE INDICATING A AS THE SUBMEDIANT

Supertonic – The second scale degree.

C MAJOR SCALE INDICATING D AS THE SUPERTONIC

Suspension – A compositional device whereby the resolution of one or more chordal notes is delayed for the sake of harmonic tension.

Tacet – A cessation of playing.

Taizé prayer – A form of prayer developed in an ecumenical community of Christian Brothers in Taizé, France. The environment for the prayer includes icons and candles, and within the prayer is mantra-style singing, Scripture, silence, intercessory prayers, and the Our Father. Any number of instruments is used to support and enhance the prayer. Taizé prayer invites people of different Christian faith traditions to gather together to pray for the needs of the world, especially for peace and reconciliation. (GIA Publications, Inc. is the American distributor for the music and materials of the Taizé prayer.)

Tempo – The speed of the rhythmic pulse of the music, often indicated by a metronome mark.

Tenuto – A style of articulation, indicating a sustained quality for each note.

NOTES WITH TENUTO MARKS

Tessitura – The quality of the sound of a particular register of an instrument or voice.

Tetrachord – A four-note scale pattern, consisting of the following intervals: whole step between the lowest two notes, whole step between the second and third notes, and half step between the third and fourth notes.

Through-composed – A piece of music that evolves without melodic repetition (e.g., a hymn).

Tie – A curved line above or below two or more notes of the same pitch, indicating that only the first of these notes is articulated (tongued), with the others following in a non-articulated, smooth style, played in one breath.

TIED NOTES

Timbre – The unique sound of any particular instrument, determined by its overtone series.

Tonic – The first scale degree.

C Major Scale

Tonic

C MAJOR SCALE INDICATING C AS THE TONIC

Treble clef – The symbol at the beginning of every line of music for high-pitched instruments—i.e., flute (piccolo), oboe, clarinet, trumpet, violin, and high notes on keyboard instruments (usually played by the right hand).

TREBLE CLEF

Triad – A chord of three notes, based on the first, third, and fifth scale degrees.

Trill – A form of ornamentation, symbolized by *tr*, that involves the printed note and its upper neighboring note, fluctuating between these two notes as fast as possible.

Tuner – A tool that checks the accuracy of the musician's intonation, allowing an auditory and/or visual indication of flatness or sharpness of pitch.

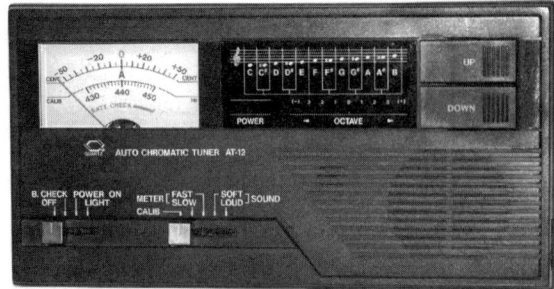

TUNER

Turn – A form of ornamentation, symbolized by ∾, that involves a total of five different notes. The first, third, and fifth notes are the same pitch: the principal note; the second is its upper neighboring note; and the fourth is its lower neighboring note.

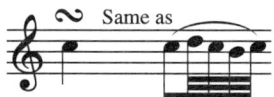

TURN (GRUPETTO)

Vatican II – One of the Councils of the Roman Catholic Church. Pope John XXIII gathered to Rome the Bishops of the Church as well as other advisors and observers, including representatives from other faith denominations and even some women and lay persons. Vatican II was convened by the Pope in 1962 and lasted until 1965, ending under the leadership of a new pope, Paul VI. The documents that were written by the Vatican Council II Fathers and their successors have shaped the worship life of the Roman Catholic Church since that time. Vatican II was also the First Ecumenical Council, having as one of its primary intentions to begin to bridge the separation between other faith traditions and the Roman Catholic Church. (The Council prior to this, Vatican Council I, occurred between 1869 and 1870, having been summoned by Pope Pius IX.)

Verse – A term used to convey a section of a piece of music that expresses one part of the text of the song—comparable to a single stanza of prose within a poem. In liturgical music, an oft-used pattern is a sung refrain between multiple verses.

Vibrato – That element of tone that pertains to the pulsation of the airstream.

Whole step – An interval consisting of two half steps.

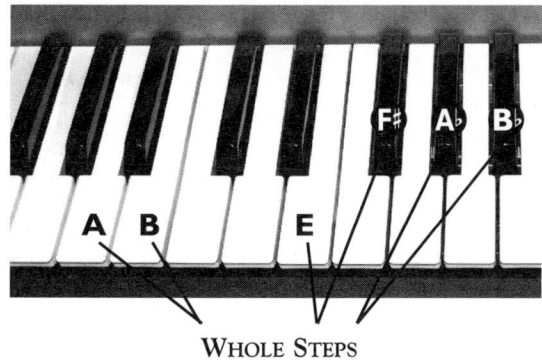

WHOLE STEPS

Listing of CD Tracks

CHAPTER 1

TRACK #	DESCRIPTION OF TRACK

TRACK #   **DESCRIPTION OF TRACK**

1   **a. Effect of Good Standing Posture on Intonation**

"God of Day and God of Darkness" – mm. 1–4, flute and piano

b. Effect of Poor Standing Posture on Intonation

"God of Day and God of Darkness" – mm. 1–4, flute and piano

2   **Slow Inhalation and Sustained Exhalation**

Metronome set at quarter = 60; voice command "Inhale" followed by sound of inhalation for 4 beats; voice command "Exhale" followed by sound of exhalation for 4 beats

3   **Fast Inhalation and Sustained Exhalation**

Metronome set at quarter = 60; voice command "Breathe" followed by sound of quick inhalation and 4-beat exhalation

4   **Breathing Exercises with the Flute**

Metronome set at quarter = 60; flute alone playing middle B♭, low B♭, and high F, each for 4 counts

5   **Effect of Playing with Too Much Tonehole Covered**

"God of Day and God of Darkness" – mm. 1–4, flute only

6   **Effect of Playing with Too Little Tonehole Covered**

"God of Day and God of Darkness" – mm. 1–4, flute only

7   **a. Application of Good Posture, Breathing, and Intonation**

"Deep Within" – piano introduction; refrain with flute and piano

b. Application of Good Posture, Breathing, and Intonation with Accompaniment Only

"Deep Within" – piano introduction; refrain with piano only

8   **Legato Style**

"Joyful, Joyful, We Adore You" – mm. 1–4, flute alone

9   **Marcato Style**

"Joyful, Joyful, We Adore You" – mm. 1–4, flute alone

10   **Slurring Patterns**

"Joyful, Joyful, We Adore You" – mm. 1–4, flute alone

11   **Listening Exercise for Major and Minor Scales**

G, D melodic minor, A♭, C, F♯ natural minor scales – 1 octave each (ascending and descending), flute alone

12   **Listening for Major Key**

"Gloria" from *Mass of Remembrance* – refrain, piano alone

TRACK #	DESCRIPTION OF TRACK
13	**Listening for Minor Key**
	"Kyrie" from *Mass of Remembrance* – refrain, piano alone
14	**Listening Exercise for Major and Minor Keys**
	"Let All Mortal Flesh Keep Silence" – mm. 7–19; "Alleluia! Sing to Jesus" – mm. 1–8 and 17–32; "Song of Farewell" – refrain; "Shepherd Me, O God" – refrain; "We Three Kings" – verse; flute alone
15	**Listening Exercise for Major and Minor Chords**
	G, Cm, Fm, A♭, Dm chords – piano alone
16	**Chord Exercise I**
	Major and minor chords – piano alone
17	**Chord Exercise II**
	Diminished and augmented chords in block and broken forms – piano alone
18	**Chord Exercise III**
	Four-part harmony of major, minor, diminished, and augmented chords – piano alone
19	**Chord Exercise IV**
	Broken chords – flute alone
20	**Vibrato Exercise on F Scale**
	Metronome set at quarter = 60; first four notes of scale played in following patterns: 1 vibrato pulse per beat, then 2, then 3, and then 4 – flute alone
21	**Vibrato Exercise I on a Tune**
	"I Know That My Redeemer Lives" – metronome set at quarter = 120; first phrase; 1 vibrato pulse per beat; flute alone
22	**Vibrato Exercise II on a Tune**
	"I Know That My Redeemer Lives" – metronome set at quarter = 120; first phrase; 2 vibrato pulses per beat; flute alone
23	**Vibrato Exercise III on a Tune**
	"I Know That My Redeemer Lives" – metronome set at quarter = 104; first phrase; 3 vibrato pulses per beat; flute alone
24	**Vibrato Exercise IV on a Tune**
	"I Know That My Redeemer Lives" – metronome set at quarter = 88; first phrase; 4 vibrato pulses per beat; flute alone
25	**Exercise Using No Vibrato**
	"I Know That My Redeemer Lives" – first phrase; no vibrato; flute alone
26	**Varying Vibrato Speeds**
	"I Know That My Redeemer Lives" – piano introduction and one verse; flute and piano
27	**Focus on Vibrato with Accompaniment Only**
	"I Know That My Redeemer Lives" – piano introduction and one verse; piano only

TRACK #	DESCRIPTION OF TRACK
28	**Scale Exercise for Tone Color, Vibrato Speed, and Dynamic Level** G scale – metronome set at quarter = 72; one octave (ascending only); flute alone
29	**Solo Exercise for Tone Color, Vibrato Speed, and Dynamic Level** "Sinfonia" from *Cantata No. 156* by J. S. Bach – mm. 1–13, flute alone

CHAPTER 4

30	**Playing the Melody as Written** "Good Christian Friends, Rejoice" – piano introduction; mm. 1–8, flute and piano
31	**Playing the Melody 8va** "Good Christian Friends, Rejoice" – piano introduction; mm. 1–8, flute and piano
32	**Playing the Alto Line 8va** "Good Christian Friends, Rejoice" – piano introduction; mm. 1–8, flute and piano
33	**Playing the Tenor Line 8va** "Good Christian Friends, Rejoice" – piano introduction; mm. 1–8, flute and piano
34	**Playing the Tenor Line Two Octaves Higher** "Good Christian Friends, Rejoice" – piano introduction; mm. 1–8, flute and piano
35	**Playing the Bass Line Two Octaves Higher** "Good Christian Friends, Rejoice" – piano introduction; mm. 1–8, flute and piano
36	**Playing from Written Instrumental Parts** "Good Christian Friends, Rejoice" – verse 1, mm. 25–32, piano alone; verse 2, flute on melody 8va with piano; verse 3, flute on descant 8va with piano
37	**Chord Resolution** Two examples of the following chords: C7 to F, piano alone
38	**Playing from Guitar Score: Descant #1** "We Are Many Parts" – guitar introduction; refrain with flute descant, cantor, and guitar
39	**Playing from Guitar Score: Descant #2** "We Are Many Parts" – guitar introduction; refrain with flute descant, cantor, and guitar
40	**Playing from Guitar Score: Descant #3** "We Are Many Parts" – guitar introduction; refrain with flute descant, cantor, and guitar
41	**Transposing Melody, Harmony, and Descant Lines One Half Step Lower** "To You, O Lord" (key of D) – refrain with four flutes
42	**Transposing Melody Line One Half Step Higher** "Taste and See" (key of F) – mm. 1–7 of refrain, flute alone
43	**Transposing All Parts One Half Step Higher** "Taste and See" (key of F) – mm. 1–7 of refrain, three flutes

TRACK #	DESCRIPTION OF TRACK
55	**Improvisation 3: How *Not* to Write a Descant**
	"We Are Called" – mm. 1–4 of refrain, one flute on melody and one flute on descant #3
56	**Improvisation 4: How *Not* to Write a Descant**
	"We Are Called" – mm. 1–4 of refrain, one flute on melody and one flute on descant #4
57	**Improvisation 5**
	"Holy, Holy, Holy! Lord God Almighty" – piano introduction and one verse, piano alone
58	**Ending a Piece without a Picardy Third**
	"I Heard the Voice of Jesus Say" – final 4 measures, flute and piano
59	**Ending a Piece with a Picardy Third**
	"I Heard the Voice of Jesus Say" – final 4 measures, flute and piano
60	**Plagal Cadence**
	"Amen" cadence (IV–I), piano alone
61	**Create Your Own Descant Using Tendency Tones**
	Harmonization of G major scale, piano alone
62	**Melodic Considerations for a Well-Written Descant**
	"The God of All Eternity" – one verse, flute on descant from Example 126 with piano
63	**Create and Play a Descant**
	"The God of All Eternity" – piano introduction; one verse, piano alone
64	**Short Grace Notes**
	Haydn's *Serenade* – mm. 59–66, flute alone
65	**Long and Short Grace Notes**
	Mozart's *Allegro alla Turca* – flute alone
66	**Varieties of Short Grace Notes**
	"The King of Love My Shepherd Is" – one verse, one flute on melody and one flute on descant in Example 140
67	**Varieties of Embellishments**
	"The King of Love My Shepherd Is" – one verse, one flute on melody and one flute on descant in Example 141
68	**Add Your Own Embellishments**
	"Onward to the Kingdom" – piano introduction and one refrain, piano alone
69	**Rhythmic Patterns**
	"Holy, Holy, Holy! Lord God Almighty" – one verse, one flute on melody and one flute on descant in triplets
70	**Compose Your Own Descant: Focus on Rhythmic Patterns**
	"Holy, Holy, Holy! Lord God Almighty" – one verse, flute alone on melody

TRACK #	DESCRIPTION OF TRACK

84   **Weaving Music and Spoken Text I**

"O Spirit All-Embracing," stanza 1; "Prayer in Alleluia," Form II, mm. 1–8; "O Spirit All-Embracing," stanza 2; "Prayer in Alleluia," Form II, mm. 9–14; "O Spirit All-Embracing," stanza 3; "Prayer in Alleluia," Form II, mm. 15–22 – spoken voice in alternation with flute

85   **Weaving Music and Spoken Text II**

"Canticle of Daniel" – recited verses underscored with free improvisation, flute and spoken voice

86   **Try Your Own Interpretive Playing**

"Canticle of Daniel" – 4 verses, spoken voice alone

87   **Interpreting the Psalms**

Proulx's "Psalm 116," Antiphon and Psalm tone – refrain and 3 verses, flute, cantor, and guitar

APPENDIX V

88   **Embodying the Prayer**

"Take, O Take Me As I Am" – flute, voice, and piano

Music and Poetry Index

Index

About the Authors

Denise La Giglia is a pastoral musician and spiritual director. She is a part-time staff member at the Institute for Spiritual Leadership (ISL) in Chicago as administrator/coordinator of ISL's weekend training programs focusing on spirituality for self and service. Denise also teaches and does supervision work in the programs.

Denise earned a master of arts in pastoral studies from the Institute for Pastoral Studies (IPS) of Loyola University, Chicago. She graduated with a bachelor of arts in music from Mundelein College in 1970, the same year she began ministering as a pastoral musician, both as cantor and ensemble director. She continues to serve regularly as instrumentalist or cantor at several Chicago archdiocesan parishes. Her interest in liturgy led to a completion of study at the Liturgy Institute of Chicago (also known as the Parish Liturgy Program of the Office for Divine Worship); several years of parish work as a liturgy coordinator; approximately fourteen years as a member of the auxiliary music staff of the Chicago Archdiocesan Office for Divine Worship (ODW); and ten years as staff member and program coordinator at ODW. She also worked for several years as program coordinator for GIA *Presents*, an offering of GIA Publications, Inc., and has served as an adjunct teacher at IPS.

In May of 2001 Denise completed a certificate program in spiritual direction training and personal transformation at the Institute for Spiritual Leadership in Chicago, and then served as an intern in the program for the next two years. She also completed a course of study at the Women's Leadership Institute in Holland, Michigan.

La Giglia has a breadth of experience as a liturgical musician as well as a leader of prayer and a planning team member for parish liturgies, archdiocesan and national conference liturgies, small group prayer, and ritual experiences for health care institutions. Denise has collaborated in presenting a number of evenings of reflection, retreats, and parish missions. Besides membership in several professional organizations, La Giglia is on the board of a Franciscan performing arts center called *Chiesa Nuova* and works regularly with *Harmony, Hope and Healing*, a creative music program to the homeless and underserved. In addition to THE LITURGICAL FLUTIST (GIA), her publications include *Mystic Vista*, a recording with Fr. Robert Hutmacher, OFM, for harp and flute (GIA); *Journey of the Sacred*, a series of session guides for small faith communities (GIA); and *Window to Peace*, a recording of piano and flute reflections with Jerry Galipeau (World Library Publications).

Denise and her husband, Frank, have five children and seven grandchildren.

Anna Belle O'Shea is the Director of Liturgy and a member of the Theology Faculty at Mother McAuley Liberal Arts High School in Chicago. She is also a freelance flutist in the Chicago area and a member of the music staff of the Archdiocese of Chicago. As a liturgical musician, she has played flute for church functions throughout the United States as well as Europe. She can be heard as the flutist on more than twenty albums of contemporary and traditional sacred music. An active member of the National Association of Pastoral Musicians, she has served that organization as workshop clinician, member of the

Board of Directors of their Ensemble Section, and flutist for numerous liturgies and events at their regional and national conventions. She has also composed C instrument descants for World Library Publications' *People's Mass Book.*

In addition to maintaining a large private student clientele, O'Shea cofounded and directed Flutes Unlimited, a community ensemble comprised of fifty members in three different flute choirs ranging from elementary level through semi-professional. Under her direction, Flutes Unlimited became a leader among musical ensembles in the Chicago area, performing at St. Xavier University, Navy Pier, Rockefeller Chapel, and Holy Name Cathedral, as well as the Chicago Flute Fair, the Milwaukee Flute Fair, and the NPM Chicago Regional Convention in 2004.

For twelve years, O'Shea was principal flutist with the Northwest Indiana Symphony and was the featured soloist with that orchestra on several occasions at the Star Plaza Theatre in Merrillville, Indiana. She also performed at the 1992 and 1997 conventions of the National Flute Association as a member of the Professional Flute Choir.

O'Shea holds a Master of Arts Degree in Church Music and Liturgy from St. Joseph College in Rensselaer, Indiana, the first flutist to achieve such a degree there. In addition she earned a Diploma in Pastoral Liturgy from the same school. She is also a graduate of DePaul University, where she earned a Bachelor of Music, magna cum laude. Her flute teachers have included Phil Sieburg, Donald Peck, Kaye Clements, and Julius Baker.